# Ancient Wisdom for Today's Christian Dissidents

## The Epistle of James Through New Eyes

―❧❦☙―

### Jeffrey J. Meyers

WEST MONROE, LOUISIANA

Wisdom for Dissidents: The Epistle of James Through New Eyes
By Jeffrey J. Meyers
Copyright © 2022 by Athanasius Press
715 Cypress Street
West Monroe, Louisiana 71291
www.athanasiuspress.org

ISBN: 978-1-7351690-9-5 (softcover)

All rights reserved. No part of this publication may be reproduced, stored in a retrieval system, or transmitted in any form or by any means—electronic, mechanical, photocopy, recording, or any other—except for brief quotations in printed reviews, without the prior permission of the publisher.

This publication contains The Holy Bible, English Standard Version®, copyright © 2001 by Crossway Bibles, a publishing ministry of Good News Publishers. The ESV® text appearing in this publication is reproduced and published by cooperation between Good News Publishers and Athanasius Press and by permission of Good News Publishers. Unauthorized reproduction of this publication is prohibited.

The Holy Bible, English Standard Version (ESV) is adapted from the Revised Standard Version of the Bible, copyright Division of Christian Education of the National Council of the Churches of Christ in the U.S.A. All rights reserved.

English Standard Version®, ESV®, and the ESV® logo are trademarks of Good News Publishers located in Wheaton, Illinois. Used by permission.

# Contents

|   | | |
|---|---|---|
|   | Acknowledgments | v |
| 1 | Introduction: So You Want to Change the World? | 1 |
| 2 | Authorship, Dating, & Structure | 13 |
| 3 | How James Came to be Written | 25 |
| 4 | Suffering, Wisdom, & Maturity | 31 |
| 5 | How God Makes Things Right | 75 |
| 6 | Currying Favor or Cultivating Faithfulness | 119 |
| 7 | Deliverance & Vindication | 161 |
| 8 | The Potent Power of the Tongue | 201 |
| 9 | Exposing the Contagion of Mimetic Violence | 245 |
| 10 | The Prophet James | 281 |
| 11 | Patience, Prayer, & Restoration | 305 |
| 12 | Final Reflections & Summary | 331 |
|   | Epilogue: Fire From Heaven | 345 |
|   | Appendix: Dating the Epistle of James | 351 |
|   | Bibliography | 365 |

# Acknowledgments

*What do you have that you did not receive? If then you
received it, why do you boast as if you didn't receive it?*
–1 Corinthians 4:7

This commentary has been a long time coming. A long time. Sixteen years ago, I preached through the book of James. The series was well-received and shortly thereafter I was considering writing a popular commentary on the letter. Five years ago, I preached through James again. It didn't take long for me to see that the key to understanding the unity of James was getting the first-century context correct. What has often been expounded as a series of loosely connected wisdom sayings turned out to have a surprising unity once I began to discern both the terrible situation forced upon the recipients as well as the dangerous temptations to retaliatory violence that plagued these exiled Christians. The more I studied James the more I learned how crucial the context was for understanding what seemed like random sections of the letter—for example, what I call "the parable of the traveling merchant" (4:13-17). Once I saw the thread that held everything together, I determined to write this commentary on James. But the process took time, more time than I anticipated.

Over the past sixteen years I have been privileged to deliver lectures, talks, and sermons on James at quite a few churches, conferences, Bible studies, and men's retreats. These have been vital to me because of the productive questions, comments, and criticisms I have received from so many people. I thank my congregation for listening to two sermon series on James and at least one adult Sunday school class. Their comments and criticisms over the years have been invaluable. After my first sermon series, one of my seminary interns at the time, Joshua Anderson, was commissioned by our elders to begin transcribing my sermons on James and transforming them into suitable language for a popular commentary. His faithful and creative work has been foundational for the finished commentary. His independent essay on the dating of James, with some modifications from me, has been included as an appendix to this commentary. Pastor Wayne Larson offered helpful editorial corrections and content suggestions on a very early version of this commentary. My good friend Randy Stone spent his COVID quarantine reading through the entire finished manuscript looking for errors and making helpful suggestions about the content. Pastor Steve Wilkins has repeatedly encouraged me to finish the project. Without his support I might have let the manuscript lie on my desks for a few more years.

Lastly, I dedicate this commentary to my mentor of many years, James B. Jordan. As I have told many people over the years, Jim knows the Bible, particularly the Hebrew Scriptures, better than anyone I have ever encountered, seminary professors included. As a young man aspiring to be a pastor, I was privileged to study under him in the mid-1980s. But that was just the beginning of a long, fruitful relationship. I have continued to learn from him over the past four decades as we have interacted with one another in many contexts, but especially the annual Biblical Horizons conference held in Florida for so many years. Of course, the "Through New Eyes" commentaries published by Athanasius Press have all been inspired by Jim's book of the same name.

A few years ago, Jim suffered through several strokes. Because of those health issues, he has not been able to be as productive in his writing and lecturing as he had been in the past. This has been a huge loss for the Church. Nevertheless, Jim's biblical and theological influence continues to inspire the work of the Theopolis Institute. I encourage everyone who wants to deepen

## Introduction

their understanding of the Bible to follow the lectures, podcasts, and essays produced by Theopolis. Start with some of the audio lectures by James B. Jordan. You will not be disappointed.

Jeff Meyers
All Saints Day
November 1, 2021

# 1

# INTRODUCTION

## So You Want to Change the World?

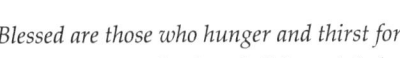

*Blessed are those who hunger and thirst for
righteousness, for they shall be satisfied*
–Matthew 5:6

Forty years ago, I was listening to a lecture by professor John Frame in which he said something like this: What is accepted as common sense in today's culture was, just a generation or so ago, philosophical speculation in the academy among intellectuals. I'm sure that was just a throwaway comment, but it stuck with me. Because it is true.

Ideas cascade down into common culture from the academy, from the elite educational institutions, and from prominent pulpits. That may seem ominous to us, dangerous even. But it is an undeniable fact. In any community, culture, state, or nation, there are the leaders and there are the led. There are the talkers and the hearers. There are writers and their readers. There are the rulers and the ruled. There are the theologians and those that learn to think like them. There are pastors and their congregations. And short of a catastrophic upheaval, this is how cultural change normally takes place. Truth be told, many catastrophic cultural upheavals are the result of some band of intellectuals implementing their ideas—the French Revolution, the Soviet Union, Nazi Germany, the philosophy of Chairman Mao, or Fidel Castro.

Contrary to popular opinion in some Christian circles, the sixteenth-century Reformation did not originate as a groundswell among common people. It was not, as sometimes portrayed, a grassroots movement. In fact, there is overwhelming evidence to suggest that what we call the Reformation did not really have much effect among ordinary people for some decades after Martin Luther posted his theses and instigated a series of academic disputations, intellectual debates, and learned publications.

The Reformation began in the minds and lives of highly educated intellectuals in schools and churches, then spread to other scholars and well-informed dukes and princes. Professors and pastors wrote pamphlets and books, lectured and preached. Those books and sermons were consumed by literate opinion makers. And then eventually it all trickled down to change the way average people thought and lived in their everyday world. Sure, Luther was something of a national hero in the mind of the masses because they saw him as a champion of German independence from the Roman Curia. But it took a generation or so for the practical theological insights of Luther and the Reformers to begin to take hold among common folk.

James Davidson Hunter, in his book *To Change the World*, argues quite persuasively that cultures are not transformed by changing the hearts and minds of enough common people until the social order comes to reflect the values and beliefs that the majority hold.[1] The "groundswell" theory of social change does not hold up—it's naive and contrary to historical precedent. We need effective leaders to change the world.

---

1 James Davidson Hunter, *To Change the World: The Irony, Tragedy, and Possibility of Christianity in the Late Modern World* (Oxford: Oxford University Press, 2010).

Introduction

# The Righteousness of God

The epistle of James is a letter written to early Christian leaders who wanted to change the world. It is addressed to influential disciples of Jesus that believed they were called to change the world. These "brothers" (James 1:2) were "teachers" (3:1) who had a passion for justice. Or to be even more precise: the letter is addressed to Christian leaders who believed that God had promised that he would change the world through them now that he had installed his Son as Lord. They were actively engaged in working for the promised "righteousness of God" (1:20). This "righteousness" or "justice of God" was the "harvest of righteousness" (3:17) that these Jewish Christian brothers expected to be implemented now that the kingdom of God had come and Jesus had been installed as Messianic Lord over all.

But not everyone was singing from the same sheet of music at first. Truth be told, everything might have been easily sidetracked if the disciples followed the wrong sorts of brothers, zealots who mimicked their enemies in their zeal to see the righteous kingdom their Lord had promised.

James knew that the way these leading men in the Christian community spoke and acted would be critical in the transformation of their world. If the kingdom of Jesus was to grow and expand as the Lord had promised, these Christian community leaders would have to carry on what Jesus began in his training of the twelve. Jesus had called and trained twelve gifted men as his disciples, whom he groomed to write and speak in ways that would change the world. These were not illiterate, uneducated fishermen. They were not, of course, trained in the schools run by the elites in first-century Judaism. But that doesn't mean they were uninformed or illiterate. Jesus saw potential in them all and chose them to be his official, authorized spokesmen, to be in effect his educated scribes. But the apostles *alone* could not be the instruments of the growth of Jesus's kingdom. They also trained men—bishops, elders, pastors, deacons, etc.—to lead local Christian communities. A faithful "brotherhood" of Christian leaders was critical for the expansion of the new kingdom, God's new way of organizing humanity under the Lordship of the risen, ascended Messiah.

But for many, that righteous kingdom project did not appear to be going very well. The world was not changing as quickly as some thought it might, as they thought it should. In fact, it appeared to be worse for them when this letter is written than it was before Jesus ascended into heaven. James is writing his epistle to an exiled community of Messiah-believing Jews who have been literally driven out of Jerusalem (Acts 8:1; 11:19). They have been harassed and pursued by over-zealous Jewish authorities (Acts 8:1; 9:1-2). These "twelve tribes" in the recent "dispersion" of Christians from Jerusalem left their homes, their work, and their communities as exiles. More than that, they were hounded by a new cadre of Jewish inquisitors intent on bringing them back to Judaism using torture and violence. The apostle Paul will later testify:

> I persecuted this Way to the death, binding and delivering to prison both men and women, as the high priest and the whole council of elders can bear me witness. From them I received letters to the brothers . . . (Acts 22:4, 5).

We know from the unfolding story in the book of Acts that the Pharisee Saul was just one of many such inquisitors who secured authorization from the Sanhedrin to search out, imprison, torture, and even execute the disciples of Jesus. Later, Saul (Paul) himself became one of their most wanted defectors and was viciously pursued in city after city. When Paul finally appeared in Jerusalem they believed they finally had him. A riot was incited, Paul was surrounded, but was rescued by the Romans in the nick of time. Even so, the Jews were intent on killing him (Acts 22:22).

# Introduction

> "... the Jews made a plot and bound themselves by an oath neither to eat nor drink till they had killed Paul. There were more than forty who made this conspiracy. They went to the chief priests and elders and said, 'We have strictly bound ourselves by an oath to taste no food till we have killed Paul.' (Acts 23:12-14).

Paul's arrest, imprisonment, and the rage of the Jews against him happened many years after the letter of James was written. Even so, these events illustrate not only the zealous, fanatical wrath of the unbelieving Jewish leaders, but also the horrible predicament that the Christians were enmeshed in during this time. Everything was topsy-turvy. The authorities whom they formerly trusted had become their enemies. The envy and resulting violence had escalated since the time of Jesus death and resurrection. To understand James's letter, we have to put ourselves in their shoes and appreciate how disorienting all this was to these new Jewish believers.

To these frustrated Christians, James does *not* say something like, "You are *not* called to change the world. That's never going to happen. Concern yourself with *spiritual* things." He does not say, "Be content to proclaim the message of individual salvation and the promise of heaven. Don't worry about social and political issues." Rather, he tells the distressed Christian community, especially the brotherhood of leaders, about how they should go about being Jesus's agents of change and chiefly warns them against the dangerous temptations that dog the people who want to change the world. James counsels patience and "maturity" (1:4; 3:13-18) in the face of their childish, petulant anger and violent aggression (1:20; 4:1-4).

Heated speeches (3:1-12) and acts of violence motivated by anger (1:20; 4:1-3) will not produce the righteous kingdom that Jesus has promised. And neither will another tactic these believers were prone to—sucking up to their oppressors with the hope of appeasing them. That also is a perilous temptation motivated by anger at their perceived impotence compared to the riches and power of their enemies (2:1-13).

What stands out in this letter is the passionate anger of these persecuted Christians, an anger that has led to supremely foolish talk and action. They are being "lured" by their unrestrained "desire" to sinful exploits that "brings forth death" (1:14). They are full of "rampant malice" (1:21). Their actions reveal that they have become "judges with evil thoughts" (2:4). The public talk of their leaders encourages exasperated members of the body to "curse people" (3:1-9). They are harboring "hateful zeal and political ambition in their hearts" (3:14). Their fervent desire for justice is leading to "wars among their members" (4:1). What they "covet" drives them to "fight and engage in violent aggression" (4:2), and such behavior is motivated by their unrestrained "passions" (4:3). In short, they have become Christian zealots. They are "proud" and therefore "double-minded" (1:8; 4:8; 1:8). They even "boast" about the "business" of violent resistance in which they are engaged (4:16).

---

## A Better Way

Drawing on the teaching of Jesus, especially from Matthew's Gospel, particularly the Sermon on the Mount, James counsels "patience" in the experience of these severe trials, a "steadfastness under trial" that leads to "maturity" (1:2-4) as well as the royal "crown" that Jesus promised to his disciples (1:12). He commends to them the "mature instruction, the instruction that brings freedom" (2:25). They should not follow the worldly "religion" of their persecutors, but practice "pure and undefiled" piety, especially as it manifests itself in caring for the marginalized and needy, "the afflicted orphans and widows" (1:26-27). This is the "royal law, according to the Scripture" to love and show mercy (2:8-13). Genuine faith will always behave this way. It is not their fiery speeches and talk of the strength of their faith that evidences true trust, but how their actions manifest obedience (2:14-18). The

## Introduction

vindication they long for will be theirs if they have a living, active faith that accepts the sacrifices that need to be made and works to help and protect those in danger from their enemies (2:18-26).

The brothers who are leading the community need to "tame" their tongues and stop encouraging "cursing" (3:9, 10) and the ensuing "unspiritual, demonic" behavior it necessarily encourages (3:15). The "harvest of justice" and "the peace" they so long for comes when disciples of Jesus "make peace" (3:1-18). They must resist the devil's temptation to stimulate the growth of the kingdom by force and respond in kind to the apostate Jewish oppressors. Stop boasting about these insurgent forays against the enemies of the church. They are not called to be Christian "zealots" and to engage in aggressive violent behavior (4:1-12). Do the right thing (4:13-17). Be patient and trust in the prophecies of our Lord, knowing that the theocratically rich Jewish rulers, who trust in the gold and silver of the temple and their glorious priestly garments, will be judged in due time (1:9-11; 5:1-9).

Remember, "the Lord of Hosts" will not long endure those who have selfishly lived "gloriously on the land" and have refused to honor the apostolic harvesters that Jesus has sent into the fields as his servants (5:3-5; cf. Matt. 9:37-38, 13:30). Your oppressors have not repented of murdering "the righteous one" that did not resist them (5:1-6). Just like in the days of the prophets, know that the righteous Lord is at hand and he will judge his enemies. Be patient and stop swearing oaths that bind you to unrighteous, conspiratorial retaliation (5:7-12). Instead, take care of the wounded and sick, forgive those who have allowed their passions to get the better of themselves, and above all, like Elijah of old, pray for deliverance and heavenly rain to bring about the harvest you desire (5:13-16). Finally, do your best, brothers, to heed my advice in this letter and turn back those who have sinned in these matters (5:19-20).

## A LITTLE BACKGROUND

Having laid out the basic context and themes of the book, I want to back up for a moment and summarize how I came to this perspective. Over sixteen years ago, I began a sermon series on the epistle of James. I initially approached the book with the relatively popular idea that James is a general epistle and so has some sort of generalized message to everyone at all times.

Approaching the book this way means that the message and the details of the letter are de-contextualized and verses and paragraphs are made to stand alone as nuggets of Christian wisdom for the ages. And, of course, as we shall see, there is a great deal of wisdom in James for all ages. I'm not denying that. But the letter was not written to twenty-first-century American Christians. Not directly anyway. As with all of Scripture, this book is *for* us and the Spirit obviously intends for us to read and apply it. Even so, this circular letter was written to a very specific group of people—those disciples of Jesus exiled from Jerusalem by the apostate Jewish rulers (1:1, "the twelve tribes in the dispersion"). And therefore, James deals with a set of very concrete temptations that presented themselves to that generation of early Christian disciples that had been "dispersed" from Jerusalem after the martyrdom of Stephen (Acts 8:1; 11:19).

Here is a huge challenge for us modern Christians in reading and appropriating the New Testament. We are prone to forget the historical context and turn all these New Testament letters into free-floating expositions of Christine doctrine and ethical instruction. It is all too easy to do this with the New Testament epistles because they seem like they are written directly to us. When, however, we deal with the Hebrew Scriptures, we understand that there is a two-step process necessary to apply them faithfully to our own contemporary situations. But when we come to the New Testament it seems directly applicable to us. There is obviously some truth to this. The ritual and legal constraints of the old covenant have been lifted with the coming of Jesus, and that makes drawing applications to us from the Hebrew Scriptures a little more difficult. But the New Testament Scriptures must also be appropriated by us not directly, but indirectly, once we have determined the original context and message of the letter.

In my preparation to preach on James, the more I read the letter and various commentators, the more uncomfortable I became with the way it was often treated—as I have said, as if it was a loose collection of nuggets of wisdom for the ages, a jumble of aphoristic sayings. For too long, academic commentators have assumed that James was a somewhat disjointed compilation of wise sayings with no really unifying argument.

I had originally been attracted to the epistle of James after a sermon series on Ecclesiastes because I had assumed it would be the New Testament equivalent of Solomon's wisdom in Ecclesiastes. After all, the magic word "vapor" occurred in James 4:14.[2] But the more I read and reflected on the book, and when I began to read some older commentaries, I became convinced that we have missed out on getting the full force of James's wisdom because we have neglected taking seriously the actual language James used, and we have ignored the powerfully persuasive temptations to violence and political insurgency that were so attractive to these early Jewish disciples of Jesus.

For example, I came across an older commentator that took James's statement in James 4:1-3 at face value.

> What causes wars and what causes battles among you? Is it not this: that your passions are at war in your members? You desire something and you don't have it, so you kill. You are zealous and you cannot obtain, so you fight and engage in violent aggression.

---

[2] For more on the significance of the word "vapor" (Hebrew: *hebel*) see my commentary on Ecclesiastes, *A Table in the Mist* (Athanasius Press, 2006).

Could the recipients of this letter have actually engaged in physical violence, even killing? Were they being rebuked by James for violent behavior? I wondered how that could be. How could members of a Christian community be led to violent aggression, including deadly force? What would inspire them to do such things? Most modern commentators suggest that James is just using very strong language to refer to the everyday spiritual struggles of believers, maybe strife and division within the Christian community that arises from envy and jealousy. James may say that they have "killed" but commentators assure us that this is surely metaphorical exaggeration. After all, didn't Jesus in his Sermon on the Mount say that one proper interpretation of the sixth commandment implied that anger with one's brother was a kind of "murder" (Matt. 5:21, 23)? Some of that is definitely in view here, of course.

But that doesn't do justice to the very explicit, concrete language of James 4, where "violent aggression" and "battles" are repeated twice in two verses. Nor does it do justice to the severe condemnation that their behavior calls forth from James. It becomes evident when we read on in James 4 that James is talking about more than just common church arguments and quarrels. In fact, James 3 should have set us up for just this kind of rebuke. Should it surprise anyone that "cursing" one's enemies would lead to dangerous physical conflict (3:1-12)? The men in his audience are denounced as "an adulterous people" (4:4). They are in serious trouble and in danger of God's judgment (4:6-10). I suppose that someone might think that arguments over the color of the carpeting in the church sanctuary or the salary of the pastor could call for such severe language. Surely there is some application to such modern, contentious ecclesiastical debates. But is that all that is going on in these exiled communities?

It turns out that there's another, more consistent way to read this reference to violence, an interpretation that better fits the context of the very early church and how she was tempted and tried. James's language indicates something much graver and more dangerous than the kind of disputes that typically plague modern American churches. The seductive lure of revolutionary zealotry as a means of rectifying the injustice that their oppressors had made them suffer would have been a live option. It would be too easy for them to mimic the zealot-infested culture of contemporary first-century Judaism.[3]

When we get the details of the story right, I believe the meaning and application for us becomes crystal clear, especially for so many Christians suffering extreme persecution outside of the United States, but also for faithful Christians experiencing cultural exile in the West as unbelieving and apostate Christian leaders become more and more hostile to authentic disciples of Jesus. If my reading is correct, then we have in this letter some very relevant ancient wisdom for today's Christian dissidents. I will be making arguments for this context and application all through my commentary. But for now, allow me in the next chapter to propose a fictional account of what prompted James to write his epistle.

I will end this introduction with one caveat. I don't want the title to raise false expectations. This is not a *comprehensive* manual for Christian dissidents today. This is a commentary on the text of James with some contemporary reflections. For example, I don't commend or critique any of the current "options" put forward by Christian leaders about how to live faithfully in our increasing post- or anti-Christian culture. As we shall see, there are some fruitful points of contact between the situation of the exiled disciples of Jesus in the apostolic age and the challenges and temptations for Christians today. James, therefore, has some remarkably prudent wisdom for us, especially how *not* to respond to anti-Christian oppressors. Even so, in explaining and applying what James has written, I have not attempted to clarify and

---

[3] The best in-depth study of the zealots in the first century is Martin Hengel, *The Zealots: Investigations Into the Jewish Freedom Movement in the Period from Herod I until 70 A.D.*, trans. David Smith (Edinburgh: T&T Clark, 1989).

qualify everything by answering every question that may arise for a modern reader. My primary purpose has been to explain and apply the admonitions of James.

## 2

# AUTHORSHIP, DATING, & STRUCTURE

*...once we free the apostle from the strange obligation of having to address sixteenth-century issues and their contemporary spin-offs, and think our way into the genuine first-century context, the complexities remain but become comprehensible.*
–N. T. Wright[4]

Solid arguments can be made that the author of this epistle is James the apostle, John's brother, one of the "sons of Zebedee," to whom Jesus gave the nickname "sons of thunder" (Mark 3:17).[5] James was chosen by Jesus, along with his brother, when they were fishing with their father Zebedee on the Sea of Galilee (Matt. 4:21). On one occasion James's and John's mother came to Jesus requesting that her sons be given places of honor at Jesus's right and left hand in his kingdom (Matt. 10:20). But Mark tells us that it was not just the mother, but the brothers were also making the request (Mark 10:35). Peter, James, and John were favored to accompany Jesus in the Garden of Gethsemane on the evening of the Lord's betrayal (Matt. 26:37). It would not be wrong to portray Peter, James, and John as Jesus's three "mighty men," like David's trusted inner circle (2 Sam. 23:8). Clearly from this brief review of

---

4 N.T. Wright, *Galatians* (Grand Rapids, MI: Eerdmans, 2021), 31.

5 See Appendix "Dating the Epistle of James" for the argument that the author is the apostle James, not James the Just.

his place in the Gospel narratives, James had a noteworthy position among the twelve disciples. Even the apostle Paul says that James was one of three "pillars" in the church (Gal. 2:9). According to some post-apostolic accounts, James appears to have been the first "pastor" of the Jerusalem Christian community. James does appear to have been a prominent leader because "the Jews" were quite pleased when Herod killed him, according to Acts 12:2-3.

Since Jesus commissioned his disciples as his authorized spokesmen, that is, as "apostles," and promised that when he departed "the Spirit would guide them into all the truth" (John 16:13), it seems reasonable to begin with the assumption that the author is indeed James the apostle. The apostolic imprimatur would lend authority to the letter, since these were the men certified by Jesus to be "servants of the Word" (Luke 1:2; Acts 6:4).[6] Unless, of course, there are some very good reasons to think otherwise. Identifying himself here in verse 1 as a "servant (*doulos*) of God and the Lord Jesus Christ," James would appear to be signaling his association with the other apostolic "servants of the Word" (Luke 1:2).

Are there weighty reasons to reject the apostolic authorship of this letter? I don't believe so. But we should briefly consider the most common alternative. As it turns out, there is another James that would qualify as the author—James, the brother of Jesus, sometimes called "James the Just" by the post-apostolic church.[7] He was not an apostle, but he did have a prominent place in the

---

[6] It is likely that the apostles' rationale for calling out these men to manage the daily distribution should not be taken merely as an administrative move to give them more freedom to "preach." Although the ESV translation inserts the word "preaching" in verse 2, it is not there in the original. Of course, they were publicly proclaiming the Gospel, as is clear from the story recorded in the book of Acts. But we also know that Luke uses this language to refer to those engaged in collecting and writing down the Gospel narratives of Jesus's life, death, and resurrection (Luke 1:2).

[7] Eusebius, *Historia ecclesiastica*, 2.23. The earliest post-apostolic evidence related to the authorship of this epistle comes almost 200 years after the letter was written, much of it is even later, and none of it is conclusive.

Jerusalem church after the apostle James's death (Acts 12:2, 17). Peter, after he was miraculously released from imprisonment by Herod, sent some of the household of John Mark to report what had happened to "James and to the brothers" (Acts 12:17). This would be James the Just since James the apostle was said to have been martyred by Herod earlier in Acts 12. In his letter to the Galatians, the apostle Paul mentioned visiting "James, the Lord's brother" in Jerusalem three years after his conversion (Gal. 1:19). And this James seems to have presided over the Jerusalem Council (Acts 15:13) and was perhaps the chief author of the circular letter addressed to the churches regarding the status of the Gentiles (Acts 15:22-29). Moreover, when Paul makes his final journey to Jerusalem, with the contributions he has gathered from the churches for famine relief in Judea, he first reports to "James, and all the elders" (Acts 21:19).

Could the author of this letter be James the brother of Jesus, the one who presided over the Jerusalem church after the death of the apostle James? The leader who gave the definitive speech that swayed the gathered elders at the Jerusalem Council? Yes, I believe so. Nevertheless, I don't think deciding between these two possibilities is the most important factor for properly interpreting this epistle. More important than figuring out which James is the author would be appreciating the relatively early context that called forth the warnings in this letter. We will get to that in a moment.

Even so, I must say that almost every commentator, even conservative Evangelical scholars, only have one big argument against the authorship of the apostle James—it would be "too early." Apparently for most scholars, a letter like this could not have been written so early in the apostolic age. Commentators repeatedly assure us of the "improbability" of dating this epistle during the life of James the apostle. Peter Davids's dismissal is representative: "James the son of Zebedee probably died too early to leave any literary remains." He adds, "Acts 12 indicates that he died before AD 44, ruling out the probability, although not the possibility, of his writing the epistle."[8]

Why is an early date so improbable? Nobody gives definitive reasons for this assessment. It's just too early, they say. Motyer, however, gives us an honest appraisal:

> It is usually thought that James son of Zebedee was martyred at too early a date (AD 44) for him to have been the author of the letter [of James]. Even this, however, cannot be maintained for certain. Nothing in the letter absolutely forbids a date as early as James the son of Zebedee, and certainly the arguments proposed for later dates lack impressiveness.[9]

I suspect that behind the trepidation to date this epistle, as well as any of the Gospel narratives, within the first decade of the life of the church, is the assumption that the teachings of Jesus and the supervision of the fledgling Christian community was at first accomplished by means of oral communication alone. Before anything was written down, the stories and the instruction had to be passed on by means of oral tradition. That may have been true in Hellenistic cultures. But when it comes to the early Christian community we are dealing with Jews, a literary, bookish people. It is very difficult to believe that men who were convinced the promised Messiah had come—the one foretold in all their sacred writings and explicitly prophesied in the prophetic books of the Hebrew Scriptures—would wait one or two decades before recording in writing such momentous events.

And the fact that this is a circular letter makes the charge of it being "too early" even more questionable. After all, the epistles of the New Testament are all written by Paul, Peter, or John

---

8 Peter H. Davids, *The Epistle of James*, in *The New International Greek Testament Commentary* (Grand Rapids, MI: Eerdmans, 1982) 6, fn 26.

9 J. A. Motyer, *The Message of James* (Downers Grove: InterVarsity Press Academic, 1985), 18.

straightaway to deal with immediate problems and challenges in the churches. There was no intermediate oral communication. Even if there was personal, oral communication by means of representatives sent by these apostles to the various churches, they more often than not carried with them letters to be read in the assembly (e.g., 1 Thess. 5:27). These are the letters we have designated the "New Testament Epistles," and not one of them was written a decade or more after the events that precipitated the need for these written messages.

Given that James identifies the recipients of this letter (1:1, "to the twelve tribes in the dispersion"), we should consider the urgency of the communication to these Christians banished from Jerusalem by the persecuting leaders of the church. If the crisis referred to here is indeed the forced exile of Jewish Christians from Jerusalem, as recorded for us in Acts 8:1 and Acts 11:19, then it seems quite reasonable to believe that the apostle James wrote this letter soon after their banishment to challenge these Jewish Christian believers. It would make sense to distribute a circular letter like this while these disciples are still separated from Jerusalem. But a dozen years or so after the initial banishment, after the death of the apostle James (Acts 12:2), when James the brother of Jesus seems to have taken the leadership of the Jerusalem Christian community, the situation had changed. There appears to be a flourishing community again in Jerusalem (Acts 12:17; 15:1-21). If that exile from Jerusalem took place in the aftermath of Stephen's martyrdom, a year or so after Pentecost, and only the apostles remained in the city, then dating the letter sometime in the early to mid 30s makes more sense.

There are other compelling reasons to believe that this letter was composed very early in the life of the church. Many commentators have noted that 1) there is a decidedly Jewish flavor to the vocabulary and content; 2) James does not touch on common debates and controversies which occupied the apostolic church in later decades; 3) there is a "primitiveness to James's theological framework ... which is exactly what we would expect of a very early Christian writing";[10] and 4) the letter is full of clear allusions to Matthew's Gospel, and the correspondences to the Sermon on the Mount are conspicuous.[11] This last feature of James fits with the post-apostolic church's understanding of the relative order of the Synoptic Gospel accounts—that the canonical order is the order in which the Gospel narratives were written.[12] Matthew's gospel was either already composed and beginning to circulate or was in the process of being written, and James, as a member of the apostolic brotherhood, had some access to Matthew's material. McCartney comes to a similar conclusion:

> It is as though James is imbued with the wisdom teaching of Jesus, but not in the written form in which we now find it. All this points to a time quite early in the life of the church, prior to the theological reflections of Paul, prior to the circulation of the Gospels, and prior to the authors of Hebrews, 1 Peter, and the Johannine materials, or at least prior to the time when these other writings began to have widespread and determinative influence . . . James represents a state of Christian thinking that has not yet been determined by them, and hence is logically prior.[13]

I would add that James is not merely grounding his admonitions on the "wisdom teaching" of Jesus, but he is also giving the persecuted community hope based on Jesus's repeated prophetic denunciations of the failed leadership of the Jewish

---

[10] Dan. G. McCartney, *James* (Grand Rapids, MI: Baker Academic, 2009), 15.

[11] For a detailed account of all the allusions to Jesus's sermon in James see Virgil V. Porter, Jr., "The Sermon on the Mount in the Book of James, Part 1," *Bibliotheca Sacra* (2005): 344-60; see also "The Sermon on the Mount in the Book of James, Part 2," *Bibliotheca Sacra* 162 (2005): 470-82.

[12] John Wenham, *Redating Matthew, Mark and Luke* (Downers Grove: Intervarsity Press, 1992).

[13] McCartney, *James*, 8.

authorities (1:9-11; 2:6-7; 5:1-6; cf. Matt. 23). Their theocratically rich oppressors will be judged shortly, "for the coming of the Lord is near" (5:8).

Earlier, I conceded that there are good arguments for the authorship of either James the apostle or James the Just, the brother of Jesus. But if James the Just is the author, it would be a mistake to date this letter after the Jerusalem Council (c. A.D. 49; Acts 15) or even during the time when Paul's missionary efforts with the Gentiles were beginning to provoke controversy among Jewish Christians. So even if we believe James the Just was the author, the letter would have been written and distributed well before the Galatian controversy. There is nothing in the letter to suggest that Paul's ministry to the Gentiles or his formulations against "the works of the law" have become controversial issues in the early Christian community. When James uses the language of "works" (James 2:14-26), he is not addressing the same errors as Paul does in his conflict against adding "the works of the law" to faith as a requirement for justification. This will be important to remember when we get to James 2 and James's warnings against the salvific impotence of a certain kind of "faith" without works. If the apostle is the author, then the circular letter could have been written in the 30s, any time after the dispersion of the Christians from Jerusalem or as late as the early 40s before his death (Acts 12:2). Alternately, James the Just would have penned it sometime after the apostle's death and before the Jerusalem Council (A.D. 44-49).

## THE STRUCTURE OF JAMES

Discerning the literary structure of the epistle of James is notoriously difficult. Most commentators suggest it is simply a loosely connected compilation of wise sayings. Some commentators have sought to discover a twelve-fold division in the text since James is writing to "the twelve tribes" (James 1:1). Since the name "James" is an anglicized version of the Hebrew and Greek name "Jacob," others have looked for a way to connect Jacob's blessing his twelve sons (Gen. 49) with twelve sections of the letter. The correlations would look something like this:[14]

> JACOB, or James (Gk. Ιακωβο), to the twelve tribes (James 1:1; Gen. 49:1)
>
> REUBEN (Gen. 49:3-4) is "unstable as water," the "firstborn. . . preeminent one," one who lost his position through unfaithfulness. James calls out "the one who doubts being like a wave of the sea, driven and tossed about" (James 1:6). Reuben is the firstfruits of Jacob's strength (Gen. 49:3) and the nascent, apostolic church is a kind of "firstfruits" (James 1:18).
>
> SIMEON & LEVI (Gen. 49:5-7) are angry, violent brothers who used the covenant to take personal revenge (Gen. 34:1-31). James warns that "the anger of man doesn't bring about God's justice" (James 1:20).
>
> JUDAH (Gen. 49:8-12) is the brother who held the "ruler's staff" and so was prince and lawgiver. James commends to his hearers "the mature law, the law of liberty" (James 1:25), calls the Lord Jesus Messiah as witness against their partiality (2:1-7), reminds them they are "heirs of the kingdom" (2:5), and are therefore bound to obey "the royal law" (2:8-14). It has been suggested that the "Judah" section extends through 2:16, but that seems tenuous. Perhaps James's admonition to care for the poor and needy relates to the royal duty of serving and caring for his people.
>
> ZEBULUN (Gen. 49:13) is "a haven for ships," so James asks us to "look at the ships" (James 3:4).

---

[14] The connection between Genesis 49 and James's epistle was first suggested by James B. Jordan, then pursued informally on a theological discussion list by John Barach and Tim Gallant. The form I have given it here is largely from Pastor Steve Jeffery's recent sermon series at All Saints Presbyterian Church in Fort Worth, Texas (allsaintskirk.com)

ISSACHAR (Gen. 49:14-15) who "saw that the resting-place was good" and that "the land was pleasant." James commends the wisdom among the brothers: "By his good conduct let him show his works...full of mercy and good fruits...a harvest of righteousness" (James 3:13-18).

DAN (Gen. 49:16-18) is characterized by Jacob as one who judged his own people like a (demonic) serpent-betrayer, biting at their heels. In James 4:1-12, the apostle inveighs against the one whose demonic ("resist the devil") desires lead to quarrels, fights, murder among the brothers ("among you"); the one who "judges his brother," "judges his neighbor." This also fits with the mention of the devil in verse 7; for he is the one who is the viper beside the path.

GAD (Gen. 49:19) has only one line: "Raiders shall raid Gad, but he shall raid back at their heels." Raiders shall raid Gad (destroying his wealth), and he'll raid in return. James 4:13-17 is a prophetic parable directed against the arrogant, "traveling merchants" who are pursuing the exiled Christians. The parable is directed against the "business" of the raiding inquisitors from apostate Jerusalem.

ASHER (Gen. 49:20) again has only one line: "his food shall be rich, and he shall yield royal delicacies." In James 5:1-4, the "rich" who live "gloriously on the land" are warned of the coming judgment: "Come now you rich, weep and howl."

NAPHTALI (Gen. 49:21) is "a doe let loose that bears beautiful fawns." Does this connect with James 5:5-6? With "fattened hearts" like sacrificial animals) prepared for slaughter?

JOSEPH'S (Gen. 49:22-26) blessing is longer than the other brothers. He is a fruitful bough who was "bitterly attacked" but persevered ("remained unmoved") and in due time was richly blessed. James 5:7-18 commends the patient farmer who waits for the crop, the prophets who remained patient in suffering, steadfast Job who experienced the Lord's mercy, the repentant sinner who is healed/saved, and Elijah who waited for the rain. And James 5:12 warns against oaths. Remember how Joseph was let down by the cup-bearer who did not keep his word in Genesis 40, but remembered him later in Genesis 41.

BENJAMIN (Gen. 49:27) is called "a ravenous wolf" (i.e., a counterfeit lion who wants to be king, like Lion-Judah, Gen. 49:9). He sought to devour what was not rightfully his and later went to war against Judah (Judg. 19-21; esp. 19:18), and was nearly wiped out before being saved from death by his brothers (Judg. 19-21; see 21:23, 28, "brothers"). James encourages his readers to rescue their Benjamin-like brothers who wander from the truth (James 5:19-20).

That James should be read in the light of Jacob's story makes a lot of sense, as we shall see in the body of this commentary. But linking the twelve sons of Jacob with the various themes in the letter still seems tenuous to me. There are connections made in the previous structural analysis that seem like a stretch (Naphtali and James 5:5-6, for example). And the way the epistle has to be broken up to accommodate the links leaves much to be desired (James 2:14-26 appears to be hanging on by a thread). But someone else may research this further and discover more points of convergence between the two texts.

One phrase does appear fifteen times in the text—the direct address "beloved brothers" or "my brothers" or simply "brothers" (1:2, 16, 19; 2:1, 5, 14; 3:1, 10, 12; 4:11; 5:7, 9, 10, 12, 19). If we combine the eighth and ninth use in 3:10-12 and the three quick occurrences in 5:7-11, we have a nice chiastic structure with matching themes in each of the paired sections.

   A. 1:2-15—Tried & Tempted Sinners Challenged

     B. 1:16-18—Gifts From Above

        C. 1:19-27—Anger & The Righteousness of God

           D. 2:1-4—Oppressors in the Assembly

              E. 2:14-26—Genuine Faith Works

                 F. 3:1-10a—The Power of the Tongue for Good and Evil

              E' 3:10b–4:10—Adulterous Works

           D' 4:11–5:6—Oppressors Judged by the Lord

## Authorship, Dating, & Structure

    C' 5:7-11 — Patience Suffering Yields Rain from Above

   B' 5:12-18 — Sinners Healed & Rescued

  A' 5:19-20 — Wandering Brothers Restored

If that seems forced, there is another chiastic option, which nearly matches the one based on the distribution of "brothers" in the text.

  A. 1:2-8 — Trials, Faith, Steadfastness

    B. 1:9-27 — Suffering, Patience, Piety

      C. 2:1-7 — The Rich and "the Poor Man"

        D. 2:8-13 — Love, Liberty, & Mercy

          E. 2:14-26 — Justification & Works

            F. 3:1-12 — The Teacher's Tongue

          E' 3:13-18 — Wisdom & Works

        D' 4:1-12 — Enmity, Adultery, & Pride

      C' 4:13-5:6 — The Rich & "the Righteous One"

    B' 5:7-18 — Suffering, Patience, & Fruit

  A' 5:19-20 — Wandering, Sin, Death

At any rate, what is clear is that James's exposition of the power and influence of the tongue in the Christian community is at the literary center of this epistle. That brings us back to where we began. James is writing to the "brothers," those who are leading the fledgling Christian communities after the dispersion from Jerusalem following Stephen's execution. James is exhorting them to maturity in the way they guide their people with wise words designed to foster mercy, service, and patience, rather than anger, cursing, and fanatical violent action. Whatever one thinks of the literary structure, as we move through the epistle, we shall see that what holds everything together is the call to mature leadership in the context of exile, persecution, and the temptations to aggressive violence against their oppressors.

## 3

# How James Came to be Written

*When the Spirit of truth comes, he will guide you into all truth*
— John 16:13

*We will devote ourselves to prayer and to the service of the Word*
— Acts 6:4

Somewhere in the city of Jerusalem on a rooftop just a few years after the ascension of Jesus and the outpouring of the Spirit at Pentecost...

"...and just when are you men going to live up to your 'Sons of Thunder' reputation? Huh? A lot of us are wondering about you two." With that, the young man spat on the ground, turned away from James and John, climbed down the ladder, and stalked down the street toward the old city.

James turned from watching the young man and looked at his brother John. This was not the first time he saw that expression on John's face. What was it? Bewilderment mixed with sadness maybe, but then too, a hint of fear. James empathized. For months now they had been hearing similar angry speeches. The younger men especially were given to reacting to the persecution with a show of strength, even force. Every apostle in Jerusalem had been approached with similar proposals. But now the situation appeared to have gotten worse. This man had reported on recent activity that crossed the line. He shamelessly urged John and James to join with the violent resistance.

James was the first to speak. "John, do you think his report is credible? Or might he have been exaggerating in an attempt to get us to join the cause, so to speak? What do you think?"

John said, "Well, I don't think he's making it up. Perhaps he's embellished the incident somewhat, but I've heard similar stories this week from other brothers who've been driven out of Jerusalem."

"Wait. Similar stories?" James asked. "Do you mean different accounts of this one incident or similar incidents in different places?

"The latter, James. Many of the brothers are losing patience. They tell me they are no longer able to control angry disciples. I guess we should have seen this coming. As you know, since Jesus's disciples were driven out of Jerusalem last year, there has been a steady deterioration of order in our assemblies...Look, James, here comes brother Matthew, Peter, and Peter's deacon Mark. They don't look very happy."

James went to the ladder and called for the three to come up. After arranging a few more cushions for their friends to recline with them, John called down to his wife and asked whether there was an extra bottle of wine downstairs for the five of them. She said there wasn't, but that she would send Joseph down to the market before it closed to purchase a bottle of that wonderful vintage port from the Negev. "Thank you, dear," John said.

James turned toward the three visitors. "Why the dour looks, brothers?"

Matthew (Levi) spoke first. "You would think that as my account of our Lord's life circulates among the disciples, they would connect the dots with their own situation. But I don't see it happening. The brothers that do see the connection are being drowned out with these loudmouth young wannabes who counsel violent action against our persecutors."

James held up his hands and said, "Violent action? You've heard about it, too? We just heard a report from a brother who claims it has moved beyond mere talk. That the angry speeches are stirring up real violence against the Jerusalem authorities. John just now tells me that he's heard similar reports. I can see from your expressions that it must be true."

Peter said, "Yes, it's awful. In Bethel, the servant of an agent of the Sanhedrin who was on a mission to find disciples of Jesus has been killed. I don't know all the details. But the reliable word on the street is that the deed was done by a band of disciples that are being described as zealots of the Way."

"We've also heard," Mark added, "that some brothers are cursing the persecutors in their assemblies and privately organizing bands of men bound by oaths to establish the righteous rule of Jesus. What a mess."

Everyone was quiet for a while. Peter spoke up.

"Too many brothers apparently believe that the success of the Lord Jesus's cause must be measured as our apostate Jewish nation measures success. The logic runs something like this: If an assembly of disciples has no political influence or power, no material wealth or visible signs of prosperity, then how can they claim to be the Messiah's new people? So they mimic their rich, violent persecutors and think that by responding in kind they will prevail."

James said, "But this kind of attitude and behavior is diametrically opposed to the way of our Lord Jesus! If we disciples are going to covet the power and wealth of apostate Jerusalem, then we may as well just become pagan Romans. After all, Jerusalem simply mimics Rome these days. Can't the brothers at least discern what's going on? Such pride will cause the Lord's judgment to fall on us, not just Jerusalem and Rome. Friendship with the world is enmity with God!"

Peter said, "So we are all feeling the same way, I see. This must be a sign to us from the Spirit that something needs to be done."

"I agree," said Matthew. "Remember how we came to a consensus about this when I was commissioned to write my account of Jesus's ministry?" Everyone nodded. "Okay. I believe we need to write something to the scattered disciples now, specifically to our brothers who are shepherding the assemblies that have been formed outside of Jerusalem since the persecution and dispersion. Do you men agree?"

Peter: "Yes, Matthew, I believe this is exactly the right thing to do. And since your account of our Lord's ministry is now being copied and circulated, the new work ought to draw out the implications of our Lord's life and teaching for the persecuted church. People should be able to see the connection between Matthew's account and this new work's presentation of proper behavior for disciples of Jesus. Does everyone agree?"

John said, "Yes, I think the Spirit is moving us in precisely that direction. May I add something to the discussion?" Everyone paused to listen to John. "Good, thank you. This work ought to be a circular letter written to our brothers, the pastors and leaders of the persecuted assemblies. Every disciple will be able to learn from it, of course, but if we write the leaders and ask them to read and explain it to their people, we will be addressing the source of the most of our problems. These brothers are supposed to be mature, able to lead their people with meekness and mercy. They seem to want to rule like the Gentiles. Someone needs to remind them of the royal instruction given by our Lord in his mountainside sermon! If we want to continue to reign with the Lord Jesus, we better start acting like true kings and leave off imitating apostate Jewish blowhards and pagan Roman warmongers."

Peter: "Good idea, John. We need to make sure that this concern for how the brothers lead the congregations by means of their words is at the heart our exhortation. Words are powerful, but words will not save us. Our Lord told us 'wisdom is justified by her works.' We need to make sure that our appointed teachers understand this."

"Speaking of words," James interjected, "I would like to see us address the true heart and soul of faithful Christian piety during this time of affliction—caring for the needy, especially widows and orphans. The apostate Jewish authorities have imprisoned and even executed too many of our men, leaving behind their wives and children. Taking care of them now is our greatest need.

But the churches are being sidetracked from this by focusing on bringing down our persecutors. Stephen was a great example of how to address our enemies with faithful arguments, but also take care of the widows and needy. But I think that some bigmouths think that Stephen's death proved his ministry was ineffective. They don't seem to remember that Stephen was following in the footsteps of our Lord. Both Jesus and Stephen were murdered by envious Jewish rulers whose own failures were illuminated by Jesus and Stephen's righteous service to the poor. Our people can talk about faith all they want, but putting one's faith in Jesus means doing the kinds of works Jesus did. Stephen understood and practiced that. Perhaps we need to remind everyone of the uselessness of empty talk, even empty confessions of faith."

"Well, men, do we have anyone more passionately concerned about this than our brother James?" Peter asked. "I think not. After hearing James speak, I believe it is especially appropriate that James write this pastoral letter given that he now functions as the chief pastor of the assemblies in Jerusalem. Most of the men and congregations that have been displaced last year were under his shepherding care. It only makes sense to have him write these brothers. What do you all think?"

Everyone nodded vigorously, while James looked a bit apprehensive. "I'll need your help, men. For I'll need to avoid just the kind of angry speech that I wish to warn the brothers against. This is an honor, but I don't feel up to it."

Peter got to his feet and motioned everyone to gather around James. They did so, laying hands on him, and praying fervently. Peter petitioned the Lord to grant them all humility and patience during these great trials. He prayed that they would have the grace to count even these tribulations as blessings.

Mark prayed that the Lord would judge those apostate Jewish leaders who failed to honor the apostles and disciples of the Messiah. He prayed that the cries of the laborers that were sent to harvest the fields of Israel would reach the Lord of Armies and that he would act swiftly to bring in the reign of righteousness he promised.

Matthew prayed that the disciples of the Messiah would remember the suffering and patience of the prophets, and that the Lord would reward their steadfast faith with the harvest of righteousness they all longed for.

Finally, John prayed for his brother, that God would grant that through his words many who are wandering from the truth might be rescued and that this pastoral letter might be the means whereby the Lord would cover a multitude of sins.

When they had finished praying, James got up from his knees and saw his son Joseph standing by the ladder with the promised bottle of wine. After everyone had a glass, he raised his cup and blessed the God and Father of our Lord Jesus Christ. Everyone shouted, "Amen." They enjoyed each other's company for a little while longer, but James's mind was already busy composing the letter. He would begin to write early the next morning. He kept hearing the prayers that were spoken over him a few moments ago. The letter was taking shape in his mind.

4

# SUFFERING, WISDOM, & MATURITY

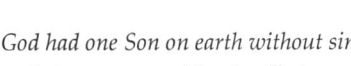

*God had one Son on earth without sin,*
*but never one without suffering.*
- Saint Augustine

*James 1:1*

¹James, a servant of God and of the Lord Jesus Christ, To the twelve tribes in the dispersion:

Greetings.

I have argued that there is strong evidence to believe that the James (Greek: *Jacob*) who pens this epistle is James the son of Zebedee—who, along with Peter and his brother John, was one of the three mighty men of Jesus, accompanying him in some of the most decisive and intimate moments in his ministry (Matt. 17:1; Mark 5:37; 9:2; 13:3; 14:33; Luke 8:51), and forming the cornerstones of the house that he built through his apostles (Eph. 2:20). It is possible that the author was James the brother of Jesus, but if so, this letter must have been written very early in his ministry, before the Jerusalem Council, and only a few years after the great persecution of the apostolic church that is described in Acts 8:1 and following.

Whether one believes James the brother of Jesus or James the son of Zebedee authored this epistle ought not to be a matter of orthodoxy. The epistle has been read and expounded with profit by those scholars, pastors, and simple Christians who took James the brother of Jesus to be the author. Both men were leaders of the early persecuted church, and both would have commanded the authority necessary to pen an epistle that would eventually be canonized as part of the inspired corpus of writings we call the New Testament. James the son of Zebedee, however, is ultimately preferred because his authority is likely to have been more significant in the early period which this letter seems to originate from, and he would have had firsthand access to the words of Jesus, whose sayings form a deeply significant backdrop to this letter (arguably more so than any other New Testament epistle). As I hope to show, reading this epistle as one of the earliest Christian documents written to the infant church in the throes of a severe crisis only a few years after Pentecost provides surprisingly productive insights into some otherwise opaque passages.

James writes to the "twelve tribes in the Dispersion (*diaspora*)." There are convincing reasons to believe that he is writing to an early group of Jewish converts to the Christian faith who are experiencing brutal persecution for their new allegiance to Jesus.

First, the Greek word *diaspora* also occurs in Acts 8:1,4 and 11:19, each time referring to the group of Jewish Christians driven out of Jerusalem because of the violent Jewish persecution following the murder of Stephen. This Christian *diaspora* is not merely a "spiritual" dispersion, but those who have experienced a specific event in the early history of the church. Because of the persecution that followed the martyrdom of Stephen, the Jerusalem church became a *dispersed* church. James's audience would, in the nature of the case, be a predominantly Jewish audience because the early Christians were converts from Judaism in Jerusalem, disciples driven out of that city by the leaders of the Jews. But James addresses them as the "twelve tribes of the *diaspora*" not because they are exiled Jews but because they are members of the new Israel who have been driven from their city.

Second, in verse 18, James refers to his audience as being "a kind of firstfruits." The Greek word *aparkea* (απαρχην) is also used in Romans 16:5 and 1 Corinthians 16:15 to refer to the first converts in a region. Its use here most likely indicates that James addresses his letter to some of the first converts of Christ's church from among the Jews. As we shall see, their behavior at this early stage of the Christian history will set the pattern for the future of the church. The way they behave in these difficult times will either set the whole future church on the path to maturity and victory as followers of the crucified and risen Christ or their failure to patiently endure their present trials will take them off the narrow path blazed first by their Lord and Savior Jesus. The stakes were extremely high.[15]

Third, the references to trials and sufferings throughout James's epistle point to a context of severe persecution (James 1:2, 12; 2:6b-7; 5:4, 6, 10, 14). Because of the other textual reasons to take this as an early letter, the best explanation for that persecution is the early opposition of the Jews instead of a later period of local or Roman persecution.

Fourth, as we shall argue in the body of the commentary, the way James the son of Zebedee addresses the question of faith and works in 2:14-26 makes more sense in a context other than that which Paul addresses in his epistles. It is also different than the way James the Just resolves the conflict when he presides over the Jerusalem Council recorded in Acts 15. If James is writing before the Jerusalem Council and before Paul's clarification of the freedom of Christians from specific legal requirements of the Old Covenant ("works of the law" such as circumcision, food laws, sabbaths, etc.), this would account for James's use of the language of "justification by works" (James 2:21, 25). The later controversy dealt with by Paul had to do with the place of distinctively Jewish "works of the law" and their place in the new order established by Jesus. In James 2, however, the "works" are not "works of the law"

---

15 As it turned out, the apostolic and post-apostolic church did heed the warning of James. The patience and perseverance of the church resulted in their cultural ascendency. See Alan Kreider, *The Patient Ferment of the Early Church: The Improbable Rise of Christianity in the Roman Empire* (Grand Rapids: Baker Academic, 2016).

but rather common Christian acts of love and service required of all believers—works that evidence a genuine "faith that saves" (2:14). Those who claim to have "faith" without following Jesus's way of life are shown to be fools that cherish a useless and dead "faith" (2:20-22). James is addressing a completely different problem than Paul.

Though there is much more that might be said on this issue of author, audience and setting for James's epistle (and you may refer to the introduction and the appendix in this commentary for more detailed arguments), it is most likely that in these first verses of his epistle James the son of Zebedee, the presiding elder in Jerusalem, greets the early church, acknowledging their dispersion and persecution but also asserting his pastoral authority to address their situation. James wrote to the scattered members of his church to warn them that, during their geographic *diaspora*, they had to take care not to wander from the way marked out by Jesus himself. James's letter performs the kind of restorative act he commends at the close of his letter: He is attempting to turn wandering "brothers" from the errors of their ways (5:19-20).

James uses the direct address "my brothers" more than twelve times. Some modern English translations feel the need to add "and sisters." But if James wanted to, he could have easily written "my brothers and sisters." In his discussion of faith and works in James 2 he writes, "If a brother or sister..." (2:15). These "brothers" are the male leaders of the church. The leadership of these Christian communities was considered a "brotherhood" of elders, pastors, deacons, etc. (Acts 15:23). We can see this in any number of places in the New Testament. For example, Paul ends his first letter to the Corinthian church this way:

> Now concerning our brother Apollos, I strongly urged him to visit you with the other brothers, but it was not at all his will....

It is true that theologically speaking the entire church is a brotherhood. John's first letter is filled with examples of this idea. And so often "brothers" refers to the entire church family. Even so, there are many times in the New Testament when "brother" or "brothers" refers to the male leadership of the various churches (Acts 15:23; Rom. 16:14, 17, 23; 2 Cor. 8:18, 23, 12:18; Col. 4:7; 2 Thess. 3:6; 1 Pet. 5:12; 3 John 3, 5, 10; Rev. 22:9). As we shall see throughout the epistle, James addresses the leaders of his scattered church in order to call them to maturity in the way they lead their communities, by their words and by their actions.

It may be helpful at this point to pause and imagine the kinds of people that James is addressing, the place in life they found themselves in. We may assume that at least the very great majority of his audience were converted Jews. Born into the world of first-century Judaism, these men and women grew up steeped in the stories of the Hebrew Scriptures and the ritual life and worship of Israel. They felt the tension of the glorious promises of the prophets and the reality of their lives under the oppression of their faithless Jewish leaders. They lived in a community that longed for redemption, and vindication before the nations by their God. And they had every reason to hope that the new Lord of heaven and earth (Matt. 28:18-20) would shortly begin to set things right in the world.

At some point, through different circumstances, each of them began to believe that Jesus of Nazareth was the one through whom that redemption and vindication had come. In his death, and especially his resurrection, they saw the righteousness of God enacted in history and believed that the latter days which the prophets had spoken of were coming to pass in their own times. Throughout the literature of the New Testament, there are numerous references to "the last days" (Acts 2:17; Heb. 1:2), "the end time(s)" (1 Pet. 1:20; 1 John 2:18; Jude 18), "the last hour" (1 John 2:18), "the latter days (or times)" (1 Tim. 4:1), and "the end of the world" (1 Cor. 10:11; Heb. 9:26). They did not expect the end of the physical world and human history, but the end of the old age. The apostolic leaders of the Christian church taught that they were living in an era that would see the end of the entire Old World. Jesus had taught them to expect this in their generation (Matt. 23:36; 24:34; Mark 13:30; Luke 21:32). The kingdom of God was at hand, as Jesus had proclaimed repeatedly in his three-year ministry (Matt. 3:2; 4:17; 10:7; etc.).

On the day of Pentecost, when it is likely that at least some of the audience of this letter first bowed the knee to their new Lord, they saw the power of God demonstrated in their own lives and before their very eyes. Surely, it would be surprising if the hearts of these men and women, who now tasted what they and their fathers and mothers had waited so patiently for, as promised by the prophets, soon began to swell with expectation for the new age that the resurrection and ascension of Jesus and the pouring out of the Holy Spirit on all flesh would surely bring. At the very least, it would be a time of repentance for Israel. But even more than that, Israel's repentance and acceptance of the Gospel would result in the world-wide victory of Jesus's kingdom (Dan. 7:13-24; Matt. 28:18-20). The true God, the Father of Jesus the Messiah, who had vindicated Jesus so decisively in his victory over death, would also vindicate his church. To understand the admonitions of the New Testament writers, especially James, we must appreciate the heightened expectations of these early believers.

But in those early days after Pentecost, when the last words of Jesus were still ringing in the ears of his followers ("All authority has been given to me…therefore go and make disciples of all nations…"), things did not happen the way many of them expected. Instead of repentance and trust from the Jewish leaders and people, after an initial period of growth and conversions, the followers of Jesus, beginning with Stephen in Acts 7, were oppressed, abused, and murdered by leaders of the religion and culture in which they had grown up. Before long, the Jewish persecution in Jerusalem dispersed these young disciples of Jesus across Israel and even as far as Phoenicia, Cyprus, and Antioch (Acts 11:19), forcing them to leave their families, homes, synagogues, culture, and livelihoods. It is this confused, angry, and refugee people that James greets in this letter, huddled in small communities across the ancient world.

## Maturity is the Goal

*James 1:2-4*

²Count it all joy, my brothers, when you meet trials of various kinds, ³for you know that the testing of your faith produces steadfastness. ⁴And let steadfastness have its mature effect, that you may be mature and complete, lacking in nothing.

These statements serve as a sort of summing up of the purpose of James's epistle. His desire for the dispersed, persecuted Christian communities to which he writes is that they would reckon their trials as joy, for it is their trials and the testing of their faith that will lead to their steadfastness, and finally to their individual and communal maturity and completion. "Trials" (πειρασμοις) does not refer to specific kinds of suffering, but rather to the process of testing itself. The sense of verse 2-3 is generic with reference to the type of suffering that is experienced, but specific in pinpointing the process of suffering, trials, and testing as the experience which the James's audience should count as joy.

Therefore, even though our suffering and trials may be different in kind than those of James's first audience, his words still speak to us, for the process of our suffering and trials are the same. The primary example for us in this regard is Jesus, who "learned obedience through the things he suffered" (Heb. 5:8), who endured the cross itself for "the joy that was set before him" (Heb. 12:2). Like Christ, we are to see our trials with the eyes of faith and consider them to be part of God's good plan for our lives, embracing and even rejoicing during them. When we "look to Jesus" and see how his story ended, how his loving Father was behind everything he suffered, then we by faith understand that Jesus has become "the founder and maturer (τελειωτην) of our faith" (Heb. 12:2).

The Greek word translated "full" and "perfect" in many English versions in verse 4 is *telios* (τελειον), and it has to do more with maturity than some kind of moral perfection. Indeed, in this context, the *telios* that James desires for the church to which he writes might simply be described as reaching *the end* that God has designed for them: "let steadfastness have its mature (*telios*) effect." The testing and trials which James describes in this section might be compared to a smelting fire, which purifies (and thus completes, or makes perfect) pieces of metals that enter its heat (1 Pet. 1:7).

James's purpose is not to encourage his audience to enter into the fire, but rather to rejoice when they feel its flames. He takes the existence of their testing and trials for granted, recognizing that God is the one who purifies and makes complete his sons and daughters—not to confirm or deny the genuineness of their faith, but rather *to lovingly bring their trust in him to maturity*. James refers to "maturity" at least five times in the opening sections of his epistle (James 1:4, 17, 25; 2:22; 3:2). Unfortunately, this is often mistranslated as "perfect." But it is not perfection but maturity that is in view here. If these newborn believers want to participate in the coming of Jesus's righteous kingdom, they must "be mature and complete" in order to effectively reign with Christ as his agents of world transformation. And that will only come about when they follow Jesus's way of humility and self-effacing service during severe persecution.

As we will find so often throughout this epistle, in his admonition to rejoice in the midst of trials, James echoes the words of Jesus, who said to James and the other disciples:

> "Blessed are you when others revile you and persecute you and utter all kinds of evil against you falsely on my account. Rejoice and be glad, for your reward is great in heaven, for so they persecuted the prophets who were before you" (Matt. 5:11-12).

## Suffering, Wisdom, & Maturity

In echoing the words of his teacher, James is not only locating the authority for his exhortation in the words of Christ, but he also calls to their mind the suffering of their Messiah. Jesus predicted that those who followed after him would suffer as he suffered:

> Then Jesus told his disciples, "If anyone would come after me, let him deny himself and take up his cross and follow me" (Matt. 16:24).

This is exactly what is happening in the lives of James and those to whom he is writing. But far from being simply a morbid parallel between the life of Jesus and those who follow him, James echoes the words of Jesus in order to exhort his readers to remember that it was through suffering that the Christ also reached the end (*telos*) that God had designed for him.

> Although he was a son, he learned obedience through what he suffered, and once made mature (*telios*)...he was ordained by God a high priest after the order of Melchizedek [King of Righteousness] (Heb. 5:8).

Notice how Jesus's endurance of suffering led to maturity that resulted in his being given kingly rule. Indeed, the vindication of Jesus by God in his resurrection and his coronation as King in his ascension is the reason James can exhort his flock to count suffering as joy. For the follower of Christ, suffering is not a gift simply because it "builds character" (as our culture might say), but because suffering and death (physically, spiritually, emotionally) is the Christ-appointed path to vindication, maturity, and a new empowered life. And Christians are called to be co-rulers with Christ: "if we remain steadfast (υπομενομεν), we will also reign with him" (2 Tim. 2:12).

In the path toward maturity and completeness, steadfastness is a necessary part of the journey for the follower of Jesus. According to James's logic, it is in the testing (i.e., smelting fire) of faith that steadfastness is produced, and when that steadfastness has its effect upon the believer, he is mature and complete, lacking in nothing. *Hupomone* (υπομονη), the Greek word for "steadfastness," appears twice in the teaching of Jesus in the Gospels, and the way he uses the word is helpful for understanding James's meaning. In Luke 8, Jesus explains the meaning of the parable of the sower (or soils) to his disciples. After describing the fate of the seed that fell on the path, the rocks, and among the thorns, Jesus explains:

> As for that in the good soil, they are those who, hearing the word, hold it fast in an honest and good heart, and bear fruit with patience (υπομονη) (Luke 8:15).

In Luke 21, Jesus describes the judgment that is to come upon Jerusalem in its destruction at the hands of Rome in 21:10-11, 20-24. But he warns his disciples in 21:12-19:

> Before all this they will lay their hands on you and persecute you, delivering you up to the synagogues and prisons, and you will be brought before kings and governors for my name's sake. This will be your opportunity to bear witness. Settle it therefore in your minds not to meditate beforehand how to answer, for I will give you a mouth and wisdom, which none of your adversaries will be able to withstand or contradict. You will be delivered up even by parents and brothers and relatives and friends, and some of you they will put to death. You will be hated by all for my name's sake. But not a hair of your head will perish. By your endurance (υπομονη) you will gain your lives.

The setting that Jesus prophesies for his disciples so closely resembles the context of the audience to which James writes that it is difficult to believe he does not have the words of Jesus in his mind as he writes James 1:2-4. Just as the Messiah had predicted, persecution and suffering and even death have come upon the followers of Jesus after his death and resurrection. Now James writes to Jesus's church, not flinching away from the reality of their suffering, but echoing Jesus's words and exhorting his flock to steadfastness. For steadfastness is the only way to travel the path of which Jesus prophesied and walked himself. Indeed, as Jesus said, it is in steadfastness that his followers will gain their lives, for it is only as suffering and death are embraced and endured that resurrection and vindication may come.

But, like the seed thrown upon the good soil, steadfastness is also what it means to be complete and whole as a disciple of Jesus, the one who bears fruit, the one whose faith is mature and vibrant and strong. At the end of his letter, James uses *hupomone* to refer to an Old Testament saint who is paradigmatic for the processes of testing and maturity that both James and Jesus describe—Job (5:11). The connection between the life of Job and the steadfastness described in 1:3-4 will be taken up in a later section, but it is significant that James's letter begins and ends with an exhortation for his audience to remain steadfast. Taken together with the way that the words of Jesus illumine the meaning of *hupomone*, we might say that to encourage steadfastness in those to whom he writes is the primary goal of James's epistle (both for the original audience as well those who hear his words today), and the rest of James's letter is both an exposition of what it means to *"let steadfastness have its full effect, that you may be mature and complete, lacking in nothing"* as well as a warning about all the ways their misbehavior is a betrayal of mature steadfastness.

---

## WISDOM FOR THE ASKING

*James 1:5-8*

⁵If any of you lacks wisdom, let him ask God, who gives generously to all without reproach, and it will be given him. ⁶But let him ask in faith, with no doubting, for the one who doubts is like a wave of the sea that is driven and tossed by the wind. ⁷For that person must not suppose that he will receive anything from the Lord; ⁸ he is a double-minded man, unstable in all his ways.

Note well that James does not say to ask for freedom from trials or for an easy life of wealth and comfort. Rather, in the face of his difficult exhortation in 1:2-4, he instructs his listeners to ask for wisdom—wisdom to know how to endure trials and suffering by rejoicing in them.

James here draws on the biblical tradition of the nature of wisdom, which has among its primary concerns teaching how to suffer, how to endure trouble and even death with trust in the vindication of God. This kind of wisdom is found most clearly in the book of Job, who endures the worst kind of suffering with steadfast faith in God's righteousness. The path of joy in suffering that Jesus walked and calls his church to follow behind him is not an easy road, and James exhorts us to plead for wisdom from God to embrace our calling with endurance.

The wisdom that James says comes from God is not some mystical insight or a Zen-like detachment from suffering by transcendentally focusing on heaven. Rather, we should assume that James understood wisdom in the same way the Old Testament saints did—the art of living righteously in light of the fear of Yahweh. This is a wisdom that does not deny suffering or persecution but admits its reality while also affirming the deeper reality of the kingship of Jesus Christ. And godly wisdom is certainly not the skill or ability to overcome all suffering and trouble in one's life. Ecclesiastes, Solomon's book of wisdom, is all about the limitations of wisdom in a vaporous world that is beyond our ability to leverage or control. Everything is "vapor" and we cannot hope to "shepherd the wind" (Eccl. 1:2, 14, 17).[16] Only the Lord has that kind of all-encompassing control. Suffering and persecution belong to a class of experiences that cannot always be fixed. Modern Americans need to learn this.

Of course, wisdom is not only needed to endure suffering well. Wisdom is also gained *through* such endurance. In this sense, it can be understood to be parallel to *telios* in James 1:4.

---

[16] See my *A Table in the Mist: Ecclesiastes Through New Eyes* (Monroe, LA: Athanasius Press, 2006) for a fuller exposition of this theme in Ecclesiastes.

That is, the man who is mature and complete is also wise, and his wisdom and maturity is a gift from God who preserves him in his suffering. Thus, the way God gives wisdom to the one who asks is intrinsically linked to the *nature* of wisdom itself—it is learned through the practice of suffering, not through miraculous implantation of knowledge. This is why there is often little or no connection between raw intellectual prowess and biblical wisdom, and the wisest person in a congregation is more often than not one of the oldest and simplest—because wisdom is a both a gift from God (not something which can be simply acquired by reading a book or taking a class), and because the only way for the gift to be appropriated is through fearing Yahweh in midst of trouble and strife.

We know that obedience in suffering is the way that wisdom is given by God because it is the manner in which Jesus himself learned maturity. The author of Hebrews tells us that Jesus was "made mature (*telios*) through suffering" (Heb. 2:10), and again that Jesus learned obedience and was made mature through suffering (Heb. 5:8-9). Since Jesus is the embodiment of true humanity, he demonstrates the path to maturity and wisdom to those who follow him. When Jesus calls us to "follow him," we should be ready and willing to learn wisdom through suffering. This pattern is a crucial dimension of Christian discipleship.

There are no shortcuts in the quest for wisdom. Mature wisdom is not so much an attribute we either have or don't have, but rather a many-layered character trait formed over time—a spiritual muscle built up by many periods of steadfast resistance. Like a football coach who leads his team in two-a-day summer practices, God gives the gift of wisdom by bringing us safely through trials, preserving and upholding us while also calling us on to go further than we thought we might. When I was in high school, I never really understood or appreciated why football practice had to be so excruciatingly painful. It wasn't until I was much older that I understood the sign above the entrance to our locker room: No Pain, No Gain.

Consider a child that is nourished by his mother's milk and must move on to solid food as he grows older. Wisdom requires that he use his mouth and teeth, grinding down his bones as he consumes stronger and better food. Indeed, it is wisdom and maturity that the writer of Hebrews has in mind when he writes, "Everyone who lives on milk is unskilled in the word of righteousness, since he is a child. But solid food is for the mature (*telios*), for those who have their powers of discernment trained by constant practice to discern good and evil" (Heb 5:13-14).

James 1:6 tells us that the one who asks for wisdom should ask "in faith," without doubting. Though most standard English translations render this "Let him ask in faith," it is probably better understood to mean, "Let him ask in (or with) faithfulness." Understanding the manner in which wisdom is given (through sustained trust and obedience in God in the midst of trials) helps us to see why one crucial requirement for reception of the gift of maturity is *faithfulness without doubting*.

When speaking of faith and doubt here, James does not refer to constant intellectual assent on the one hand and wavering intellectual assent on the other, as these words are commonly used in Christian circles today. Rather, by faith or faithfulness, he means a simple fear of Yahweh that shows itself in obedience to his Word through enduring life's troubles. We should understand "doubt" to mean asking for wisdom from God with the expectation that it will be given quickly and easily and without the commitment to endure the process of being mature and wise by learning obedience through suffering that Jesus has shown us. One who asks for wisdom in this naive way is indeed like a wave of the sea that is tossed by the wind, unable to sustain itself, driven in every way by his circumstances without the steady commitment of trust in God.

The one who doubts in this way may also be compared to the fool in Proverbs, who believes that wisdom is quickly and easily acquired and does not care for the hard process of correction and submissive obedience. A fool can be crushed like grain "in a mortar with a pestle" and yet his folly will not depart from him because he does not accept the discipline of suffering and trials (Prov. 27:22). One who accepts suffering as from the loving hand of God the Father will faithfully endure the trials because he believes they are paradoxical evidence of God's loving purpose. The Father matures his sons in just this way. We have already noted how the author of Hebrews sets before his readers Jesus as the true Son of the Father who "learned obedience" and was "made mature" through suffering (Heb. 2:10; 5:8-9). Later in that same epistle, he links Jesus's experience with the experience of all believers:

> Consider him who endured from sinners such hostility against himself, so that you may not grow weary or fainthearted. In your struggle against sin you have not yet resisted to the point of shedding your blood. And have you forgotten the exhortation that addresses you as sons?
>
> "My son, do not regard lightly the discipline of the Lord,
>
> nor be weary when reproved by him.
>
> For the Lord disciplines the one he loves,
>
> and chastises every son whom he receives."
>
> It is for discipline that you have to endure. God is treating you as sons. For what son is there whom his father does not discipline? If you are left without discipline, in which all have participated, then you are illegitimate children and not sons. Besides this, we have had earthly fathers who disciplined us and we respected them. Shall we not much more be subject to the Father of spirits and live? For they disciplined us for a short time as it seemed best to them, but he disciplines us for our good, that we may share his holiness. For the moment all discipline seems painful rather than pleasant, but later it yields the peaceful fruit of righteousness to those who have been trained by it (Heb. 12:3-11).

A person who asks for wisdom and maturity without the faithfulness to endure the hard process of learning "will not receive anything" from God, not because of God's stinginess, but because of the person's own unwillingness to participate in the reception of the gift. Yahweh is a good and liberal God (James 1:16-17), who longs to give the gift of wisdom to his sons and daughters (Prov. 2:7). But as Christian parents eventually learn, the gift of wisdom and maturity can only be given to our children through discipline and love as they grow into men and women—not protecting them forever from struggles and hardship, but faithfully loving them as they acquire the gift of wisdom during trials.

The person who doubts is "double-minded" and "unstable" because he is inconsistent in his behavior. He asks for wisdom but is unwilling to endure and remain steadfast in order to receive it. He is, as it were, of two minds—he desires wisdom, but wants it on his own terms and so does not truly desire the gift for which he asks. The Proverbs of Solomon contain instruction for his sons in the acquisition of wisdom. And he repeatedly warns them that one must fear Yahweh, accept rebuke and discipline, before one can hope to be wise. Only the humble, faithful son who humbly endures trials can hope to gain the honor of being judged as a wise man (Prov. 15:33).

Like a man who desires a good marriage but constantly tears down his wife and spends his evenings in front of the television or computer without conversation, he longs for something he himself is preventing by his actions. It is important to note the difference between the man who asks in faith for wisdom and the one who is double-minded is not merely their internal posture toward God as much as it is the way their hearts are demonstrated in their behavior toward him. To ask for wisdom with faithfulness does not mean that there will not be times when we struggle to believe that God is good and faithful, but rather that we persevere in faith despite these feelings. Job's unfaithful wife nagged him to "curse God and die." But Job wisely rejected that option: "You speak as one of the foolish women would speak. Shall we receive good from God, and shall we not receive calamity" (Job 2:9). Later on, berated by his faithless friends, Job will confess, "Though he slay me, yet will I trust him" (Job 13:15).

## Encouragement for the Impoverished Believer

*James 1:9-11*

⁹Let the lowly brother boast in his exaltation, ¹⁰and the rich in his humiliation, because like a flower of the grass he will pass away. ¹¹For the sun rises with its scorching heat and withers the grass; its flower falls, and its beauty perishes. So also will the rich man fade away in the midst of his pursuits.

The double mindedness that James speaks of in verse 8 is made concrete in verses 9-11. He warns against seeking an escape from persecution and suffering by striving for earthly power and possessions. It would have been easy for James's readers to envy and long for the wealth and strength of the Jews who were coming against them in power and had driven them from Jerusalem. It is important to note that throughout this epistle "the rich" are the *theocratically* rich, not just generic wealthy people. The affluent Jewish authorities are the ones in possession of the "gold and silver" (of the Temple) and have lived gloriously on the land (5:3, 5). These early disciples are tempted to cater to their persecutors in order to engineer some relief from their suffering (James 2:1-7). Here James provides some initial encouragement to the humble to be patient and wait for God's coming righteous judgment against their seemingly invincible enemies.

Many of these persecuted, dispersed disciples had likely sold their possessions in the early days of the Church, recorded in Acts 2:42-47, because of the need of those in their midst, as well as their belief in Jesus's prophetic warning that Jerusalem would destroyed (Matt. 24; Mark 13; and Luke 21). In addition, all of those to whom James wrote left behind families, homes, and their livelihoods to flee the persecution of the Jews after the murder of Stephen (Acts 8:1-3; 11:19). Many of them were tempted with by a perverse vision: if only we could acquire wealth and power, the Church would gain the ability to resist the oppression of the Jews. But James warns them against the danger of trusting in these earthly means of security by reminding them that riches do not last and man's power will fade. This is particularly true of the apostate Jews, whose coming demise John the Baptist and Jesus had clearly prophesied throughout their ministries (Matt. 3:7-12; 23:29-39, to cite two explicit examples).

In reading James's words here, we should be reminded of Paul's warning against riches in 1 Timothy 6:9-10, where he writes,

> But those who desire to be rich fall into temptation, into a snare, into many senseless and harmful desires that plunge people into ruin and destruction. For the love of money is a root of all kinds of evil. It is through this craving that some have wandered away from the faith and pierced themselves with many pangs.

James does not speak here against riches in and of themselves, but rather the desire to acquire riches (or an unwillingness to relinquish wealth) for the purpose of escaping the way of suffering that Jesus has marked out for those who follow him. In his description of the fate of human trust in riches, James echoes the vocabulary of Jesus's image of the rocky ground in the parable of the soils:

> Other seeds fell on rocky ground, where they did not have much soil, and immediately they sprang up, since they had no depth of soil, but when the sun rose they were scorched. And since they had no root they withered away (Matt. 13:5-6).

To most readers of this commentary, James's words should cause us to pause and consider the ways in which our heart's commitments are revealed in the way that we think about wealth and possessions. Even more pointed, however, is the lesson we should learn about ecclesiastical wealth and power politics. Are we double-minded in our requests to God for maturity and wisdom? Are we willing to give up our wealth and power to follow Jesus, or are we torn between placing our trust in riches instead of God? Do we long for all the wealth, power, and influence that apostate, unorthodox churches seem to enjoy? Are we willing to put aside comfort, knowing that human wealth will fade away, and trust in God's vindication in history and at the Last Day? The Lord's people have had to learn this lesson repeatedly throughout history. Psalm 73 is a wonderful example of the kinds of struggles which believers faced under arrogant oppressors.

James 1:9-11 is not only a warning to his readers against the dangers and temptations involved in envying their wealthy persecutors. His words are also an encouragement to them in their lowliness and poverty—a prophetic warning that the power and influence of those who oppress the Church will fade away in the searing heat of God's judgment. For at this early time in the history of the Church, the Jews who are murdering and imprisoning the Christians are the ones who have all the resources, all the property, the temple itself, and the power structure of a well-organized religion under the protection of Rome (Matt. 10:17; 23:34; Acts 22:19; 26:11). As we shall see at the end of James's epistle, these theocratically rich and powerful oppressors have "condemned" and "murdered the righteous one" (James 5:6).

In contrast, the Jewish Christian converts to whom James writes have no power, no property, and very little money, for they have left behind their homes, possessions, and families to flee the violence of the Jews after the death of Stephen. But James writes these words to encourage the Christians to base their confidence in the future, not on material or physical power, but rather in God's promises to judge their oppressors and vindicate them in their faithfulness. At the end of his epistle, James promises that "the coming of the Lord is near" (5:7). They should therefore be patient and wait for the Lord who is "standing at the door" ready to execute justice for his oppressed church (5:9).

Of course, the problem with the Jews whom James addresses is not simply their riches and power, but the way they are using their riches and power to persecute the defenseless Bride of Christ. Rather than viewing this passage as a blanket condemnation of the rich, we should understand it rather as an encouragement to a suffering church and a word of judgment against those who would use their positions and wealth to abuse her. Like the grass withers in the heat of summer and the flower fades without rain, these rich Jews who have set themselves against God by persecuting his Church will fade away and not stand under the heat of God's judgment (1:11).

The fulfillment of these forecasts comes in the events of A.D. 70, when Jesus uses the Roman Empire to destroy apostate Judaism. In that day, the apostate Jewish nation was struck down for their rebellion against the Messiah and their violence against his followers, and both Jesus's prophetic promise (Matt. 24) and James's words here were vindicated. But at the time which James wrote his letter, the Church would have been strongly tempted to believe that their lack of power and poverty and suffering was an indication that they had been mistaken to leave the relative comfort and safety of traditional Judaism. And so James exhorts his readers to boast, or glory (*kauchaomai*), in their lowliness—for God will lift them up and vindicate them over against their powerful oppressors. "Blessed are the poor in spirit for theirs is the kingdom of heaven....Blessed are the meek, for they shall inherit the earth" (Matt. 5:3, 5).

James's words have a clear application for Christians today in nations like the Sudan, Saudi Arabia, Afghanistan, or India, where the Church is marginalized and persecuted and the temptation to return to the fold of Islam or Hinduism must be very strong for those who convert to Christianity. Members of the body of Christ in those countries should be encouraged by the words of James, because the promise that he gives to his readers is also applicable today—though the Church may be pressed down by the rich and powerful ones who oppose it, Islamic and Hindu oppressors will also fade away and wither under the heat of God's judgment, just as the Jewish oppressors of James's day did. And for American Christians who are increasingly marginalized by a wealthy and powerful ruling class, the message is the same.

## The Promise of Ruling With Jesus

*James 1:12*

> ¹²Blessed is the man who remains steadfast under trial, for when he has stood the test he will receive the crown of life, which God has promised to those who love him.

Evoking the words of Jesus at the Sermon on the Mount, James gives his readers a beatitude that flows from the teaching of his master and addresses their situation perfectly: *"Blessed is the man who remains steadfast under trial, for when he has stood the test he will receive the crown of life, which God has promised to those who love him."* Though James is echoing the form of Jesus's beatitudes, he is also changing the content for his own purposes. Instead of using a plural noun to refer to the one who is blessed in his beatitude, James uses the singular word for "man." In using this singular form, James also reminds his readers of Psalm 1 and the description of the blessed man there. Indeed, in a sense, James is giving a new perspective on the blessed man from that Psalm, a new way of thinking of his blessedness—not only is he one who avoids wickedness and meditates on the law of Yahweh, but he is also one who remains steadfast under persecution and receives the crown of life.

Who then is this blessed man? There may be some intentional ambiguity here, for there is certainly a sense in which James is giving his readers this beatitude with the expectation that they will seek to conform their lives to its pattern. But there is only one man who truly fits this description—Jesus himself. It is Jesus who faithfully endured the trial of persecution at the hands of powerful Jewish oppressors throughout his ministry, culminating in his torture and murder at the hands of wicked men. It is Jesus who waited patiently for God to vindicate him in his suffering without uttering a bitter or vengeful word, going to his death like a lamb to the slaughter. And it is Jesus who burst forth from the tomb three days after his violent death, receiving the crown of life from his Father in his ascension to heaven's throne.

In modern evangelicalism, the letter of James is often categorized as focused nearly exclusively on the relationship between works and faith and having a minimalist conception of Christ and his work. But perhaps part of the reason James is often understood in that way is because we have a truncated view of Jesus. In this brief and concise statement, James gives his readers a deeply complex and powerful Christology, suggesting a more nuanced understanding of the purpose of Jesus's death and life. When theologians have studied Jesus, one of the questions most often asked is, "Why did Jesus live and die?" Of course, the most common answer to this question is summed up by simply quoting Jesus's words in John 3:16: *"For God so loved the world, he gave his only Son, that whoever believes in him should not perish but have eternal life."* In other words, Jesus lived and died because God loved the world, and so that individual men and women might believe in Jesus and go to heaven. Of course, there is a sense in which this answer is perfectly right.

But there is more we can say on this subject, and James suggests here one of the ways we might further answer this question. James is saying that at least one of the reasons Jesus lived and died was to steadfastly endure trials and suffering, thus receiving the crown of life and God's blessing. In this way, Jesus, acting as the fulfillment of humanity, was enthroned as the mature and complete man, a new Adamic king, and as such brings those who are united to him to maturity as well. "In bringing many sons to glory it was fitting that God made the Forerunner [αρχηγο] of their deliverance mature through suffering" (Heb. 2:10). For God's purpose in sending his Son to the world was not simply to reconcile individual creatures to himself despite their sin and rebellion, but to bring about the completion and maturity of humanity through the decisive and faithful actions of Jesus.

In the life of Jesus, the story of the Old Testament is fulfilled — simply put, God created man to rule the earth with him as kings. But Adam was not content to wait patiently, to endure steadfastly the maturing process God set for him, and in eating from the fruit of the tree of knowledge of good and evil Adam grasped for kingship before it was given to him. The rest of the story of the Old Testament can be seen as God faithfully training and maturing humanity—preparing man for his created place as king, ruling with God himself. But again and again, mankind failed to endure steadfastly the trials and suffering that are a necessary part of his maturation.

There are a few glimpses of mature men in the Old Testament—men who faithfully and patiently endured suffering, waiting for God to vindicate them and make them kings. David is the best example of the mature man that God desired. Anointed king of Israel as a boy, David was content to wait and faithfully submit to God's discipline and correction, never lifting his hand against Saul, even at the risk of his life. Through those years of suffering and running for his life, David was matured and made into the man who would rule God's kingdom. And even though in the end, David was not the one in whom humanity would be definitively matured, God promised him that it would be from his line that the mature man, the king, would come. And that man was Jesus. Like Adam, Jesus was tempted by Satan to grasp his throne before his time had come (Matt. 4:8-10). Like David, Jesus endured faithfully and waited for God to grant him the gift of ruling over humanity. Like the prophets before him, Jesus endured violence and conspiracies against him, finally going meekly and humbly to his death at the hand of violent, immature humanity. And in his resurrection, Jesus's maturity was completed, and he was finally and decisively made King (see Phil. 2:5-10).

And now, James is saying to his hearers, especially the "brothers," blessed are you when you faithfully endure trials, for you will receive "the crown of life"—we will be made mature and complete and we too will rule with Jesus our King. Is it simply an accident or incidental coincidence that the Greek word James uses for crown here is *stephanos*? For the life of Stephen ("the crowned one") is a paradigm for the life of suffering and maturation that James is exhorting these early Christians to pursue. Stephen was a faithful follower of Jesus, and when the same men who put Jesus to death conspired against Stephen as well, he patiently endured their threats and in his last breath forgave them for their violence, faithfully following Jesus until the end. By invoking the name of Stephen, James invites his readers to endure as Stephen did, to follow him as he followed Jesus. Remember, too, the death of Stephen was the catalyst for the persecution that exiled and dispersed the Jewish disciples from Jerusalem (Acts 8:1; 11:19; James 1:1).

God's gift of maturity for his children through steadfast endurance of trials for the purpose of ruling is the central theme of James. Spoken into a context of suffering and persecution, James commands his flock to regard their trials with joy, knowing that in their troubles God is disciplining them, bringing them to maturity, and making them complete as they endure. Therefore, James calls the new instruction and example of Jesus "the royal" or "the kingly law" (James 2:8). Self-effacing service to others, as exemplified in King Jesus, is the end for all who are being transformed into his image.

What does this mean for us today? God's purposes for his church has not changed. Even though dramatic and systematic persecution is largely absent from the Western church today, we still encounter God's disciplining hand in our lives, and we still suffer trials and trouble. Today in formerly Christian cultures, believers are being marginalized and ostracized in many ways. When suffering comes into our lives (and come it must, if we are to be presented mature and complete, as sons and daughters of the King), how will we respond? Will we look forward to the blessed outcome of maturity and sonship with joy, trusting in the good God who gives the gift of wisdom to his children through their endurance during troubles? Will we follow Jesus and learn obedience from our Father, so that we will be made complete? Or will we respond to troubles with utter disappointment and hopelessness? Will we give in to bitter envy of others whose lives seem so tranquil and easy? These questions are difficult to ask, and harder to answer honestly. But they point down the road away from drowning in our bitterness and toward the road of wisdom, toward the path that leads to maturity and ruling and the crown of life, where David and Stephen and Jesus wait for us.

# God's Good Gifts

*James 1:13-18*

<sup>13</sup>Let no one say when he is tempted, "I am being tempted by God," for God cannot be tempted with evil, and he himself tempts no one. <sup>14</sup>But each person is tempted when he is lured and enticed by his own desire. <sup>15</sup>Then desire when it has conceived gives birth to sin, and sin when it is fully grown brings forth death. <sup>16</sup>Do not be deceived, my beloved brothers. <sup>17</sup>Every good gift and every perfect gift is from above, coming down from the Father of lights with whom there is no variation or shadow due to change. <sup>18</sup>Of his own will he brought us forth by the word of truth, that we should be a kind of firstfruits of his creatures.

As we have said, the road to maturity is not easy—indeed, it is full of pitfalls and temptations. One of the primary temptations that James's audience faced was the tendency to blame God for their testing and trials, to assume that God was acting maliciously and he was tormenting them in their time of trouble. This response to suffering reminds us of the story of Job's wife, who bitterly advised her husband after the destruction of their family and Job's physical torment, "Curse God and die!" (Job 2:9). James's audience also faced a similar temptation in the midst to their struggle—to curse Jesus and return to the traditional Jewish religion they had left behind.

Consider how difficult it was for them to remain steadfast in their trials, to count it all joy. They were the first disciples of Jesus. They were a little band of nobodies, in the midst of a nation of Jews with institutions and authority and robes of office and priests and elders and a beautiful baroque temple that reminded them of all the past glories of their history. Nevertheless, they were leaving all this glory and tradition behind to follow the Way. They had no place to worship, no safe place even to meet and pray together and plan for the future, because of the persecution of the Jews.

The leaders of this nascent church were men unaccredited by the ruling Jewish elites—plain men like Peter, James, and John. These people to whom James writes have no Bible outside of the Hebrew Scriptures, and perhaps the gospel of Matthew. And these manuscripts would have been kept by their local Levites (and now deacons) to be read aloud during their assemblies. And now the official word from the Jerusalem authorities and the hallowed halls of their Temple is that Jesus was a hoax (Matt. 28:11-15), that Jesus was just another insurrectionist rebel, another failed messiah, and his followers are not to be trusted (Acts 5:33-39). The resurrection? It was a trick, orchestrated by Jesus's disciples, merely a power play by fanatics who couldn't give up on their dream of a true Messiah (Matt. 28:11-15). We can almost imagine the conversations that might have happened between the Jewish leaders and these early Jewish followers of Jesus when they were dragged into prison and pressured to turn back to Judaism:

"Did you see Jesus after his miserable death?"

"No, but we were told about his resurrection. We heard stories…"

"But you didn't see him. He only 'appeared' to a few, to select people. Isn't that suspicious?"

"But his disciples, they told us they saw him with their own eyes."

"His disciples! Ha! After all, how can you trust these disreputable men, these Galilean disciples? They left everything behind to follow that fool. Of course, they're not going to give up now. And how can you claim to start something new, when we are the elders and official teachers of Israel, Yahweh's appointed leaders?"

"But Jesus, he said that…"

"Jesus? Don't even talk to us about him. Are you going to tell us that this simple man Jesus, who died on a cross, is the Anointed One? The Messiah? The King of Israel? This man Jesus was a failure. Rome remains untouched by him. She still reigns supreme, we're still under her thumb. Your religion is nothing but old wives' tales and the ramblings of disenfranchised common folk. Come back to us—we're the true Israel, we're God's people."

This infant community of dissenters was set upon by the official Old Covenant people of God, the Jews. And not just set upon, but they were flogged and beaten and run out of the synagogue, and some even stoned. Stephen is stoned to death, for the sin of blasphemy, for saying that Jesus is Messiah. After his death, the persecution begins in earnest, and the followers of Jesus are scattered from Jerusalem. Saul, with his agents, is finding out who is a Christian, and who is not. Women and children are being dragged off to prison and tortured and executed (Acts 8:3; 9:1-2; 22:3-5; 26:4-12).

We have to imagine how disorienting all this would be. How very difficult it would be to get our bearings when everything we've considered solid ground is all just washed away, and it appears that we must start anew. And what a seduction, what a temptation, the lure of coming back into Judaism would be. This is the kind of thing they had to live with. This is the kind of life they had to accept. This is kind of life they had to believe was God's will, and therefore "to count it all joy." Perhaps we can begin to see why James writes these words, why he feels the need to remind them that God is not evil, and that it would be an awful mistake to become bitter and curse God, or to give in and renounce Jesus.

If we take James's warning in these verses seriously, some of James's readers were beginning to believe the lie that God was intentionally tempting them to curse him, or to turn away from Jesus. Here was a powerful, deceptive story: God was playing games with them, and their suffering wasn't part of a fatherly process of bringing them to maturity, but rather a malicious game of cat and mouse.

And the temptation to believe this lie rings true to our own experience, doesn't it? All of us know what it is like to believe that God is not good, and that some hardship in our lives is evidence, not of his care for us, but rather of an evil attempt to disrupt our faith and maliciously cause us to suffer. Even the psalmist cries out, "Why?" in the midst of his suffering. "Why, O Lord, do you cast my soul away? Why do you hide your face from me?" (Ps. 88:14).

This is a normal and understandable reaction to suffering. But the psalmist's question always leads to two answers—we suffer because God is sovereign and because God is good. But sometimes, when we are suffering or experiencing times of trouble, when we cry out to the heavens and wonder, "Why?" we can be tempted to answer that question by believing either that God is not sovereign or that God is not good. And when we begin to give into this temptation, another temptation arises—to blaspheme Jesus, to reject our Lord and to turn away and live our lives as though all that comes to us is not from our Father's hand. Even if the intensity of our temptation may not equal that of James's first readers, the manner of the temptation is the same. We need to hear James's defense of God, to apply it to our own hearts and situations.

James's first response to his readers' temptation is to assure them that God is not evil, and God is not the source of their temptation to embrace bitterness and curse their maker. God tempts no one (James 1:13). Rather, James says, their temptation comes from within their own hearts. We don't need to look to God to find a reason for our temptation for sin. Instead, our temptation flows out of our own fallen desires—our desire for shortcuts on the path to maturity, our pride, and hatred of discomfort as well as our desire to grasp the promised fruit from the tree of the knowledge of good and evil without having to endure the hard task of obedience and endurance that must precede our enjoyment of the fruit of maturity.

As James tells us, when we harbor and nurture these desires within us, they conceive and "give birth to sin" (v. 15). So that like a worm in our heart, we begin to be eaten inside by bitterness and soon come to hate the gifts of God and the discipline and suffering that we find when we follow Jesus. And the end of this sin is, of course, death. If we allow bitterness to grow in us without check, it will lead to abandoning our Lord. If we really allow our hearts to believe that God is evil and wicked and plays games with us by sending curses and suffering into our life, then we cannot expect that we will continue to love and serve such a God. If we allow ourselves to truly believe that God is evil, then we will eventually serve our own definition of good, which will ultimately be ourselves.

But James does not stop at merely asserting that God is not evil, that he is not the source of their temptations. Rather he calls to his brothers to put away their deception, their temptation to believe that God is wicked, and assures them that every good gift that comes into their lives comes from their good God. "Do not be deceived, my beloved brothers" (1:16). All the blessings that come to us—sunlight and rain and bread and wine and love and sons and daughters and wives and husbands—all these good things come from God. Indeed, the only reason we know to call suffering "suffering" is because of all the good gifts that God has given us. It is because we have tasted his goodness that we know what it is to suffer.

But this is not all James says. It is not only good gifts that come from God, but also "perfect gifts" (ESV), or better understood as "mature" (τελειον) gifts. Here, James gives his readers a framework to understand their suffering and persecution, the destruction of their homes and loved ones, and their own physical and bodily troubles. They are the gifts of maturity, given by their Father, the Father of lights, who does not waver and who does not change. Though at first glance, God's good gifts of wine and laughter and friends seem different or opposed to his gifts of suffering, struggle, and disappointment, James invites his reader to embrace wisdom and maturity and see that the God that gives both pleasure and suffering does not change, and does not shift, and all his gifts, both pleasure and pain, are good. That is, they are for our good (Rom. 8:28). Instead of using times of suffering to try and determine God's disposition towards us, whether he loves us or hates us, James gently says, "Don't do that." For both pleasure and pain are gifts from our good Father—there is no shadow of turning, no inconsistency, and no wavering in all that comes to us by God's hand.

James invites us to confess today the answer to the question, "What do you understand by the providence of God?"

> God's providence is His almighty and ever present power, whereby, as with His hand, He still upholds heaven and earth and all creatures, and so governs them that leaf and blade, rain and drought, fruitful and barren years, food and drink, health and sickness, riches and poverty, indeed, all things, come not by chance but by His fatherly hand (Heidelberg Catechism, Question 27).

Every good gift, every perfect gift, every mature gift is from above, for God is the Father of lights, and he gives all things to his children. Don't be deceived. God is not a miser, and he does not withhold good gifts from his children. In every moment of our lives God is with us, bringing us to maturation and conformity to the image of his Son. Our Lord does all this because as the Father of lights, he is in the business of creating lights for the world.

Once again, James invites his readers to reflect on God's purpose of maturing man to the place where he can rule. The "lights" God created on the fourth day of creation are not simply there to help us mark time but they are also "signs," specifically symbolic of rulers—the "greater light to rule the day" and the "lesser light to rule the night" (Gen. 1:16). Powers are often symbolized as the sun, moon, and stars in the Scriptures (Gen. 37:9; Isa. 13:10; Mark 13:25; Rev. 1:16). James refers to God as the "Father of lights" to remind them of his promise to them that they will one day "shine as lights in the world" (Phil. 2:15) if they steadfastly endure the trials so as to attain the wisdom necessary to rule.

We are to be mature as God is mature, says Jesus in Matthew 5:48, so that we will image him and spread his kingdom throughout his creation. To this end, God gives us not only gifts of pleasure, but also good gifts, which are gifts of maturity and which bring us along on the path of completion, so that we will lack nothing. We are being given these mature gifts of struggles and trials so that we can be the light of the world. Jesus is the light of the world (John 8:14) and in him we also are lights (Matt. 5:14). As we have seen, lights are rulers, and in the words of Jesus, we are the lights. The city set on the hill ought to give forth light, and not be put under a bushel. And so our good God trains us and shapes us, and brings us to become the rulers and kings that he needs in his kingdom. The process is slow and hard, but there is no other path to maturity.

In verse 18, James summarizes the major themes of the first part of this letter. Whereas our inner desires, when nurtured and coddled, give birth (αποκυεω) to sin, God's will (that is, his good and mature gifts) brings forth or gives birth (αποκυεω) to sons and daughters of the King—to lights and rulers for the world.

The "word of truth," of course, is Jesus, who calls us after him on his path of suffering and resurrection, who beckons us onward, and brings us to completion. And in all this, James says to his readers, you are a "firstfruits of his creatures." Indeed, James's readers are a firstfruits church, a pattern for the rest of God's sons and daughters to follow. Just as the Israelite would bring the firstfruits of his harvest near to Yahweh and lay them on God's altar in the hopes of more fruit to come, just as Jesus is the firstfruit of the resurrection (1 Cor. 15), so also this newborn church is to be a firstfruit of God's harvest—a harvest that we ourselves are a part.

The early church sets the pattern, blazes the trail. The church that follows them will be like them, just as the one they followed. Jesus first set the pattern for them. As it happened to Jesus, so it happens to the early church, his bride. And as it happens to the early church, so it happens to the church that comes after her, which means the Christian communities James is addressing will be exemplary for the coming generations.

These are the words from the apostle James, written for the firstfruits church, but we know that they are written for us as well, not just for them. In their steadfast faithfulness under trial, in suffering they were vindicated and await their resurrection and triumph. And if we follow them, we will be like them, just as we follow Jesus. Their result of maturity and completeness ought to continue to inspire us and cause us to rejoice. We know that God is good and faithful because he was good and faithful to this early church. He brought them through their struggles and hardship and led them into victory and vindication, and he promises the same to us.

## Summary & Reflections

As is often the case in New Testament epistles, in the opening section of his letter, James has given us an introduction to the main theological and literary themes of his letter. Surveying these themes will be helpful for reviewing the overall message of James 1:1-18, as well as preparing us for the content of the rest of the letter.

The admonition of James 1:2 to "count it all joy, my brothers, when you meet trials of various kinds" is often quoted by Christians during times of difficulty. But it often seems to function superficially. The larger context is all about how suffering produces character over the long haul. And that is a very difficult lesson to learn. In the mid- and late-1970s, Aleksandr Solzhenitsyn was severely criticized by the American media for suggesting that ordinary Russian people had experienced an elevated spiritual character after having endured so much suffering at the hands of their communist oppressors.

> This is no more than the ancient truth that strength of character comes from suffering and adversity. Oppressed and driven as they are by constant poverty, it is inevitable that many of our people are crushed, debased, warped, or dehumanized....But direct oppression can give birth to a contrary process too—a process of spiritual ascent, even of soaring flight.[17]

The first major theme that we find in James's letter is his focus on the severe trials and suffering that the readers of his letter are experiencing. The importance of this historical context and background for understanding James's letter cannot be overstated. James writes to a very young church, an infant church, a church that has been set upon by the religious leaders of their childhood. Those men and women to whom James writes are subject to some of the worst kind of persecution we can imagine, beginning with the stoning of Stephen and continuing in their being driven out of Jerusalem by Jewish leaders. These early converts have left behind all the religious traditions of their youth—the temple and the priests and the sacrifices and the festivals, and everything else they have held dear for so long—all to follow Jesus.

Therefore, the church that James writes to is confused, scattered, homeless, and longing for answers about why this suffering has come upon them, and how they are to endure it. Though, for most of us, our sufferings are in many ways easier than those experienced by the original readers of this epistle, we too know suffering—whether in the serious sickness or death of a child, the collapse of a marriage, or the disappointment of losing a job. And we also know what it is like to be confused and bring our questions to God in the midst of our trials. Reading James's applications of the teaching of Jesus to the followers of Jesus during their extreme trials will help give us a framework to understand and wrestle through our own lesser struggles and trials.

---

17 Aleksandr I. Solzhenitsyn, *The Mortal Danger: How Misconceptions About Russia Imperil America* (New York: Harper & Row, 1980), 66.

The second theme of James's message in this initial section of his epistle is the necessity of maintaining a steadfast, enduring faith and trust in God when we experience severe trials. Will we trust God when there is no comfort, no experiential evidence of God's favor? Will we trust him, nonetheless? Will we trust him for the end, for the goal that he's promised? Will we count it all joy in the midst of our trials and afflictions? These are the key questions of James 1:1-18, and indeed, the key question James poses to his audience throughout his letter.

The third significant theme of James's opening section is the need for wisdom from God in order to negotiate the difficulty of maintaining trust in him throughout suffering and trials. For James, wisdom is bound up with suffering in an interconnected relationship—wisdom is necessary to endure trials, but endurance of trials is also the manner in which wisdom is learned and the sons and daughters of God are brought to maturity and receive the crown of life. Perhaps the best way of stating this relationship between wisdom and suffering is that a wisdom that begins with the fear of Yahweh (Prov. 1:7) is necessary to enter and endure trials and suffering, but the only way that initial wisdom will be tested, developed, and brought to maturity is through the path of suffering and endured trials.

The reason for the emphasis on wisdom in James's letter is that the early church is being called to *rule* with Jesus. From the history of Israel, we know that wisdom is given for ruling (Prov. 8:15), that the Hebrew wisdom literature is produced during the peak of Israel's kingship, and is written by Israel's mature rulers. In James, the early church needs wisdom, for they will receive the crown of life, they will be vindicated, and they will rule with their Lord. Just as Jesus learned obedience and was brought to maturity through the things he suffered, so those who follow after him must suffer and learn obedience and thus be brought to maturity.

One of the main ways that James helps us—contemporary readers of his letter—is by giving us a framework, an interpretive grid to understand the sufferings and trials that come into our lives. By reading James and understanding the connection between maturity and suffering, endurance in trials and the crown of life, we begin to see that suffering in the life of a follower of Jesus cannot be explained simply as a random result of sin, or even the result of life in a fallen world, but rather that our suffering is an essential component in the process of Jesus's recreation of all things, and a necessary part of our eschatological participation in the new heavens and new earth. In our sufferings, we are brought to maturity and completion and prepared for life in the kingdom of Jesus—for our service to the suffering king who also was made mature by his truly innocent and bitter sufferings.

The fourth major theme that comes from this first section of James and helps us also to understand the overall message of his epistle is that all good things—maturity, wisdom, trials and the strength to endure suffering—come from the hand of our liberal and generous Father. Throughout his letter, James is moving his people to trust in God the Father in the midst of these tribulations and troubles, for God the Father is the mature Person of the Trinity. It is in his image that we are all being transformed. Jesus, the Son, is transformed into his image *as a man*, and becomes like his Father. And so we also, the younger brothers and sisters of Jesus, are transformed after him into the image of God the Father.

Perhaps it needs to be noted that this emphasis on the growth and maturity of Jesus is not because Jesus is less than divine or that James thinks Jesus is less important than God the Father. We know this can't be true because the whole book of James is filled with the teachings of Jesus. There is no other epistle in the New Testament that has so many allusions, connections, and links to the teachings of Jesus in the synoptic Gospels, particularly the Gospel according to Matthew. Rather, what James has done is pattern his own instruction after our Lord's teaching quite carefully and deliberately.

It was Jesus who taught his disciples, James being one of them, to trust in God the Father's goodness during the experience of affliction and trial. At every point, Jesus trusted his Father, yielded to his Father, prayed to his Father, and submitted to his

Father. Even in the Garden of Gethsemane, in the most difficult of times, Jesus's prayer was "not as I will, but as you will" (Matt. 26:39). In the end, Jesus trusted the goodness of his Father, even though there wasn't any sign of it in the world. All of his disciples left him, all the people he had served for the last three years of his life, most of the people he had loved and taught and healed had cried out in one voice for his death. His life ended with hanging on a cross, with no evidence of God's favor upon him—indeed, by all appearances, he was cursed and abandoned by God.

Even so, through all of this Jesus trusted in the goodness of his Father and obediently suffered and was made mature, and three days later his trust in his Father was vindicated when God raised him from the dead and made him King over all of creation. And this trust in the goodness of God is one of the foundational truths James is trying to convey to his readers. The displaced persecuted flock to whom he writes has no evidence of God's favor upon them. Indeed, quite the opposite. And many of us who read this letter today may feel as though there is no reason to trust in God's favor or goodness in our life because of the hardship and trouble we are now experiencing. But James's message to his readers, and to us, is to trust in God the Father's liberal goodness. We ought to learn our lesson from Jesus. If we are going through trials and hard times and suffering, it does not mean that God hates us, anymore than it meant that God hated Jesus when his son hung on the cross. In truth, our suffering means that God loves us and that he is working in us his plan for our lives. Therefore, we should embrace the way of wisdom and fear Yahweh, remembering that Jesus whom we follow also tasted suffering and confusion and abandonment—but all this was for his good and God's glory.

After considering the weight of James's words and the important themes of this opening section, we may also begin to consider some concrete ways in which we should apply his teaching to our lives.

First, James's teaching should cause us to purge from our minds the unbiblical, awful idea that God is a miser, and that he is gracious and generous toward us only reluctantly, only when good things are yanked and pulled out from him. Indeed, in order to endure trials in the way that James describes, we must put to death such thoughts when they arise in our minds. The temptation to see God as fundamentally distant, miserly, and set against us is an easy trap for us to fall into, especially when we are suffering, but embracing or nurturing that attitude does not do justice to the witness of the biblical narrative and will lead to the fruit of foolish bitterness instead of maturity and wisdom when we experience trials.

James is very clear about God's goodness to us. God will "give generously" to all who ask for the gift of wisdom from him. "Generously" in the Greek may be better translated, "Without hesitation." The sense here is that God gives good gifts to his children just as we ourselves give to our sons and daughters—naturally, reflexively, and without hesitation.

Nevertheless, this does not mean that God gives us everything we want or think we need. But all good things in our life do come from him (James 1:17). He is the Father of lights—there is no change in him. He is not fickle, his goodness does not change, he does not change his colors—one moment good, another evil. The temptation to view God as miserly and reticent in his care for us was at the root of Satan's subtle temptation to Adam and Eve. He wanted them to believe that God was not good, that he was not generous, and that he was withholding good things from them—forcing them to snatch good things from God instead of waiting patiently. And Adam and Eve believed the lies of Satan, and they rebelled against God and took his good gift for themselves, instead of waiting for God to give it. And ever since then, as sons and daughters of Adam and Eve, we have fallen into believing this lie about God. We have lived as though God is stingy, closed-fisted, and miserly toward his creatures. But when we read the Bible closely, we see that everything in the Bible screams against this lie. Indeed, how could God have given us anything more? He's given himself. He's given his beloved, one and only son. How will he not, along with him, also freely give us all things?

Secondly, God's goodness toward us means that we ought not rashly to interpret our trials, our afflictions, or our sufferings as evidence of God's displeasure with us, or of his failure to graciously give to us. We must not believe the lie that because we don't have everything we want, or even everything we need, God hates us, or that we've done something wrong and now God is punishing us. Remember, the early church did nothing wrong and yet they experienced bitter suffering and persecution. They were not being punished but trained. Stephen did not die because God was displeased with him—indeed, Jesus stood to receive him into heaven (Acts 7:56).

When we meditate on the lives of the Old Testament saints, we also see that suffering is God's normal way of maturing his people. Consider Joseph, who was sold into Egyptian slavery by his jealous brothers. Despite this injustice, Joseph remained faithful and trusted in God, only to find himself thrown into prison on trumped up charges and left to rot. Did all these sufferings and trials come into Joseph's life because he had somehow sinned against God and brought his displeasure upon himself? There's no evidence of such a tit-for-tat judgment. Rather, God was teaching Joseph obedience, and making him mature so that he could set him up to rule over the people of Egypt and so that he would provide for his people Israel and maintain the promises he made to Abraham. Joseph gains wisdom from these trials and is thereby fit to serve/rule the world during the famine.

God is good and he longs to give good things to us, his children. We shouldn't interpret our trials as evidence of God's disfavor. Rather they should cause us to reflect on our union with Christ. We're suffering with him and in him (1 Pet. 4:13). We are "called" not simply to believe in Jesus but also to suffer with him. "For it has been granted to you that for the sake of Christ you should not only trust in him but also suffer for his sake" (Phil. 1:29). In this way we will also partake of his glory, his elevation, and his crown (2 Tim. 2:12; Rev. 2:10; 20:4).

Thirdly, don't think that the wisdom which God gives to endure trials is going to give us the ability to *solve* all our problems, or put an end to our afflictions. Biblical wisdom is not some special skill that enables us to fix everything. James nowhere suggests such an idea because this is not the way wisdom is portrayed in the Hebrew Scriptures. Remember, Jesus was the greater son of David, and he had all the wisdom of God, even more than Solomon; but his trials were not cut off prematurely. If, however, God provides a way out of a trial that has come into our lives, we should by all means take the path that he has given us.

When the early church leaders were in the middle of difficulties, they always sought to escape them if they could do so without compromising their faith. Jesus tells his disciples to flee Jerusalem when they discern that the situation is getting bad (Matt. 24:15-16). Paul gets lowered down in a basket outside the wall of Damascus to escape the enemies of the Gospel (Acts 9:23-25). He even uses the legal means at his disposal to try to avoid unnecessary scandal and trouble (Acts 16:37; 25:11). Nobody wants to put their family through intense suffering. Everyone wants to alleviate hardships if possible. But there are times in life when we must suffer through things that we cannot solve, no matter how much wisdom God may give us.

Unfortunately, this goes against most Americans' conception of what wisdom really is—often we see wisdom simply as practical know-how. We have all heard that wisdom is not about theory, but about knowing how and what to do and say. It is often said that a wise man knows how to do things, how to figure things out, how to fix things. Then we come to the wisdom literature in the Bible, and what do we find? It seems odd to us, almost weird. Where is the nitty-gritty practical how-to advice? It's just not there. At least not how we want it. It is a bit like the disappointment a man might feel if he goes into a hardware store, looking to find nails and screws and a screwdriver and tools to fix his shed, and there's nothing there.[18]

What, then, is the wisdom that God gives us? It is not power to fix our troubles. God's wisdom does not have the power to bring back our dead friends or family. Stephen is not brought back. People are not spared from death in the early church, or in the church today. Wisdom does not give us the power to reverse our fortunes and to end our trials. *The wisdom that God gives is the grace to discern God's promise, his curse on those that despise him, and the strength to trust him for the outcome of everything that may come to pass in our lives.* God's wisdom gives us the freedom to acknowledge that we have no ultimate control over the outcome of our lives. God's wisdom allows us to confess that all life is vapor, that we cannot hold on to it. Like the wind, we cannot shepherd our lives or make them go the way we want. True wisdom is the fear of God and the trust that he will deliver his children, regardless of how things may appear during our trials. And with these convictions, we obey his commandments, we suffer through the trial, and we believe in the end that God will vindicate his people.

The English word "James" comes from the Latin translation of the Hebrew as well as through the French translation of the Latin, and what is hidden behind the English word is clear in the Greek: "James" is simply the Greek translation of the Hebrew name "Jacob." And when we look at the Old Testament story of Jacob, we find many of the themes of James's opening section illustrated in his story.

Jacob was born to Isaac and Rebekah in the womb with his twin brother Esau (Gen. 25:19-26). And as the brothers are born, they struggled, wrestling with one another, and this was prophetic of their relationship all their lives. For God promised that Jacob would be the one who is blessed over his brother. He would be the

---

[18] For more on the nature of biblical wisdom see Meyers, *A Table in the Mist* (Monroe, LA: Athanasius Press, 2006)..

one upon whom God's covenant blessings would rest, the heir of the promises of Abraham. Even so, Jacob had to wrestle, struggle, and sweat for those blessings.

Born the younger son, Jacob wrestled away Esau's birthright through his cleverness and a pot of red stew (Gen. 25:29-34). Later, with the help of his shrewd mother he dressed himself in the skin of a goat and wrestled with Isaac, who was so blind—spiritually—that he was going to ignore God's promise and give the entire Abrahamic blessing to Esau (Gen. 27:1-40). Through his righteous deception, Jacob took the blessing away from Esau, but, fearing for his life, he was forced to flee from his home. And so the man upon whom rested the blessing of God—the promises to Abraham—went out alone, with nothing.

On his journey to Padan Aram, he laid his head on a rock, and called the place where he slept Bethel ("House of God"). That night God appeared to Jacob and told him, "All this land is yours and your sons and your sons' sons, your offspring forever" (Gen. 28). But still, Jacob had nothing to his name. He had to go up into the home of his mother's brother, Laban, who was a scoundrel. Jacob worked fourteen years for the woman he loved—slaving and working and wrestling with Laban, who was deceitful with him, who cheated Jacob every chance he got, and forced him to strive with him an additional seven years.

Finally, when Jacob was able to flee Laban and journey back home to the land of Canaan, he anticipated a dangerous meeting with Esau, convinced that he would have to wrestle with him again, but this time unto death (Gen. 31-32). Jacob is now an old man (97 years old), made mature by his suffering, and the night before he was forced into his climatic reunion with Esau, he lay down for the night, alone on the bank of the Jabbok river (Gen. 32:22-32). That night, a man came to Jacob and wrestled with him until the break of day. All night they strove together, and even though all of Jacob's life had prepared him for this moment, this night, still the wrestling was fierce and hard-fought and almost too much to bear. But Jacob would not relent and finally the man reached down to finger Jacob's hip socket and in that one small touch, Jacob's hip is put out of joint. Even though the pain was now excruciating, still Jacob would not relent, would not give up, until finally the man with whom he wrestled cried out, "Let me go, for the day is dawning!" And Jacob, with his last breath, gasped and said, "I will not let you go unless you bless me." And the man, who was the Lord himself, said to him, "You shall no longer be called Jacob, but Israel" (Gen. 32:28).

This was not Jacob's conversion. Genesis 32 is not a revival text or even an evangelistic text. This is Jacob becoming mature, a ruler. For God tells him that his name is no longer Jacob, a wrestler, but Israel, the Prince of God, "for you have striven with God and with men, and have prevailed" (Gen. 32:28). The text does not say that God finally overpowered the recalcitrant man Jacob. We are not told that God at last brought Jacob to his knees. Rather, we are told that Jacob has prevailed in his wrestling with God and with men!

Jacob was then gifted with the "crown of life." What was hidden from Jacob all his life was that he was not wrestling with Esau or with Isaac, or with Laban, or even with his wives. He was wrestling with God. That Jacob understands this meaning is made clear when he finally does meet up with his brother Esau. Jacob had named the place where he wrestled with God *Peniel* ("face of God," Gen. 32:30). Now when he sees Esau he says, "For I have seen your face, which is like seeing the face of God" (Gen. 33:10). In other words, Jacob was confessing that in all his struggles with his brother, he was grappling with God.

All Jacob's life God wrestled with him—as a father gets down on his knees and wrestles with his son in order to strengthen his son and teach him. God the Father of Jacob was wrestling with him, training him, preparing him, maturing him, perfecting him, making him into a man that would be complete and be a ruler over the twelve sons, the twelve tribes of Israel, who would become God's people. And, in the end, Jacob is that mature ruler because of all these experiences. He is given a new name: *Israel* ("Prince of God"). In that moment, Jacob knew whatever evil people or powers or troubles he had struggled and wrestled with—it was God who was behind them.[19]

As it was for Jacob, so it is for us. Though we may believe that we wrestle and struggle with wicked men or physical sickness or life's hardships that seem to have no connection to God at all. Remember the story of Jacob and remember the night when, in the darkness, the man fingered his hip and gave him a new name and opened his eyes to the one with whom he had wrestled all his life—his Father God. Indeed, we may say that reading the book of James is for us what the night on the banks of the Jabbok was for Jacob—we read his words and realize that our hardship and sufferings are not random or senseless, but they are evidence of our Father entering into our lives and striving with us, inviting us to wrestle with him, to endure in our pain and to receive the blessing that awaits us at the first light of the dawn.

And so from the story of Jacob, and the words of the New Testament apostle Jacob/James, we learn that we are to count as joy our trials and our sufferings and our afflictions—for they come down into our lives from our Father, the Father of lights, for our maturation, our development, our good, so that we will have a crown of life, so that we will be an Israel, a Ruler, a Prince of God. For God wants mature children who will grow in suffering, be given a crown of life and rule with him. He longs for us to accept his good gifts from his hand. For we will either count our trials as joy, understand that we are blessed by them, or we will become bitter, hateful, angry. There are no other paths than these to take when suffering and hardship come into our life, and there is no one whose life is not marred by affliction. The choice between wisdom and maturity on the one hand and anger and bitterness on the other is unavoidable—we must choose one or the other. James's words are written to ensure that we follow the path of wisdom, that we follow the path of Jesus and that we remain

---

[19] For more on Jacob's life see James B. Jordan, *Primeval Saints: Studies in the Patriarchs of Genesis* (Moscow, ID: Canon Press, 2001), 85-116.

steadfast, joyous, and blessed by God in the midst of hardship, sure that those who humble themselves will be lifted up, that death will be followed by resurrection, and God is making us into mature sons and daughters who will strive until the dawn and will receive the crown of life.

5

# How God Makes Things Right

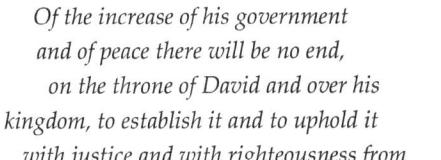

*Of the increase of his government
and of peace there will be no end,
on the throne of David and over his
kingdom, to establish it and to uphold it
with justice and with righteousness from
this time forth and forevermore.
The zeal of Yahweh of Armies will accomplish this.*
– Isaiah 9:7

*James 1:19-27*

[19]Know this, my beloved brothers: let every person be quick to hear, slow to speak, slow to anger; [20]for the anger of man does not produce the righteousness of God. [21]Therefore put away all filthiness and rampant wickedness and receive with meekness the implanted word, which is able to deliver your lives.

[22]But be doers of the word, and not hearers only, deceiving yourselves. [23]For if anyone is a hearer of the word and not a doer, he is like a man who looks intently at his beginning face in a mirror. [24]For he looks at himself and goes away and at once forgets what he was like. [25]But the one who looks into the mature law, the law of liberty, and perseveres, being no hearer who forgets but a doer who acts, he will be blessed in his doing.

> ²⁶If anyone thinks he is religious and does not bridle his tongue but deceives his heart, this person's religion is worthless. ²⁷Religion that is pure and undefiled before God, the Father, is this: to visit orphans and widows in their affliction, and to keep oneself unstained from the world.

In the first eighteen verses of his epistle, James has carefully explained to his readers the necessity of their steadfastness under trial in the persecution and violence they face. Again and again, he has reminded them of their blessed future—the vindication God promises, the crown of life they will receive, and their destination as mature sons and daughters of their heavenly Father.

In 1:19-27, James presents a series of contrasting portraits, fleshing out on the one hand the way of patient meekness, obedient perseverance, and active, pure religion, and on the other hand, the way of anger, self-deception, and worthless religion. In contrasting these two ways of living, James calls his readers to embrace the way of Christ and reject the world's wisdom as they follow their Lord in suffering and maturity. They ought to be clear about the way God will make things right in their lives and in the world at large.

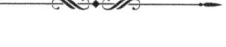

*James 1:19-21*

> ¹⁹Know this, my beloved brothers: let every person be quick to hear, slow to speak, slow to anger; ²⁰for the anger of man does not produce the righteousness of God. ²¹Therefore put away all filthiness and rampant wickedness and receive with meekness the implanted word, which is able to deliver your lives.

James contrasts the way of meekness and humility with the way of anger, exhorting his readers to embrace the blessedness of meekness as they participate in building and extending the kingdom of God. The key phrase in this section is found in verse 20: "For the anger of man does not produce the righteousness of God." This statement is meant to explain the imperatives that precede it in verse 19, "be quick to hear, slow to speak, slow to anger," and to provide the ground for the commands that follow it in verse 21: "Therefore put away all filthiness and rampant wickedness and receive with meekness the implanted word."

What does James mean by this phrase, "righteousness of God"? It may be tempting to imagine this sentence to mean something like man's anger does not produce "godly righteousness" or the "righteousness that God requires," where "righteousness" is understood to be equivalent with keeping God's law. This is the sense of the word "righteousness" that Paul has in mind in Philippians 3:6 when he writes, "as to righteousness under the law, [I was] blameless." But the New Testament writers also used the word "righteousness" in another sense, often meaning God's faithfulness to his promises to set right things in his creation. Paul's use of the phrase "righteousness of God" in Romans 3:21-26 is a good example of this sense of the phrase, and his usage there parallels the way that James uses "righteousness of God" in James 1:20. Paul writes:

> But now the righteousness of God has been manifested apart from the law, although the Law and the Prophets bear witness to it—the righteousness of God through the faithfulness of Jesus Christ for all who believe. For there is no distinction: for all have sinned and fall short of the glory of God, and are justified by his grace as a gift, through the redemption that is in Christ Jesus, whom God put forward as a propitiation by his blood, to be received by faith. This was to show God's righteousness, because in his divine forbearance he had passed over former sins. It was to show his righteousness at the present time, so that he might be just and the justifier of the one who has faith in Jesus (Rom. 3:21-26).

In Romans 3, Paul uses the phrase "the righteousness of God" to refer to God's faithful keeping of his promises in restoring man to himself through Jesus as a part of his plan to redeem and make right all things. Too often Christians think of "the righteousness of God" as his moral perfection in the abstract. That's why God's righteousness is often a scary notion. God is so righteous that he's frightening. But that is not how God's righteousness is perceived in the Bible. God's righteousness has to do with his "doing what is right" according to his covenant and promises. For Paul's readers in Romans, for example, God's absolute moral perfection was not at issue. Instead, the concern was about God's dependability, his reliability. The question for them was, how is it that God has remained true to his word, loyal to his covenant promises in the face of the failure of Israel, especially the murderous execution of the man many hoped was the Messiah? And, for the Jew, how has God done right—if, as you say, Paul—he has now turned his attention and favor on the Gentiles? What about us? What about his promises? What about Israel? Where is the evidence of God's righteousness?

Here at the end of James 1, the issue is not precisely the same as in Paul's letters to the Galatians or to the Romans. But "the righteousness of God" is nevertheless being called into question. Perhaps it would be more accurate to say that for James's readers the question was, *how* would God's righteousness be accomplished?

Israel was encouraged to appeal to God's righteousness when she was in trouble! The righteousness of God is the promise to God's people that he will deliver them from evil, just as the Psalmist prayed for deliverance, grounding his petition in God's righteousness:

> "In you, O Lord, do I take refuge; let me never be put to shame; in your righteousness deliver me!" (Ps. 31:1).

> "In your righteousness deliver me and rescue me; incline your ear to me, and save me! (Ps. 71:20).

James ends this section with the promise of deliverance in James 1:21. Doing what he counsels will lead to God's doing what is right with the result that these disciples will "deliver their lives."[20]

---

20 See the discussion of the fuller meaning of "justification" to include deliverance in Peter J. Leithart, *Delivered from the Elements of the World: Atonement, Justification, Mission* (Downers Grove: InterVarsity Press Academic, 2016), 180-188.

With this background, we might paraphrase James's words in 1:20 to mean, "the anger of man does not make things right, as God has promised to make things right in Christ." As we have seen, when God makes things right, he delivers his people. James knows that God has promised to make good on his promises, to set things right, and to deliver his people from their enemies. He knows that his readers not only know this, but since the coming of Messiah Jesus they *long* for it. God has promised through his prophets to make things right. God has promised through Jesus to make things right in the world through his church, through his people. The apostolic church rightly had high expectations. But these heightened expectations, no matter how securely grounded in God's promises, seemed diametrically opposed to the harsh reality they were experiencing after the onslaught of persecution (Acts 8:1-3; 11:19).

James's congregation was experiencing something that appeared to be contrary to this hope. Things were not yet right for a church that was scattered throughout the land because of the wrath of unbelieving Jewish authorities. These simple disciples of Jesus had correctly discerned that the righteousness of God had not yet been enacted. They were eagerly waiting for God to be true to his covenant—that is what righteousness is—God's pledge to be true to his covenant. This pledge to his covenant people appeared to be lacking. Things were not going well. The church had been run out of Jerusalem. People were being tortured, stoned, and executed by the leaders of the apostate Jews.

Into this highly charged, confusing situation, James warns against the "anger of man." In the context of verse 19, he clearly means to direct the behavior of his people so that they would be quick to hear, slow to speak, and slow to anger. Avoid the "anger of man" and the way of the fool. Be wise. Once again, the style and content of James is dependent on Hebrew wisdom literature. And great wisdom is called for in difficult circumstances like that which the apostolic church found herself. Remember the situation of James's original audience—they had been set upon from all sides, driven from their homes, and many in their community had been imprisoned or even killed. In that kind of situation, it should be easy to understand why these early Christians would have been tempted to follow the way of anger and respond to their persecutors and oppressors with hatred and even subversive violence. One can almost hear the angry speeches. "Something must be done! We can't just sit around and pray! The situation must be fixed!" Many were tempted to "rectify" (i.e., make righteous) the problem with fiery speeches and violent action (James 1:19; 3:1-11; 4:1-4). To this dangerous movement, James says, in effect, "Back off, hold on, wait just a minute. This is not the way to bring into effect God's promise to make things right."

Righteous anger and violence were the ways that the Hebrew zealots of their day had often responded to the Roman oppression of Israel, and it is likely that at least some of these early converts had earlier engaged in violence against their Roman overlords. At least one of Jesus's twelve disciples was formerly counted as a zealot (Simon the Zealot; see Luke 6:15; Acts 1:13). Even those that had not been zealots in the past would have been sorely tempted to fight their Jewish oppressors, if not with violence, then with angry words and speeches, complaining bitterly about their own shameful treatment and cursing those who persecuted them (James 3:9). Consider how hard it is for us today to avoid responding angrily when we are "oppressed" in some tiny way. We are furious when a person cuts us off in traffic or writes an unfair paragraph about us in a blog post or spreads gossip about us in our church. If these small transgressions incite our anger and bitterness so easily, how much more so would have James's audience longed to speak and act vengefully against their enemies when their lives were at stake?

But James commands his audience to abandon the way of anger and revenge because it would not bring about the hoped-for righteousness of God—the implementation of his promised deliverance and the righting of all wrongs for which they longed. If they respond with anger and vengeance, their actions will not have the desired effect and will only increase their frustration. Instead, they should respond to suffering with meekness, patience, and wisdom—not with prideful anger but rather a humble dependence and trust in God for their vindication. This way of patient suffering and meekness is the path which Jesus walked—he endured his suffering, which was even more innocent and terrible than the suffering of his followers, with the dumbness and humility of a lamb led to the slaughter (Isa. 53:7; Acts 8:32). If Jesus, who commanded the armies of heaven, avoided violence and revenge against his oppressors, how much more so must we also seek to implement the righteousness of God with humility?

But we need to be careful here, for we do not follow in Jesus's path of meekness simply because it was the way he walked (as though his path were arbitrary and we simply follow him blindly), but rather because the way in which Jesus endured suffering is in accordance with the God-ordained path for the maturity of man and the way in which the righteousness of God has always been effected in communities. In other words, we don't simply imitate Jesus because he was good. Rather, we follow him because he embodies the image of God in man, showing us God's pattern for human wisdom and maturity. That is, we ought to avoid the way of anger and embrace the way of meekness not simply because anger and violence violate God's law, but because the meekness of Jesus and those that follow him, paradoxically, accomplishes the justice/righteousness of God. To say this in yet another way, our meekness and humility in the face of suffering will bring about the end or goal for which we long—the maturity of humanity, the destruction of the Lord's enemies, and eventually the resurrection of our bodies.

Jesus and his followers resisted violence and wrath not because violence and wrath are not an appropriate reaction to innocent persecution, but because the time for violence and wrath has not yet come. This means that the way of Jesus, the way of meekness, which at face value seems passive and weak, is actually profoundly strong and subversive—because its power rests upon the power and faithfulness, that is to say, the *righteousness* of God. This is why peacemakers are called the sons of God. And why those who mourn will be comforted. Moreover, the meek inherit the earth. How? Through the righteousness of God, by the power of Yahweh, the one who is "merciful and gracious, slow to anger, and abounding in steadfast love and faithfulness...but who will by no means clear the guilty, visiting the iniquity of the fathers on the children and the children's children, to the third and the fourth generation" (Exod. 34:6-7).

What does it mean practically to follow in the path of Jesus, and to avoid the anger of man? How is it that James commands his audience as well as us to respond to the suffering that will come into our lives when we follow our Lord? James outlines five different ways we should follow Jesus and endure suffering, five ways in which we may participate in bringing in the righteousness of God. Let's examine each of them in turn, paying particular attention to how we might apply them to our own lives.

First, "Be quick to hear" (James 1:19). This particular admonition (like the two which follow it) is drawn from the Old Testament wisdom tradition, and in particular the words of Solomon to his son in Proverbs. The roots of these admonitions in wisdom literature are significant when we recall James's words in 1:5, where he writes, "If any of you lacks wisdom, let him ask God, who gives generously to all without reproach, and it will be given him." Here James instructs his readers in the wisdom that God gives, that wisdom they will need to navigate the trials that God brings into their lives in such a way that they will develop the fruit of maturity. For Solomon's son to rule wisely, he had to learn how to use his ears and tongue.

Are we quick to hear? Are we a people who are quick to listen, to hear instruction, to be taught by others? The imperative James uses here is general, and we're not quite sure what the object of "hear" is, but it is likely that James imparts a general command because he is describing a person's *character*, not their reaction to a particular situation. What he means is that we need to be the kind of people who take in the situation carefully and hear and listen before we make rash, hasty judgments—we must be slow and deliberate, careful about hearing and being sure we understand before we do or say anything. Do we strive to be that kind of person? Beyond this, being quick to hear also implies a kind of humility, a lack of self-righteousness and a rejection of the assumption that there is no one around us who is wiser than we are. Rather, a person who is quick to hear assumes he can learn from others, that he needs teaching, and that he doesn't have everything already figured out.

In some ways, it is surprising that James's advice to a church experiencing severe maltreatment is "be quick to hear." To Christian communities suffering persecution, James advocates caution and humility. But then again, maybe it is not so surprising. When we're in the kind of intense situation that James's audience found themselves in, we want to act and change things. We want to make things right. We just want to say something. But James says that if you're a wise man, you'll be deliberate, you'll be careful, and you'll be quick to hear rather than quick to speak and act.

All through Proverbs this theme is repeated—listen, hear, receive from others without responding rashly (Prov. 1:5; 8:6; 4:10; 8:32; 8:33; 19:27). This is because listening and hearing is the first posture that a wise man takes—not the posture of fighting. The path to wisdom is found in listening, not acting in anger. James, who knows that his church will need godly wisdom to endure their trials, commands them to "be quick to hear." I must admit that the older I get, the more I see the value in this command, and when I look back on my younger days as a minister and as a Christian, I realize how I didn't practice being quick to hear very well. I was far too hasty in my evaluations and far too quick with my lips and tongue. I always thought I was the righteous one and was too proud to demonstrate my humility by listening before speaking. What kind of people are we? Are we quick to hear, or quick to speak and act?

Second, "[Be] slow to speak" (James 1:19). This instruction completes the admonition that precedes it and is also part of the wisdom that God gives to those who ask (Prov. 10:19; 13:3; 21:23). To be quick to hear implies that one is also slow to speak. We can't listen if we are talking. James ensures that his readers will not miss this point by making the command explicit. James will further explain this admonition in James 3, but for now he simply notes the importance of being deliberate and cautious in our speech.

This imperative would have had special meaning to James's original audience. For if we are in chains, or if we are severely curtailed in our freedom in some way, the one thing we can wag is our tongue. But fiery speeches and bitter resentment will not produce the righteousness of God, and James warns his readers against this path, despite how easy and justified it may have seemed to them. Are we a people who restrains their lips? Are there times when we're ready to say something or type something because we're outraged or have been attacked, but we pause? If so, it's likely that after some period of time—ten minutes, two hours, a day—we realized that stopping our mouths was following the path of wisdom.

James asks his readers to receive from the Lord cool spirits instead of hot tempers. Let them ask God to give them the strength to follow the true Son of David, the greater Solomon, the one who received the admonition of his Father and walked the path of wisdom flawlessly. For Jesus, the Lord of all, the Son of God, was innocently oppressed and he was afflicted bitterly and he opened not his mouth. "He was oppressed, and he was afflicted, yet he opened not his mouth; like a lamb that is led to the slaughter, and like a sheep that before its shearers is silent, so he opened not his mouth" (Isa. 53:7). Peter writes as part of an epistle to an audience that also suffered oppression and persecution,

> To this [suffering] you have been called, because Christ also suffered for you, leaving you an example, so that you might follow in his steps. He committed no sin, neither was deceit found in his mouth. When he was reviled, he did not revile in return; when he suffered, he did not threaten, but continued entrusting himself to him who judges justly (1 Pet. 2:21-23).

Peter's words illuminate James's command for us. The only way we can follow in the path of wisdom and be quick to hear and slow to speak even in the face of unjust suffering is by following Jesus and entrusting ourselves to him who judges justly. Our willingness to endure suffering without bitterness is not based on some fatalistic view of destiny as it was for the Greek Stoics. Rather, our patience is grounded in our inability to control our situation. We trust that our Father is the one who will judge us, and he will vindicate his children with power and strength. We put aside our own power and strength, and we shut our mouths only because we have one who will act powerfully on our behalf and will speak for us in time of need. "Humble yourselves, therefore, under the mighty hand of God so that at the proper time he may exalt you" (1 Pet. 5:6).

Third, "[Be] slow to anger" (James 1:19). James now sums up at least a part of what it means for his audience to be quick to listen and slow to speak—that they will be slow to anger. As he explains in verse 20, James is warning his audience against a deafness to others, a hastiness to speak, and a baseline attitude of anger because such behavior does not produce or implement the righteousness of God. Living according to these foolish attributes is to live in a way that does not participate in the story of God, which is demonstrated most conclusively in the narrative of Jesus, who remains the model for the lifestyle that James commends.

In his warning against anger, James also reminds his readers of Jesus's words in Matthew 5:21, where the Lord gives his disciples a new commandment, saying, "But I say to you that everyone who is angry with his brother will be liable to judgment; whoever insults his brother will be liable to the council; and whoever says, 'You fool!' will be liable to the hell of fire." The seriousness with which James takes the way the early church uses its tongue and guards against its anger is fundamentally based on the seriousness which his teacher Jesus showed toward these issues. James and Jesus both understood that far from being an unimportant and inconsequential sin, the way the Christian uses his mouth and the ease with which he falls into anger reveals at least as much about his heart as a stack of pornographic magazines or a dependence on alcohol.

In commanding his audience to be "quick to hear," and "slow to speak," before he admonishes them to be "slow to anger," James also makes an important point regarding the *roots of sinful anger*. The first two commands that James gives in this section are concerned with how the follower of Christ uses his *body*—only then does he move to the emotional aspect of anger or its source in the heart. The order and combination of James's commands reveal his biblical commitment to the connection between the body and soul—far from the Gnostic tendency of the contemporary American church, which rarely imagines a character flaw that "quiet time" can't solve. *James directs his readers to root out their heart's anger by changing what they do with their ears and mouths.* By listening first and speaking only after deliberation, our body's participation in the sin of anger will be gradually shifted, and our heart's posture will follow. The goal of this shaping of body and soul is maturity, for to endure the harsh words of others without anger and to overlook offense against us is a weighty, glorious, and beautiful thing—and to live in this patient, mature way is to imitate God.

Fourth, "Put away all filthiness and rampant wickedness" (James 1:21). At first glance, this admonition may seem out of place. James has been directing his attention toward anger and the physical behavior which produces anger, but he switches to "filthiness" and "wickedness," more generic terms for evil. Ordinarily, we would be liable to interpret this warning to mean some general or moral filthiness and wickedness, and it's likely that at least on some level, this captures the meaning—James is admonishing his audience to live pure and godly lives in front of the unbelievers in the midst of their afflictions, so as to bring glory to God. Indeed, this is exactly the point which Peter makes when he writes, "Keep your conduct among the Gentiles honorable, so that when they speak against you as evildoers, they may see your good deeds and glorify God on the day of visitation" (1 Pet. 2:12).

But it is much more likely that this reference to filthiness and wickedness has to do with our behavior before those who hate us and those who accuse us and persecute us. James warns against the wickedness and filthiness that we are tempted to engage in when we get angry. If the Bible is true about its evaluation of our lives, we are at our worst, most depraved, most wicked, when we hate others. That's the filthiest, most wicked thing we can do. When we're attacked, when we're reviled, when our character is impugned, and our bodies and minds and hearts are not guided by the wisdom of Jesus, our first reaction is one of anger, and the anger which produces hatred and the scheming to do something against our attacker would only intensify sin, including that of our enemies. The rampant wickedness and filthiness that James tells his audience to put away from themselves applies to all sorts of moral misbehavior, but it finds particular expression in how this early church was tempted to respond to their attackers.

In Matthew 5:11, Jesus promised the church, "Blessed are you when others revile you and persecute you and utter all kinds of evil against you falsely on my account." He doesn't promise blessedness when we return "evil for evil" by reviling them in return. He simply promises that we will be blessed if we endure such treatment with patience. The apostle Peter says the same thing: "Do not repay evil for evil or reviling for reviling, but on the contrary, bless, for to this you were called, that you may obtain a blessing" (1 Pet. 3:9). Paul concurs: "Repay no one evil for evil, but give thought to do what is honorable in the sight of all" (Rom. 12:17). Only this kind of radical Christ-like behavior will contribute to God's promise to make things right.

Fifth, "Receive with meekness the implanted word, which is able to deliver your souls" (James 1:21). After warning against all the different ways in which his audience might act futilely to make things right, to usher in God's kingdom using the pseudo-wisdom of man, here in his closing admonition, James points toward the way in which the righteousness of God will indeed be produced—by the faithful and meek reception of the implanted word by its hearers. The "implanted word" here likely refers to the word of the gospel as it went out, and like a seed was planted in the hearts of those who heard it. The manner of implantation might also be compared to baptism, for when we are baptized, we received the word within us, and we wait expectantly for it to bear fruit.

The image of the word as a seed being planted in the ground of its hearers calls to mind Jesus's parable of the sower and the soils, especially with that parable's focus on the perseverance and endurance of those who hear the gospel. James is evoking the memory of that parable in his readers' minds, encouraging them to endure patiently, trusting in the one who can deliver them, avoiding the rocks, thorns, and birds, and bearing the fruit of the righteousness of God in and through their faithful lives of quiet trust.

James also defines the way this word is to be received as "meekness," a description that should also call to mind in his audience another famous teaching of Jesus. Like a hook, James throws out the word "meek" and reels in the entire list of Beatitudes, reminding his readers of the promises given there by their Savior as well as the manner in which those blessed promises are received—by poverty and mourning, purity and meekness.

James instructs his readers to meekly receive the word that has been implanted in them. Cultivate that seed, let it have its effect, and it will produce the righteousness of God that we long for. This is James's plan for the deliverance of his flock that's been scattered to the four winds and persecuted severely—*this is what he tells them to do if they want deliverance* (v. 21). Verse 21 is often translated, "which is able to save your souls." But that translation makes it sound like he is talking primarily about the soul's guarantee of heaven, about what we call "individual salvation." Surely that is part of it, but again, we are back to the thrust of this passage and the entire epistle: It is all about rescue from their enemies and vindication in God's righteous kingdom. If they want to see the righteousness that God has promised to manifest in the world, if they want to see God make things right through Jesus's reign, they should suffer meekly, avoiding anger and bitter speech, putting away all wickedness.

And the same is true for us, for through the righteousness of God, the reign of Jesus has expanded since the time James wrote these words, but God has not yet made everything right in all the world. So how will the righteousness of God continue to be produced in our day? How will it come to pass? By our meek reception of the implanted word, by seeking to be quick to hear, slow to speak, and slow to anger in our day-to-day lives, in our families, and in our jobs. It's not a glamorous route to victory, not a glorious parade, but rather a humble path. But after all, it is the meek who will inherit the earth (Isa. 11:4; Matt. 5:5).

If this humble path was effective for the early church, in the midst of their severe persecutions and trials, how much more ought we to follow them in our lesser sufferings, in the small persecutions we must endure? If James was able to admonish his audience to avoid anger and fiery speeches in the face of their suffering, how much more so do his words apply to us? And if these early Christians were commanded to avoid anger and bitterness against their wicked oppressors, how much more must we avoid anger and bitterness against those in our world or even in our church communities who offend us?

## The Man in the Mirror

*James 1:22-25*

²²But be doers of the word, and not hearers only, deceiving yourselves. ²³For if anyone is a hearer of the word and not a doer, he is like a man who looks intently at his natural face in a mirror. ²⁴For he looks at himself and goes away and at once forgets what he was like. ²⁵But the one who looks into the mature law, the law of liberty, and perseveres, being no hearer who forgets but a doer who acts, he will be blessed in his doing.

After contrasting the way of anger and the way of meekness, James sets up another contrast for his readers—between the one who *does* the word, persevering until the end, and the one who *hears* the word only and deceives himself into believing that he is blessed because of this. Now James turns to what may be perhaps the most difficult and frightening topic of his letter—the possibility of self-deception in the life of the Christian.

If we are honest with ourselves, there is not a single follower of Jesus who has not at some point wondered if he has deceived himself and everyone around him, and wonders if he truly believes the gospel that he professes or really belongs among the people of God. The usual response to this kind of uncertainty is to encourage the believer to examine his heart, to look inside himself and realize the vibrancy of his internal faith—to remember the gospel of individual salvation from sins and anchor himself in that hope. Thankfully, this is not James's advice.

Here James exposes the possibility of self-deception in the life of the Christian. But rather than suggesting that the means for assurance lies in correcting an internal problem or stirring up their hearts to greater faith, James gently instructs his audience to persevere, to act in obedience to the word they have received, and thus be blessed in their actions, receiving the assurance of faith.

At first, this link between the assurance of faith and the presence of good works in our lives may seem antithetical to the gospel of free, unmerited grace, but a closer look reveals this link is well attested to by the Scriptures as well as by Reformation theology. James will explain the necessity of good works for salvation later in 2:14-26. Indeed, James's brother John spoke to a congregation that had reason to doubt whether it was in Christ with these words, "And by this we know that we have come to know him [Christ], if we keep his commandments" (1 John 2:3). James's fellow apostle, Peter, also encouraged his flock to assure themselves of their faith, writing,

> Make every effort to supplement your faith with virtue, and virtue with knowledge, and knowledge with self-control, and self-control with steadfastness, and steadfastness with godliness, and godliness with brotherly affection, and brotherly affection with love. For if these qualities are yours and are increasing, they keep you from being ineffective or unfruitful in the knowledge of our Lord Jesus Christ. For whoever lacks these qualities is so nearsighted that he is blind, having forgotten that he was cleansed from his former sins. Therefore, brothers, be all the more diligent to make your calling and election sure, for if you practice these qualities, you will never fall. For in this way there will be richly provided for you an entrance into the eternal kingdom of our Lord and Savior Jesus Christ (1 Pet. 1:5-11).

In addition to the biblical witness, the Westminster Confession of Faith states, "good works, done in obedience to God's commandments, are the fruits and evidences of a true and lively faith: and by them believers manifest their thankfulness… [and] strengthen their assurance" (16.2).

It is because of this connection between the assurance of a lively faith and our good works that we must, by God's grace, be "doers of the word," responding in faithful living to the gospel of the kingship of Jesus. There is a danger in evangelical circles to simply be connoisseurs of sermons, lectures, and books. In the age of the internet and mp3s, it is easy to listen to sermons constantly and read thick, meaty books of theology and all the while think that this is the essence of being a Christian.

But if all we are doing is hearing the Word spoken to us and not *acting* in faith in response to the Word by participating in bringing about the kingdom of Jesus through love of God and our neighbor, we will eventually become self-deceived about our own status before God and our own spiritual health in his kingdom. Slowly we will begin to believe that being a follower of Jesus is demonstrated in our knowledge of his word and appreciation of the finer points of Christian history and theology. Our confidence in our knowledge and wisdom can lead to a subtle form of justification for the indulgence of our natural desires—and before long, our vanity becomes our piety.

Though we often focus on the New Testament warnings against deception through the false doctrine or teaching of others, James's words regarding the reality of self-deception ought to be taken with equal seriousness. It is possible to listen to and understand insightful teaching, to ward off deceptive doctrines, and yet to be deceived by ourselves, to be deluded in our own mind and heart about our life and status before God—and this is the danger James warns against.

Self-delusion is the most frightening and insidious kind of delusion because it is the most difficult to detect. Indeed, the very definition of self-delusion is that we are unaware it is happening. We must, however, not dwell too long on the dangers of self-deception, and we should note that the antidote for its danger is not morbid self-inspection, not a turning inward to discover evidence of a changed heart, but rather, simply hearing the word of God and doing it. The path to freedom from self-deception in the Christian life is not to think more deeply or reflect more closely upon our internal state, but rather to act in obedience to the way of Christ—giving ourselves to others by loving God and our neighbor.

With this summary in mind, let us look closer at the process of self-deception in the life of the believer as described by James. James writes, "for if anyone is a hearer and not a doer, he is like a man who looks repeatedly at his beginning face in a mirror. He looks at himself and goes away and at once forgets what he was like" (James 1:23-24). This is the way that self-deception begins—not being honest when we see ourselves reflected in the mirror. This is how self-deception takes over and blinds us to the truth.

The mirror that we examine our spiritual selves in is not a physical glass mirror, but rather the mirror of God's Word. Our self-deception takes root when we examine our lives in the light of what the Scriptures demand (or, more accurately, when we are confronted with the word of God in the liturgy and sermon of the gathered worship of God's people) and pat ourselves on the back, congratulating ourselves on our knowledge and spirituality and ignoring the practical ways we neglect to actually act out the commands of God in love toward our family, friends and neighbors.

What James is saying is that our spirituality must be defined not simply by careful attention to God's word but also a life of obedience to its demands. Indeed, James shows us here what it means to be a hearer of the word. It is not nuanced intellectual appreciation of its details but rather actually acting in humble submission to the shape of its story. This does not mean that we ought to dismiss the serious study of Scripture in favor of a consciously "simple" spirituality, but rather that the most spiritual person in a church may very well be the quiet man or woman whose life is marked by the beauty of humility and gentleness rather than the one with the most books on his shelf.

Furthermore, the self-deception that James warns against in this passage is not something that happens overnight. Rather, inoculation against the piercing of the word and sacrament is a slow process and is the fruit of a consistent refusal to allow oneself to continually repent and be shaped by the demands of Jesus. Every time we look in the mirror of the Word and refuse to allow the sword of the Spirit to carve us up, we build up a resistance to his work. Over time, the image we see reflected back at us in the mirror will cease to match reality and will only reflect what we imagine.

But we must not misread the intention of James's words in this passage. He does not write to his flock so that they will be filled with morbid suspicion of themselves and others around them. Remember that James opens this section with an exhortation: "Be doers of the word, and not hearers only!" (1:22). The antidote to self-deception is not self-suspicion, but rather an obedient participation in the life of the people of God and a life pattern of humble repentance that marks those who have received with meekness the implanted Word.

Indeed, day after day and week after week, we who belong to the people of God are given the opportunity to have our ears opened to the word of God through our participation in the worship of the church. Each time we hear the word in a sermon spoken by a servant of Christ, speak the word in the liturgy in response to the call of Christ, eat the word in the Lord's Supper, and see the word implanted in the baptism of one of God's children, we are called to be shaped by the ritual that we inhabit. "Shape" ought not to be misunderstood to mean simply "think differently." Rather the meek and humble are shaped by their participation in the ritual life of the church almost without their realization of it. It is actually more normal and natural that only after we begin to "do" God's word that we will be able to consciously articulate its effect on our hearts, rather than the other way round. Indeed, if we allow our definition of repentance and sanctification to be understood as simply the manner in which the word of God affects our conscious thoughts and then trickles down to informing the way we speak and act, we will have missed the point of James's admonition. For James defines the one who truly "hears" the word as the one who "looks into the mature law, the law of liberty, and perseveres, being no hearer who forgets but a doer who acts" (1:25).

In the life of the follower of Jesus, there is no standing still. We are always walking in the Christian life either away from or towards our destination as mature sons and daughters of God. There are no plateaus in our journey—the nature of our humility and the manner of our participation in the life of the people of God is always shaping us to become like Christ in his maturity or like someone or something else that is less than that.

Several more comments are in order regarding the pattern of self-deception as described by James. For example, notice that the reason the hearer of the word falls into self-deception is because he looks into the mirror and immediately *forgets* his appearance. When he returns the next day to gaze at himself again, he has forgotten what he looked like yesterday and soon begins to believe that his appearance is improving, unaware that nothing is happening, because he has no context to judge his progress. Spiritual self-deception is linked to a fundamental lack of self-honesty.

When we examine the original Greek of the passage, we see that in verse 23, the one who is a hearer of the word only examines his "genesis face"—translated in the ESV as "natural face," but perhaps better rendered as his "beginning face." In contrast, the doer of the word in verse 25 examines the "*telios* law," that is, the perfect, complete, or the mature law. Thus, James links this passage back to his epistle's overall theme of suffering and maturity. This is the law that when followed brings the hearer and doer to his God-appointed end or goal (*telios*). James has been talking about "maturity" (*teleios*) a great deal already (1:4: 17) and he will continue to do so (2:22; 3:2). What James advises here will be what produces maturity. Follow the "mature instruction" (a better translation than "perfect law") and one will find blessedness and peace (1:25).

The one who hears the word only but does not act does not grow into maturity, but remains rooted in his "beginning face." We should see this as another perspective on the double-minded man who asks for wisdom in verses 6-8, or the rich man who will fade away under the scorching heat in verses 11-12. This immature man is unable to endure the suffering necessary for wisdom and maturity, because he hears the word only but does not act—he is self-deceived, forgetful, and double-minded, and he will fade under the fire of persecution.

In contrast to the image of the foolish and self-deceived man, James calls his readers to be like the man who is a "doer of the word," the one who looks into the mature law of liberty, perseveres and acts in obedience—and thus is blessed. But what is this mature law, this law of liberty? James certainly refers here to the Old Testament law, but more than that, it is likely that he also intends his readers to understand that this law of liberty is the mature, complete instruction/law given in the teachings of Jesus (as will be examined later, in 2:11-12 James explicitly ties "the law of liberty" to the teachings of Christ).

James locates the path of maturity and blessedness squarely in the context of the commandments or instruction of God. The biblical law, summed up and clarified in the words of Jesus, is not a hindrance to our maturity and growth as Christians (that is, serving *only* the purpose of helping us to realize our sin and need for Christ), but it rather outlines how it is that we are to grow and mature. James calls this law the law of liberty because it is his belief that it is through meditation on and acting in accordance with God's law that men and women may live in the freedom that God intended for them—it is only through obedience to the commands of Jesus that humanity will grow into maturity and image God in the fulfillment of his creation purpose.

This discussion of the law sets the context for how we understand James's discussion of faith and works in James 2. Obedience to the law (that is, "works") is an essential component of faith not simply because it verifies the existence of intellectual assent to the promises of Jesus, but rather because it is the Christ-appointed path to maturity and righteousness—to proclaim faith in Jesus and fail to meditate on and keep his instruction is to demonstrate the lack of faith, for faith and obedience are inseparable from one another.

To shun the instruction of Jesus and to avoid the path he walked in perseverance and suffering is to fail to trust in him, and it is for this reason that such a person's "faith is dead," because he trusts in something other than Christ himself. Jesus is the mature man, the model, and the goal of the Christian life. Jesus is the true image of God towards which we are all being drawn and into which we are all being transformed. And James clearly here outlines the only way that transformation may happen—through meditation upon and acting in response to his law. To fail to live in the way Jesus lived or to resist the life-altering demands of his teaching is to prove our resistance to his lordship. Maturity in the Christian life is not an extra requirement for the super spiritual; rather it is God's intention for all those that follow his son. To fail to grow in maturity and to persevere is to fail to trust in Jesus, since to hear the word only and not act in obedience is to reject the pattern of Jesus's life.

James finishes his portrait of the mature doer of the word by writing that such a disciple is one who, "perseveres, being no hearer who forgets but a doer who acts, [and] he will be blessed in his doing" (v. 25b). James here describes not only the path for those who follow Jesus but also the character and life of Jesus himself. As we who follow Christ meditate and gaze upon his mature law, we are transformed into his image—and as we are transformed, we participate more and more in his way of life, which was one of obedience, submission and perseverance in the face of suffering.

And in the end, the result of this kind of life is "blessedness." This was the point of Jesus's teaching during his Sermon on the Mount, and this is the point of James's words to the embattled and suffering church of Jesus, as they struggle to pursue his ways in their own lives. What is the nature of this blessedness?

To be sure, our blessedness is based fundamentally in God's eschatological vindication of his people and his restoration of all things. But perhaps even more at its core, the blessedness of the doer of the word as he or she perseveres in obedience and is made mature as a son or daughter of God is their participation in the life of Jesus, acting as he acted, obeying as he obeyed—more and more completely following Jesus, who lived as the fulfillment of God's intention for the crown of his creation, humanity. That is, when we hear the word and act upon it, steadfast in our perseverance despite suffering, we are living as God created men and women to live—through Christ, we are patient and obedient where Adam was arrogant and rebellious, and we receive the maturity and blessing that he failed to enjoy because he was unable to remain steadfast.

In all of this we see that James is in no way advocating a "works-righteousness" gospel—rather he is proclaiming the consistent biblical message that reception of the blessings of God is tied up with acting in cooperation and in enjoyment of God's story for the world (and not simply giving intellectual assent to the story). This lack of cooperation was the failure of Adam, but through the greater Adam we are drawn into obedience of the law of liberty and a participation in the blessedness of Jesus as we obey his commands and persevere in his ways.

Biblical righteousness in the Old or New Testaments never separates internal love of God from external submission to his pattern for life (except in commenting on the perverseness of having one without the other). If we approach the letter of James expecting that he will declare either the internal assent or external obedience to be more essential to faith than the other, we miss the basic point of his letter. For in James's understanding of the kingdom of God, obedience to God's law (or "works") does not serve to merely verify or prove our internal faith (as though only our internal faith was important) but rather obedience and perseverance are part and parcel of faith, since in our obedience and perseverance we act out our belief that living as Jesus lived will result not in death but resurrection, not in ridicule but in the fullness of maturity.

In James's view, we are not blessed in our works because we earn points with God, nor because we simply prove the veracity of our inner faith—rather we are blessed because we are living out the God-created narrative of humanity—indeed, at its core, it is our participation in the story which is our most significant blessing as sons of God, for in our participation, we are made like the greater Son as we follow him.

What is the path to maturity and blessedness? How may we avoid the pitfalls of self-deception? The way that James paints here is not complicated or difficult to understand. He simply argues that we must be careful to not only hear God's word, but also to act in response to it and to continually gaze into its mysteries and beauty, honestly evaluating the areas where we fall short, confessing our sins and pursuing repentance. This is the way to life and fullness, to maturity and blessedness—trust, repentance, and obedience to the exemplary life of Jesus.

## Worthless Religion

*James 1:26-27*

<sup>26</sup>If anyone seems to be religious and does not bridle his tongue but deceives his heart, this person's religion is worthless. <sup>27</sup>Religion that is pure and undefiled before God, the Father, is this: to visit orphans and widows in their affliction, and to keep oneself unstained from the world.

At the end of his epistle's first chapter, James describes in greater detail exactly what it means to be one who is a doer of the word, boiling it all down into three key actions: bridling one's tongue, visiting orphans and widows in their affliction, and keeping oneself unstained from the world.

For James, these actions comprise a three-fold test of "true religion," and when we lead lives that are characterized by these key attributes, we can add to our assurance that we are not self-deceived, and not one who is a hearer of the word only. It is significant that for James, true religion is not merely thinking the right thoughts or believing the correct doctrinal statements (as modern evangelicalism has often defined true religion) but rather by living in submission to the law of Christ and acting in accordance with his commands.

Again, this is a powerful rebuke to the tendency in some churches to view the most spiritual members of our congregations as those who excel in theological knowledge. In contrast to this, James provides another measure of true spirituality—those whose lives are marked by quiet and humble obedience, by small and seemingly insignificant acts of service are genuinely pious. As he does throughout his epistle, James's words form a stubborn counterpoint to our instinctual assumptions regarding the essence of the Christian life, reminding us that assurance of faith is found not primarily in the stability of our affections for Christ, and our maturity is not measured by the number of sermons we have turned our ear toward or how many fat theological tomes we have read, and surprisingly, spiritual vitality should not be judged by the frequency or quality of our devotional life.

The first test James describes for true religion is the bridling of the tongue. Interestingly, James defines religion without the bridling of the tongue as "empty" or "worthless" (ματαιος), the same word that Paul uses in 1 Corinthians 15:17 to describe the emptiness of our faith without the resurrection of Christ, writing, "And if Christ has not been raised, your faith is futile (ματαιος), and you are still in your sins." What James says is that without a bridled tongue, our religion is groundless—there is no reason to have confidence that we trust in Christ (because we are not walking the path Jesus has marked out for us). Though at first this admonition may seem harsh in its condemnation of those who profess faith in Christ and are unwilling to control their tongues, it is worth considering for what reason James makes this strong connection between vital religion and bridled speech.

At least one reason James is so concerned about speech in his letter (i.e., 1:19-20, 26; 2:2-3, 12, 14; 3:1-12; 4:11, 13-16; 5:12) is because his epistle is written to encourage his readers to remain steadfast in their suffering so that they will be made mature, and in their maturity, they will participate in Christ's kingdom by ruling alongside him. This connection with maturity and ruling is significant because one of the most fundamental ways in which men and women rule with Christ is by speaking righteously—that is, in using their tongue in service to their king.

In Genesis, when Yahweh appoints Adam over all creation, one of his first tasks was to name each of the animals, thus establishing his rule over them. Just as God named the Earth and the Heavens, the Day and the Night, Adam spoke each of the names of the animals, "and whatever man called every living creature, that was its name" (Gen. 2:19). Later, when Eve is brought to Adam as his helper, he continues to speak wisely, naming her with these words, "This at last is bone of my bones and flesh of my flesh; she shall be called Woman, because she was taken out of Man" (Gen. 2:23).

In Genesis 4, this theme of ruling by speaking is depicted vividly, as Lamech speaks these words, "Adah and Zillah, hear my voice; you wives of Lamech, listen to what I say: I have killed a man for wounding me, a young man for striking me. If Cain's revenge is sevenfold, then Lamech's is seventy-fold" (Gen. 4:23-24). Eve, however, righteously responds by calling her new son, "Seth, for she said, 'God has appointed for me another offspring instead of Abel, for Cain killed him'" (Gen. 5:25). And so the seed of the serpent and the seed of the women both rule by their speech, one using his tongue foolishly and the other wisely—one boasting in his own strength and the other speaking words of gratitude and praise to God.

This theme of ruling righteously by speaking continues throughout the Hebrew Scriptures (for example, in the wisdom literature and poetry of Israel's righteous kings, David and Solomon). James is able to speak so strongly about the necessity of bridling the tongue for true religion because he understands that speaking rightly is at the heart of what it means to rule God's creation, which is at the heart of what it means to be human.

It is in Jesus that this biblical theme of ruling by speaking wisely reaches its fullest expression. According to the Servant prophecies of Isaiah, God made Jesus's "mouth like a sharp sword," (Isa. 49:2), and he would rule with his tongue, "strik[ing] the earth with the rod of his mouth" (Isa. 11:4). But the way Jesus would rule with his mouth in Isaiah's prophecies is instructive. Though there would come a time when the Servant would rule with his mouth in power, he first would endure a time when he would rule by bridling his tongue. Indeed, according to Isaiah, the Servant would "not cry aloud or lift up his voice, or make it heard in the street," (Isa. 42:2) and, "he was oppressed, and he was afflicted, yet he opened not his mouth; like a lamb that is led to the slaughter, and like a sheep before its shearers is silent, so he opened not his mouth" (Isa. 53:7).

When Jesus took on flesh and was made man, he followed the pattern that was prophesied for him. Though Jesus spoke out strongly against those who opposed him during his ministry (see, for example, his woes against the scribes and Pharisees in Matthew 23), during his passion, as he endured accusations, threats and violence against him, Jesus chose to bridle his tongue, neglecting to rebuke his oppressors and instead remain silent in the face of their evil. Again, and again, the gospel writers record Jesus as giving his persecutors "no answer" in the face of their threats and lies (Matt. 27:12, 14; Mark 14:61; 15:5; Luke 23:9; John 19:9).

Of course, the way that Jesus used his mouth in the face of persecution directed the rest of his body as well. Explicitly rejecting violence in response to his enemies' violence against him (Matt. 26:52-53), Jesus confidently put his trust in his father to righteously vindicate him, even in the midst of his humiliating and excruciating death on a cross.

After his resurrection from the dead, Jesus was "declared to be the Son of God in power" (Rom. 1:4) and was given "all authority in heaven and on earth" (Matt. 28:18). But in his post-resurrection appearances, Jesus does not rule his kingdom or his subjects by violence or a sword. Rather, when Jesus appears to his disciples after his resurrection, he rules by *speaking*. The one who was once silent in the face of violence and evil now speaks words of authority, explaining the whole of the Scriptures in their relationship to himself (Luke 24:13-35), admonishing and encouraging his closest followers (John 20:24-29; 21:15-19), breathing upon them the gift of the Holy Spirit (John 20:21-22), and issuing to his apostles their marching orders in order that they would go out in his name to spread his kingdom (Matt. 28:18-20; Mark 15:15-18).

When Jesus appears to John in his vision recorded in the book of Revelation, he also rules by speaking (as he did at creation, when he spoke the world into existence and named the earth and heavens). John describes Jesus in terms that echo Isaiah's prophecies—in the first chapter, "from his mouth came a sharp two-edged sword" (Rev. 1:16) and later in his vision, "from his mouth comes a sharp sword with which to strike down the nations" (Rev. 20:15).

Throughout the vision, Jesus is always portrayed as speaking—first Jesus speaks as a king to the seven churches, issuing words of judgment and encouragement as he deals with his subjects (Rev. 2-3), later judging the dead from his throne (Rev. 20:11-15), prophetically speaking the future world into existence (Rev. 21:3-8), and encouraging John that he will come again (Rev. 22:6-16). Elsewhere, angels are described by John as being in violent and physical combat with Satan and his followers, and bringing judgment to the earth (for example, Rev. 8:5; 12:7; 16:1-21; 20:1-3), but the consistent way that Jesus rules the world in Revelation is through speaking—that is, with the sword of his tongue.

In understanding James's words throughout his epistle regarding speech and the use of the tongue by the followers of Jesus, we must remember the context of this epistle. The original readers of this epistle faced violent, systematic, and brutal persecution (Acts 8:1-3; 11:2). Mindful of the prophecies and life of king Jesus, when James warns his readers that in order to practice true religion they must bridle their tongue, he is not simply giving them a wise rule to live by, one that will help them to live at peace with their neighbor. Rather, he is telling them, in no uncertain terms, that there is but one path to maturity and a place as a ruler in the kingdom of Jesus.

If they trust in Jesus, they will walk the path he walked before them—as he was silent in the face of violence, so they ought to be silent, as he bridled his tongue when evil came against him, so also his followers must bridle their tongues. In this way James explains what it means to count it joy in the midst of trials, what it means to remain steadfast so that the work of maturation may be completed—it means to shut one's mouth instead of crying out words of vengeance in response to persecution. To remain silent, even in the face of ultimate evil, is not to be passive or pliable—rather it is to reject one means of resistance and to embrace another, to put our trust in your Father's power to vindicate instead of our own, and to follow Jesus on the long and lonely road to kingship and resurrection, which comes only by suffering and death.

So what does this command to bridle our tongues mean for wealthy Americans who enjoy religious liberty and have little fear of persecution? First, it should help us put in proper perspective the (by comparison) small ways we are sinned against by those in our lives. If James could command his readers to bridle their tongues in the face of violence and death, how much more must we control our speech when someone mocks or slights us?

When we experience "persecution," such as it is, we should follow the admonition of James and the example of Jesus and be willing to suffer without verbal retaliation. Of course, this does not mean that we need to remain absolutely silent. Consider the story of Stephen in Acts 7, who spoke honestly and boldly to his accusers, and in the end, asked Jesus to forgive them. The main thrust of James's words is not that we endure suffering in absolute silence, but that we refrain from cursing our enemies and instead love, bless and forgive them. As we shall see the brothers James addresses are, by their fiery speeches, instigating aggressive, retributive violence against their oppressors (James 4:1-4).

James's words also help us to understand the significance of our battle of control over our words (like bridling a wild animal, to borrow James's metaphor). Refusing to speak, biting our tongue—these are not simply the habits of a highly effective Christian, or a baptized version of nice manners. Rather, when we eschew speaking in anger and choose to trust God for our vindication instead of seizing it for ourselves, we are learning to act like kings. When we practice humility with our words, when we wrestle with and bridle our tongues so that they speak in righteousness and not evil, we are learning to live as Jesus lived, participating in what it means to be fully human—to name the world according to God's law and not our own.

After describing what "worthless religion" looks like, James writes, "Religion that is pure [καθαρος] and undefiled before God, the Father, is this: to visit orphans and widows in their affliction, and to keep oneself unstained from the world." Significantly, *katharos* (καθαρος) is another echo of the Sermon on the Mount, where Jesus said to his disciples, "Blessed are the pure [*katharos*] in heart, for they shall see God."

James is explicating what it means to be pure in heart—to care for those in need and to keep from being corrupted by the world. Again, James points his readers back to the "instruction of liberty," which is the commands and teaching of Jesus, and explains for them what their Lord demands.

It should be noted that the Greek word for "visit" (επισκεπτομαι) is the translation of the Hebrew word that is used whenever God is described as "visiting" his people—that is, saving them, or delivering them from their trouble or hardship. The command that James gives here regarding orphans and widows is not simply going by and spending an hour cheering up a lonely widow—rather it means to enter her life and care for her, ensuring that she has food to eat, a roof over her head, and is safe in her bed at night.

Does it seem odd that we have a command to care for the poor and helpless in an epistle written to persecuted Christian communities? First, consider the fact that it is likely that there were many orphans and widows in the Christian community that James writes to—not because of famine, but because of the persecution of the Jews. During their own suffering, James calls these followers of Jesus to remember the suffering of those around them and act in profoundly unselfish ways by expanding their own families to care for the wives and sons and daughters of those who had been imprisoned or even killed because of their confession that Jesus is Lord.

Beyond this reality, we need to also consider how remembering the purpose of this epistle will help us to understand this command. James writes to his flock so that they will endure their trials joyfully and with steadfastness and will be made mature, so that they will follow Christ and rule with him. In this command to visit orphans and widows in their distress, James is encouraging his readers to fulfill their role as co-rulers with Christ—because to care for orphans and widows is a part of what it means to exercise biblical kingship. Consider the example of David's kindness to the orphan Mephibosheth, who was lame in both legs, but ate every day at the king's table. Also consider the generosity of Solomon's table, recorded in 1 Kings 4. At their best, both kings acted according to the biblical conception of kingship, serving their people with wisdom and abundant generosity. Kingship and ruling in the Bible is always about "service" not "lording it over others" (Mark 10:43-45).

Perhaps, however, the best example of an Israelite figure that serves others with his wealth is found in the story of Boaz, and his actions form a helpful pattern for our own lives as wealthy followers of Jesus. In the beginning of the book of Ruth, Naomi and her daughter-in-law Ruth have lost both of their husbands and are in a precarious situation. Without the protection and care of their husbands, the welfare of these widows is uncertain, especially in the pagan land of Moab. Hearing that the famine in Judah has ended, they journey back to Naomi's homeland together, as Ruth, a Moabitess, refuses to leave her mother-in-law alone and uncared for.

After returning to Bethlehem, Ruth volunteers to glean (that is, gather grain that fell to the ground during the first harvest, a practice that was established for the poor in Israel) from the fields belonging to Boaz, a wealthy relative of Naomi. Boaz is described as a valorous, strong man (Ruth 2:1) and he is one the elders who sits and rules at the gate in the city of Bethlehem (Ruth 4:10). When Boaz discovers that a poor foreigner is gathering grain in his fields, he responds not with indignation, but protection and care. Warning his workers to help Ruth in her work and not obstruct her, Boaz goes out of his way to make sure this widow is welcomed and given food and water.

In time, of course, Boaz would care for and protect Ruth in a more intimate and personal way, taking her into his household and making her his wife. But their later romance grew out of Boaz's initial righteous response to the biblical emphasis on caring for orphans and widows. Acting as a mature and royal follower of Yahweh, Boaz sacrificed grain to personally "visit" this foreign widow that God brought into his fields. In this way, he is a striking fulfillment of the intention of James's exhortations in this verse.

What does James's instruction mean for us today? How are we to imitate Boaz's example and act in obedience to the words of James? First, this is not an isolated command. To care for the physically poor and needy is to act in accordance with the stream of biblical spirituality (e.g., Exod. 22:22; Deut. 10:18; 16:11; 24:19-21; 26:12; Job 29:12; Ps. 10:18; 146:9; Zech. 7:10; Mal. 3:5; Acts 6:1; 1 Tim. 5:3-16). After all, Yahweh is "the Father of the fatherless and the protector of widows" (Ps. 68:5).

As we sacrificially act and give our money, time, and lives to those in need, we obey the royal law of liberty given to us by our Lord Jesus, and we act as his faithful and mature followers. Indeed, James again gives us another mark by which to judge those who model "true religion" and spiritual maturity in our congregations and communities—not by articulate words or teaching skill, and certainly not by their ability to incite violence against their persecutors, but rather simple and consistent actions on behalf of the poor and needy.

To "visit" those in poverty, to protect the unprotected, and to befriend the fatherless and the widow is not a special gifting given only to some members of the church—rather it is a lifestyle we are each called to live out and demonstrate as we grow in maturity in Christ (though our expressions of obedience to this command will vary depending on our particular gifting and callings). James's words do not proscribe a detailed standard by which his readers might fulfill his commands, and we would be misguided if we attempted to enforce a law that Scripture does not give.

Though the specifics of our obedience to James's words in this verse may differ based upon our various callings and situations, James expects those who follow Christ to be people who care for, serve, and protect those widows and orphans that are brought into our lives by God. It also means that we are people who do not ignore the widows and orphans who are already in our congregations and communities, who do not wait for a knock on the door requesting help but seek to proactively reach out to those in need in their neighborhood, city and church.

Though we may at first think that widows and orphans might be difficult to find in our modern and wealthy society, it is worth considering that to be a "widow" does not necessarily mean that your husband is deceased but can also include women who have been divorced or deserted by their husbands and must now fend for themselves in the world. There may not be too many women and children who are literal widows and orphans in our communities, but nearly every neighborhood and congregation include women who have been left alone by men who were duty-bound to care for them. Surely James's words call us to proactively engage and care for these women and children in our churches and neighborhoods, serving them physically as well as spiritually.

Remember that James is here again expounding upon the words of Jesus his teacher, for it was Jesus who taught that the righteous and wicked will be separated in judgment based upon whether they fed the hungry, clothed the naked, and visited those in need (Matt. 25:31-46). James's emphasis upon the necessity of deeds of love for those who belong to the kingdom of God is not a novel or radical teaching, but rather one that fits into the broad narrative of biblical salvation and redemption. This is what it means to trust in Jesus—to live as he lived, to follow his path, trusting that his vindication and resurrection is a foreshadowing of our own. And so just as Jesus loved and served the innocent, helpless, and needy so also must we care for those in our churches and communities who find themselves in need.

Finally, consider James's admonition to "keep oneself unstained from the world" (James 2:27). It may be tempting to take James's words to mean that those who follow Christ ought to separate themselves from the outside and unbelieving world. But we must read this command in its immediate context, and James has also just instructed his readers to care for widows and orphans, without any indication that this care should be restricted only to believers—so James is not interested in physical separation from the world, but something else.

It is better to understand James to mean that his readers are to keep themselves from being unstained from the ways of the world—the world's wisdom, the world's understanding of reality and suffering. Indeed, this passage can be considered a parallel to James 4:4, where James warns his readers against "friendship with the world." James is reminding his readers that they are called to live not in submission to the rules and expectations of their world, but rather their allegiance and friendship is due to another—to their Lord and Savior, Jesus.

It is in this command to remain unstained by the world that the highly political nature of the gospel that is proclaimed by the apostles is revealed. These early followers of Jesus were persecuted and killed not simply because of the evil nature of the Jews who pursued them but because of a real understanding that in the proclamation of Jesus as Messiah, these Christians were threatening the very foundation of the Jewish religion. It was for this reason that Jesus himself was put to death, and for this reason his followers were put to the sword for their claim that Jesus had been brought back from the dead by God himself.

But of course, the announcement of good news that these Christians made with their lives and their innocent deaths was not simply that Jesus was the Jewish Messiah, but that this man from Nazareth was the king of the entire world, and that no other, even Caesar himself could lay claim to his title. These early followers of Jesus were not simply practicing a new religion in a world that was full of new religions. If this had been the case, then none would have sought them out for imprisonment and death. Rather, those who bore the name Christian proclaimed a new social order, a new kingdom, and lived as though what they believed had actually come to pass in time and space.

In commanding his flock to remain unstained from the world, James is not simply maintaining the innocence of his church. Rather he is taking seriously the reality of Jesus's ultimate kingship and reminding his followers that they are no longer beholden to the authority of the old world, but are in the business of bringing in a new one.

It is difficult to know exactly how to apply the political nature of this command in a world that has largely forgotten or grown immune to the radical nature of the Church's purpose and aims. Of course, this immunity is due in large part to the Church's own amnesia regarding her fundamental reason for existence. Perhaps the best application of these passages in our own lives is to meditate anew upon the deep reality of the truths we proclaim when we gather for the liturgy and word, when we feast with Christ and taste the firstfruits of the new earth on our tongue, or watch the water trickle down the face of our sons and daughters and are reminded that we are promised a share not only in the death of Jesus but also in his glorious resurrection.

After all, Jesus's claim that the meek shall inherit the earth is not some pie in the sky oath made by a fiery-eyed prophet who faded away and was never heard from again. Rather, this radical declaration regarding the identity of the future rulers of this world was made by a man who was violently killed and then would not stay dead. We who follow the Christ are caught up in a story that is larger than we dare dream, and to live as though the One who created all things is unable or unwilling to keep all his promises is to make allegiance with the losing side. We are not of the world, and our inheritance will not be as the world inherits. But in the end, make no mistake, the meek shall inherit the earth, and the pure in the heart shall see God.

## Summary & Reflections

In James 1:2-4, the apostle explained the basic purpose of his letter: to exhort and encourage his dispersed flock to remain steadfast and joyful under trial and suffering, knowing that the testing of their faith will result in their maturity. When we read the entire book of James through this lens of suffering and maturity, it helpfully opens the rest of the book's meaning, cohering it around a single theme. Indeed, James 1:19-27 fits nicely with the overall thrust of 1:2-4 and examining this section briefly as an explication of the book's main purpose will help us to understand and apply their meaning. So how does reading James 1:19-27 through the lens of 1:2-4 help us to understand these verses?

We might put it this way: in verses 19-21, James explains further what it means to "count it all joy" when we encounter trials and suffering in our lives. In verses 22-25, James deals more closely with the concept of "steadfastness"—teaching how we may persevere in the midst of trials and examining the way of steadfastness so that his readers will continue in the faith. In verses 26-27, James briefly explains in more detail what it means for his readers to be mature and complete in their faith, explaining the character and lifestyle of the mature follower of Jesus. Let's now take a brief look at each of these sections in turn, considering how reading them in light of James 1:2-4 helps our understanding.

In James 1:2, James instructs his readers to "Count it all joy, my brothers, when you meet trials of various kinds." But what does James mean by "count it all joy"? Does this simply mean that we should remain happy and optimistic when tragedy and suffering enter our lives? Does it mean when suffering comes upon us that we simply grit our teeth and intellectually acknowledge that it is for our good (i.e count it as joy), and then enter a state of detached stoicism? Not at all.

James admonishes his readers to be quick to listen, slow in their speaking and slow in their anger, for their anger will not bring about the righteousness (that is, the justice and promises) of God. In verse 20, James reminds his readers that it is for this reason they should put away wickedness and receive with meekness the gospel of Christ. And so, we begin to see what it means to "count it all joy" when we suffer trials and tribulations, whether through persecution and oppression or simply in the sickness and trouble of this broken world.

To count our sufferings as joy is to stop our mouths before we speak in haste against those who trouble us, to listen humbly to the word of God before we raise our fists to the sky in righteous indignation, and to put off self-indulgent and worldly anger against the reality of our sufferings, or against whom or whatever we consider to be their author. To count our sufferings as joy is to shed our own anger because we trust that it is not in our strength or ability that God's righteousness will be accomplished, but rather through the vindication and renewal effected by God himself.

Therefore, to count our sufferings as joy is to put aside wicked aspirations of revenge against our tormentors, and trust, with meekness (that is, patient and humble faithfulness), the power of the gospel of our Lord to save us and make us new. Far from simply an optimistic approach toward life or a stoic resignation to the harshness of this world, James teaches us in 1:19-21 that to count our sufferings as joy is to embrace a full-bodied trust in Jesus by rejecting worldly responses to suffering and confessing in our hearts, words and lives that despite what we may see before us, God will bring his righteousness into this world, that all things will be made new, and our participation in this renewal is helped by our endurance of trials and suffering.

Looking further in James's introduction to his letter, we find that to receive blessing and maturity through our trials and suffering, we have to remain faithful and steadfast during them. As James writes in 1:12, "Blessed is the man who remains steadfast under trial, for when he has stood the test he will receive the crown of life, which God has promised to those who love him." But how can we remain steadfast while experiencing severe suffering and persecution? James answers this question in 22-25 by writing that we may avoid self-deception only by meditating upon and obeying the law of liberty—acting in accordance to the words and teaching of Jesus. The path of perseverance is not found in our quantity of theological knowledge or our mastery of biblical minutia, but simply in our embodied obedience to the commands and example of our Lord.

James's introduction examines the fruit that our steadfast endurance of trials will bear in our lives—maturity and completeness. But what does it mean to be mature and complete, to lack nothing? Of course, there is a sense in which this maturity is only found in the coming age of the renewed heavens and earth, but we must not miss the fact that James holds out *the promise of a maturity to be found in this life as well*, as we faithfully endure our Father's discipline and instruction for us, meekly following Jesus in obedience and in suffering.

Then, in verses 26-27, James describes what this maturity looks like, and by giving us a picture of the goal of our obedience, he helps to persevere towards that goal. First, the mature man or woman is someone who bridles their tongue, one who follows the commands of 1:19, and is slow to speak, quick to listen and slow to anger. This mature humility should not be confused with passivity, but rather is a quiet patience based upon a strong confidence in the power and faithfulness of God to protect and vindicate them. Allowing "love to cover a multitude of sins" (1 Pet. 4:8), the mature man guards his mouth and is careful with his words, mindful of the power of his tongue to control his heart and mind and its proclivity for inflicting unrighteous injury upon others.

The mature person described in verse 27 is also someone who proactively reaches out to those in need around him, neither ignoring the existence of the defenseless nor excusing himself from aiding and protecting them by pointing to his busyness or other important responsibilities. As he cares for and serves orphans and widows in his neighborhood and congregation, the mature man or woman imitates Christ and images God, acting as a ruler who has gazed upon the law of liberty and lives in accordance to its demands.

We should remember that James is writing first to the "brothers," that is to the leaders of the community. As we read on in the letter, we will discover that these men have fallen into certain predictable "worldly" traps often common to leaders, especially intellectuals. Educated pastors and professors come to believe that they exist on a higher plane than ordinary people because they consider themselves to be the heralds of a social vision for peace and justice. But when they seek to implement that vision, they act as if they are above the law, above common morality. Since their cause is righteous and, in their minds, would benefit the masses, some liberties can be taken in the pursuit of their righteous ends.

But more troubling still is when Christian leaders love to spin out grand theories about why things have gone wrong, what needs to be changed, and how to inspire others to action for the sake of the kingdom. . . but then they themselves will ignore the more common, ordinary acts of charity and obedience, as if such concerns are below them. It is too easy for Christian professors, theologians, teachers, and pastors to exult in rhetoric designed to move others to act, but then we ourselves ignore obedience in common life, if you will, because we are called to greater deeds. Worse still is when we look down our noses at these ordinary activities as ineffective distractions from the larger theatre of political and governmental affairs. But rather than being distractions, these ordinary acts of self-denial, sacrifice, of treating others as better than ourselves, loving those whom God has put in our path—all of this is precisely characteristic of the new social reality we call the kingdom of God. It is, as James will remind us in James 3, a kingdom characterized by loving, charitable, peaceful speech and behavior. This is the "harvest of righteousness" (3:18) that Christian leaders must model and encourage in others.

Finally, according to verse 27, the one who has persevered and has learned obedience will live in the world but will also be distinct from it—having rejected the world's wisdom, he confidently conforms his life to the pattern set forth by Jesus. Living as one who is unstained by the world does not mean that we are separate from and fearful of the world's agenda and values—indeed, this an immature shadow of faithful obedience to James's commands.

Rather, to be truly unstained by the world means that we will speak the world's language, enjoy its good pleasures and love its beauty, but subversively pattern our steps after Jesus, beating a counterpoint to the world's accepted rhythm. In our quiet lives of humility and service we proclaim that Jesus is both risen and king, and it is he who owns all authority, not the United Nations or States or any other human invention.

Indeed, if we believe that to live unstained by the world is to protect ourselves or our children from its wiles, then we have missed the point of the words of James and the life of Jesus—for our faithful purity, properly understood and practiced, threatens to shake the foundations of the world's power because we refuse to accept its validity or hold over our lives. This is how we change the world.

At the end of the last chapter, I quoted from Aleksandr Solzhenitsyn's response to the American media's mocking criticism of his praise for how many of the Russian people were spiritually transformed by their experience of suffering. He notes how, in the absence of anything close to love from their ruling elites, the common people expressed their love for one another in concrete ways.

> Russian faces seldom if ever wear a token smile, but we are more generous in our support of one another. This is all done voluntarily and informally, and such sacrifices are in no sense tax deductible; indeed, no such system even exists in our country. Taking risks for the sake of others is part of the moral climate in which we live, and I have more than once had occasion to witness the transformation which people from the West have undergone after living and working for a long period in Soviet conditions.[21]

In closing, consider the word that James uses repeatedly to describe the man or woman who guards his or her tongue, who perseveres in obedience and is made mature. James writes, "But

---

21 Solzhenitsyn, *The Mortal Danger*, 67.

the one who looks into the mature law, the law of liberty, and perseveres, being no hearer who forgets but a doer who acts, he will be *blessed* in his doing" (v. 25). It is worth pausing for a moment to consider how counterintuitive this statement is in our world. In the epistle's first chapter, James claims that person who bears suffering through no fault of his own, who endures trials without anger but joy, who holds his tongue in the face of unjust oppression, and spends his days in meditation and submission to the law of a dead man who claims to have risen again—according to James, this man is not a fool, he is *blessed*.

And what is this blessing? It is God's loving, good purposes for our lives, his comprehensive well-being in all its fullness, whatever that means and wherever that takes us. Simply put, blessedness is our participation in the *shalom* of God, in the fulfillment of his promise to renew and remake all things, and to put all things under the rule of his ascended Son and to bodily live with him forevermore.

As in the first chapter of this book when we considered how the life of Jacob demonstrated and foreshadowed the promises and themes of the opening verses of James's epistle, it may now be helpful to consider the way another prophetic preview of Jesus epitomizes the themes of James 1:19-27.

Born the favored son of Jacob, the God-wrestler, Joseph began to dream dreams when he was seventeen and still in his father's house. In the night, Joseph was given visions of his authority and power over his family, but in the mornings when he awoke, he was greeted only by the derision of his older brothers who jealously longed for his place of favor. In many families of power, the favored son and heir is pampered and protected until the day when he assumes the authority from his father. Though Joseph's dreams of his royal future were prophetic of his future rule, his path to kingship would not be through pampering and pleasure. Instead, Joseph would walk the path of Jacob, the path of David, the path of Jesus—the downward road to kingship.

## How God Makes Things Right

Sold into slavery by his brothers because of their jealousy and hatred, Joseph found himself working in the house of an Egyptian officer, far from home and dead to his family. But instead of crying out because of the injustice of his situation, Joseph humbly accepts his plight and becomes a prosperous worker for his new owner. However, sometime later, after resisting his owner's wife's sexual advances, Joseph is falsely accused of attempting to rape his mistress and thrown into an Egyptian prison. It seems impossible to imagine that there in that cold and dark prison, hungry and sore from his beatings, the fleeting memory of his dreams of ruling did not come back into Joseph's mind, haunting him with their promises.

Falling from his status as the favored son of a tribal leader to a slave in a foreign land all the way to slave's prison with no hope of release, Joseph endured a series of trials we can only begin to imagine. And yet, even in that cold prison, Joseph bridled his tongue and did not speak in anger. Instead, he humbly began to serve his captors and soon he was put in charge of all the prisoners. Years later, Joseph was still serving humbly in prison when Pharaoh, the king of Egypt, had his own dream. Unable to understand its meaning, Pharaoh heard of a faithful Hebrew slave with the strange ability to interpret dreams and called Joseph into his presence. Faced with the opportunity to voice his anger and bitterness directly to the king himself, Joseph chose instead to explain Pharaoh's dream and wisely suggest how the disaster of famine in Egypt might be avoided. In this way the young boy's dreams would begin to be fulfilled through his interpretation of the dream of this foreign king.

Struck with the wisdom and ability of the freshly shaved and cleanly dressed Hebrew slave, Pharaoh made the astonishing decision not only to believe Joseph's interpretation but also to appoint him as the ruler over all of Egypt, in order that Joseph might prepare Egypt for the famine to come. For seven years, Joseph faithfully served Egypt, ruling over them with wisdom and humility, and when the promised famine came upon the land, all the earth came to Egypt to buy grain for themselves.

Indeed, even Joseph's brothers were forced to visit Egypt, looking for food in their time of hunger. And in that moment, faced with his brothers on their knees asking for mercy from the one brother they thought they would never see again, Joseph was given the opportunity to take his revenge, to angrily berate his brothers for their hatred and violence against their own blood. But instead of anger, Joseph wept tears of joy. And instead of curses, he spoke only these words: "You meant evil against me, but God meant it for good, to bring it about that many people should be kept alive" (Gen. 50:20). And Joseph, the ruler made mature by these trials, bridled his tongue and served those in need whom God had brought to him, even his brothers who had sought to kill him so long ago.

Like Joseph, we are sons of the living God, destined for maturity and kingship alongside his greater Son. But, also like Joseph, our path to maturity is the path of trials and suffering. But as we count our trials as joy, being quick to listen and slow to anger, as we persevere in obedience to the law of liberty, we will also be lifted up and made into mature sons and daughters of God with bridled tongues, caring for those in need, living pure and unstained by the world.[22]

---

22 For more on Joseph's life of faithful service see Jordan, *Primeval Saints*, 117-149.

## 6

# CURRYING FAVOR OR CULTIVATING FAITHFULNESS

*Jesus said to them, "Watch and beware of the leaven of the Pharisees and Sadducees."*
*"If anyone would come after me, let him deny himself and take up his cross and follow me"*
– Matthew 16:16, 24

### James 2:1-13

¹My brothers, show no partiality as you hold the faith in our Lord Jesus Christ, the Lord of glory. ²For if a man wearing a gold ring and fine clothing comes into your assembly, and a poor man in shabby clothing also comes in, ³and if you pay attention to the one who wears the fine clothing and say, "You sit here in a good place," while you say to the poor man, "You stand over there," or, "Sit down at my feet," ⁴have you not then made distinctions among yourselves and become judges with evil thoughts? ⁵Listen, my beloved brothers, has not God chosen those who are poor in the world to be rich in faith and heirs of the kingdom, which he has promised to those who love him? ⁶But you have dishonored the poor man. Are not the rich the ones who oppress you, and the ones who drag you into court? ⁷Are they not the ones who blaspheme the honorable name by which you were called?

⁸If you really fulfill the royal law according to the Scripture, "You shall love your neighbor as yourself," you are doing well. ⁹But if you show partiality, you are committing sin and

are convicted by the law as transgressors. ¹⁰For whoever keeps the whole law but fails in one point has become accountable for all of it. ¹¹For he who said, "Do not commit adultery," also said, "Do not murder." If you do not commit adultery but do murder, you have become a transgressor of the law. ¹²So speak and so act as those who are to be judged under the law of liberty. ¹³For judgment is without mercy to one who has shown no mercy. Mercy triumphs over judgment.

In the first chapter of his epistle, James exhorts his readers to endure their suffering with perseverance and joy so that they will be made mature. At the end of his letter's first chapter, James begins to describe in detail the nature and behavior of the mature person, concluding that he is a man who bridles his tongue, cares for the poor and defenseless and keeps himself unstained by the world. Here in the second chapter of his epistle, James continues to teach his disciples regarding the maturity in Christ for which they are being shaped and are called to embrace, beginning with an illustrative parable (2:1-7), and then meditating upon the teaching of Jesus (2:8-13), focusing on impartiality, a thoroughly Biblical expectation for rulers.

*James 2:1*

¹My brothers, show no partiality as you cling to faithfulness of our Lord Jesus Christ, the glory.

This might better be translated as "My brothers, not in partiality hold [to] the faithfulness of our Lord Jesus Christ, the glory." The question is whether to translate *pistis* as "the faith in" or "the faithfulness of" of Jesus. Both are possible exegetically, but the latter is more likely given the context of this verse, which comes in the middle of James teaching his disciples how best to imitate the mature Christ in their own lives. The meaning might then be paraphrased this way: "My brothers, be impartial in your dealings with others as you hold to the pattern of our Lord Jesus Christ in your own lives, who is himself the glory—that is, the one who has been made mature."

The thrust of this verse is to urge the readers of this epistle to commit themselves to follow the faithful example of Jesus as they endure suffering and trials, for through imitating him they will be made mature. Understanding this passage through the lens of the purpose of the letter in 1:2-4, we might say that James is encouraging his readers to rejoice in their sufferings as Jesus rejoiced, to persevere as he persevered, and to be made mature as he also was made mature (not only in fact, but also in the same manner).

Significantly, Jesus is called "the glory." This is because Jesus is the glorious man, the one who learned obedience and was made mature through his suffering and death (Heb. 5:8-9) and was therefore declared to be superior to the angels and called "the radiance of the glory of God" (Heb. 1:3-4). Though Jesus was certainly made man in order to live a sinless life and die an innocent death in order to atone for the sins of man and pacify God's wrath, this verse focuses upon another part of Jesus's mission. He was called to obey where Adam rebelled, and to patiently wait for the Father to bestow upon him the glory of kingship, in contrast to Adam, who impetuously grasped glory for himself when he ate from the fruit of the tree of the knowledge of good and evil.

Though Adam failed to mature into glory and damned all his seed, those who have been united to Christ share also in his glory and maturity, both in this age (incompletely) as well as the next (completely). When we are called by the New Testament writers to "be like Jesus," it is this maturity in obedience and submission that we are being called into. Here James is claiming that a part of the maturity that his readers are called into is to "show no partiality."

But why does James emphasize impartiality with such force here? Because our calling as followers of Jesus is to be "mature as your heavenly Father is mature" (Matt. 5:48)—that is, to imitate and be like God (Eph. 5:1). It is for this reason that we are called to guard our tongues, eschew anger, and serve and deliver those in need—because this is how God deals with his people. It is also for this reason that we are called to be impartial, for showing impartiality toward others is one of the fundamental ways in which God and man are distinct.

It is the consistent witness of Scripture that God "shows no partiality" (Rom. 2:11), and that he "judges impartially" (1 Pet. 1:17) between men. Indeed, a prominent theme of the Mosaic law is Israel's responsibility to deal impartially in judgment between men because to act in this way is to mirror and imitate God (Exod. 23:3; Deut. 1:17; 10:17; 16:19). One of the most significant locations of this command is in Leviticus 19:15, which reads, "You shall do no injustice in court. You shall not be partial to the poor or defer to the great, but in righteousness shall you judge your neighbor." A few verses later, Moses connects this command to the more general admonition, "You shall love your neighbor as yourself" (Lev. 19:18). Significantly, James, who has studied and meditated upon the Old Testament law as well as the instruction of Jesus, also connects impartiality to love of neighbor in James 2:8-9.

James is exhorting his readers to consider the full implications of Jesus's distillation of the entire law into two commands: loving God and loving neighbor (Matt. 22:37-40). Just as we would expect in an epistle that is concerned with maturity in its readers, James is working out for his flock a more complete understanding of what it means to live in submission to Christ's law. But there is an important difference between James's application of this principle (show impartiality as a way of loving our neighbors) and the Mosaic application.

When impartiality is commended to Israel in the Torah (Exod. 23:3; Lev. 19:15; Deut. 1:17; 16:19), it is always in the context of rendering judgment in a court setting. However, in James 2, the context shifts to gathered worship, and indeed, to all of life. Beyond this shift of setting, James's commands also have more to do with correcting the more subtle sin of how a person is discriminated against informally rather than the justice of a formally rendered legal judgment. For example, James's commands concern whom his readers "pay attention to" (James 2:3a), the words they use to address different kinds of people (2:3b), and their inner thoughts (2:4). Just as James's teacher, Jesus, delivered an expansion of the Old Testament law in his Sermon on the Mount which called his disciples to a more mature and complete keeping of God's ways (so that they would be mature as God is mature), James applies the Old Testament expectation that God's people would render impartial judgment and requires his church to be loving and impartial in all their dealings with men.

*James 2:2-4*

²For if a man wearing a gold ring and fine clothing comes into your assembly, and a poor man in shabby clothing also comes in, ³and if you pay attention to the one who wears the fine clothing and say, "You sit here in a good place," while you say to the poor man, "You stand over there," or, "Sit down at my feet," ⁴have you not then made distinctions among yourselves and become judges with evil thoughts?

James illustrates and applies his general exhortation to avoid partiality as we follow the life-pattern of Jesus by telling his readers a simple and brief story. In James's parable, a rich man and a poor man come into a worship gathering of the church, one with expensive clothing and gold jewelry and the other dressed in worn-out garb. Noticing the rich man, the church members hurry over and quickly give up their own favorite seats so that he can rest comfortably and enjoy the service and singing. In contrast, the poor man is hardly given a second glance and offhandedly offered one of the few, unwanted places left in the assembly. After describing these events, James then turns back upon his readers and accuses them, arguing that if they behave in this way, they "have made distinctions among [them]selves," and have violated his command in 2:1.

But why did James use this story to illustrate his command regarding partiality? Considering again the context of the situation of the church to which James wrote will help us to understand his intentions. The early Christians who were the recipients of this letter were Jewish believers exiled from Jerusalem, leaving behind their possessions and livelihoods. Though they fled to escape persecution, we know from the story of Saul in Acts 8-9 that the Jews were sending out men from Jerusalem to track down baptized followers of Jesus. Poor and persecuted, these Christians met in hiding, and were largely powerless against their enemies. Perhaps many of them were still gathering at the local synagogue available to them where they had been exiled. If a rich man had come into one of their assemblies, the immediate reaction would likely have been excitement and hope—hope that if this man, who obviously had money, authority, and power were treated well, then perhaps he would influence others to end or slow the persecution the church was experiencing. This wealthy man has a ring and a robe of office. James will shortly identify this rich man as a blasphemous oppressor (James 2:7), so it makes no sense to think he is referring to wealthy Roman aristocrats. Gentiles would not be strolling into their synagogues. This rich man is no random visitor, but an emissary from the Jewish authorities. He wears a gold signet ring and a robe of authority.

It is not insignificant that this story of discriminately favoring the rich and powerful comes directly after James warns his followers against being stained by the world in 1:27—to leap at the entrance of a person into your assembly who has power and authority, and to hasten to serve him in order to gain his favor and thus manipulate the political situation that you are caught up in—that is the very definition of living according to the wisdom of the world. If James's flock decided to live in this way, it would have been offensive to God not simply because of their impartiality, but what their impartiality revealed—a lack of trust in the way of Jesus and the power of God to vindicate and rescue his people. As James will later warn them, "Friendship with the world is enmity with God" (4:4).

Though rich, powerful men at times courted his favor, Jesus refused to cooperate with their machinations, choosing instead to faithfully obey his father and trust in him alone. Jesus was not interested in currying the favor of the rich, powerful authorities in Jerusalem. He did not attempt to sidetrack their plans to kill him by trying to get them to like him. To walk in the way of Jesus means not only to live as he lived but also to trust as he did, and in this story, James is asking his readers to forsake the political wisdom of the world and instead serve the world's true king (and this itself is of course a highly political demand).

Here in the beginning of James 2, James adds to his command, showing that the coddling of the rich does not produce the righteousness of God either. Both actions—revolutionary anger and political manipulation—have in common their root in the world's assumptions regarding power and authority. Again and again, throughout his epistle, James demands that his readers put aside worldly political assumptions and wisdom and embrace instead the kingdom of God—to "receive with meekness the implanted word." In this he is not asking them to reject politics altogether, but to exchange one kind of politics for another—to join with him in the politics of Jesus, in which the power of the rich oppressor is ignored and the only power that is honored is the authority located in the world's true Lord.

Of course, James's wisdom here in the beginning of James 2 also fits well with his expectation in 1:27 that mature followers of Jesus will care for those in need, for widows and orphans and all those who are valueless in the eyes of the world. When the church goes out of its way to welcome and serve the poor and shabby as James requires, they participate in the kingdom of God and live according to the way of Jesus. To act in this manner, to serve both the rich and the poor without distinction requires not only maturity but that we view the world through the eyes of faith and cease to make value judgments according to our culture's standards, but rather according to the standards of a new culture and kingdom—one that will indeed produce the righteousness of God as we meekly live according to his subversive narrative.

In our own contemporary situation, the temptation for the church to behave according to the world's definitions of power and wisdom has not dissipated. Indeed, if anything, recent history has seen an age when the American church has become more and more politically and media savvy. As we follow Jesus in the modern world, we should be careful not to withdraw from the political or cultural spheres of our society, but we must also operate in those realms with special care, behaving with meekness and godly wisdom and never forgetting that our political power is not located in how well we mold our popular image or make inroads with the rich and powerful. Rather, the modern church would do well to remember that her most powerful political action is in her gathered Sunday worship, in the liturgy and preached word, and most especially, in the sacramental meals and washings which mark out the new and reborn humanity.

Those who have been marked by Christ in baptism and feast with him in the Lord's Supper are a new race that encompasses and overcomes the distinction between all ethnicities and social classes, and her manner of producing the righteousness of God must be according to the rhythms of his kingdom and not the world's demands. This means that we welcome all who come into our community regardless of their power or social status, and that our ultimate hope for survival and social reform lies not in the latest candidate for president or ballot initiative, but in our faithfulness to our king's command to disciple the nations, teaching them the ways of Jesus and baptizing them in the name of the Father, Son, and Holy Spirit.

James provides this critique of the church when it behaves in the way he has described, favoring the rich and powerful at the expense of the weak and helpless: "have you not then made distinctions among yourselves and become judges with evil thoughts?"(v. 4). James makes explicit the way the church breaks his command to reject partiality in their community is by making distinctions among themselves. Though James's example in James 2 deals explicitly with the distinction made between the rich and poor, we can easily see that James's concern can be extended to other superficial differences in the makeup of our communities, be it race, age, education, physical attractiveness or any other variation that may cause us to favor one over another, whether in formal and standardized ways or informal and subtle ones.

As the new community of Jesus we are called to conform to his image both personally and corporately, and so we are a people who are characterized not by cliques and power politics but by joyful fellowship and self-giving love. Living in a broader society that constantly differentiates between its members and segregates itself into smaller groups of common interests, backgrounds, and social classes, the church is meant to be the place where these distinctions are overshadowed by our common allegiance to our king and our shared participation in his story of the redemption and renewal of all things. In a world that assumes and acts according to the belief that money, skin color, and family history determine the extent to which we share our lives, the community of the bride of Christ ought to demonstrate that it is water, not blood, which is thicker and more fundamentally determines the corporate life of our communities.

The rebuke is not only that the church has violated his command to show no partiality but also that they have become evil judges. To "judge" the rich oppressor as someone more deserving of special care than the poor believer is "to become judges engaging in an evil conspiracy" (2:4). That evaluation from James is not just about individual "evil thoughts" but about the way the brothers have conspired together to appease their rich enemies. They have thereby dishonored those poorer disciples whom "God has chosen . . . to be rich in faith and heirs of the kingdom" (2:5).

Moreover, James echoes the commands of the Old Testament for Israel to judge without partiality those who come into her courts and reminds his readers that their subtle favoring of the rich over the poor in their assembly may violate the letter of the Old Testament law (Exod. 23:3) and run counter to a mature obedience demanded by our Lord—an impartiality in all things. In this we see demonstrated the reality that Jesus and his disciples did not come to do away with the law of Moses but rather to fulfill it by calling the new people of God into a mature obedience of its requirements. It is a temptation for many Christians to see the Hebrew Scriptures as antiquated or backwards in its many demands. But the instruction given to Israel in the law is the backstory of the New Testament, and we would be mistaken to believe that God has reneged on his purpose of creating a new society in the midst of a rebellious world that would reflect his righteous character in its patterned life. James calls his church into maturity as they obey God's law and reject partiality in all parts of their community and mirror God's own love and care for mankind.

## Consorting With the Enemy

*James 2:5-7*

> [5]Listen, my beloved brothers, has not God chosen those who are poor in the world to be rich in faith and heirs of the kingdom, which he has promised to those who love him? [6]But you have dishonored the poor man. Are not the rich the ones who oppress you, and the ones who drag you into court? [7]Are they not the ones who blaspheme the honorable name by which you were called?

Previously, James has charged his readers with "becoming judges with evil thoughts," and breaking the Old Testament laws of impartiality when they favor the rich over the poor in their assemblies. Now, in verses 5-7, he gives two further reasons for rejecting this kind of favoritism—God's regard and love for the poor believers, and the oppression of the church by their rich enemies.

It is difficult to read James's words in verse 5 concerning God's election of the poor of the world to be heirs of the kingdom without recalling Jesus's teaching that "blessed are the poor in spirit, for theirs is the kingdom of heaven" (Matt. 5:3). Once again, James echoes the words of his teacher, confronting his readers with the continued authority of Jesus's teaching (due to his resurrection from the dead), but also developing and explaining some of the full implications of Jesus's instruction.

But what does it mean that "God has chosen those who are poor in the world to be rich in faith and heirs of the kingdom"? First, given the reference to the "poor man in shabby clothing" (v. 2), James is talking here about disciples who are materially impoverished. We should, however, be careful here. For it would be a mistake to understand that this verse means that God has chosen the poor at the exclusion of the rich (after all, in 2:1, James prohibits partiality in his reader's lives, and we know from Rom. 2:11 that God himself "shows no partiality"). There are many wealthy believers commended in the Scriptures. It would also be a mistake to think that this passage forbade rich Christians from patronizing the church with gifts. Or that receiving such gifts was a violation of James's injunctions. Such patronage was received by the Jews and by the early Christians (Acts 10:1-2). For example, the fledgling churches needed houses in which to hold their meetings. Wealthy homeowners often allowed their large homes to be used as meeting places (Acts 18:7; Rom. 16:5; 1 Cor. 16:19; Col. 4:15, etc.). The rhetorical point James is making here regarding the poor is not that God prefers the poor to the rich, but that God has indeed chosen poor people as well as rich people to be heirs in his kingdom, especially the impoverished, exiled Christian communities to which James writes.

Moreover, we must note the astonishing implications of God's election of the poor and his impartiality in calling heirs of his kingdom in the context of the culture of the first century Greco-Roman world. Society at that time was rigidly stratified, with a few rich at the very top of the heap, and many poor at the bottom. The only hope for a poor person to climb the social ladder was in finding a rich sponsor who would give him an education and money or land. Though most of the population was poor, the rich controlled the inner workings of society and diligently protected their interests. Essentially, in the Greco-Roman world, only the rich could choose a poor person and make him an heir of the kingdom and part of the powerful elite. But in these verses, James claims that it is God who has this power, and that he also freely chooses whomever he pleases to be an heir in his kingdom, without regard to wealth or social class.

Again, we can begin to see the radical implications of impartiality in the kingdom of God. For within the larger society that was rigidly divided into social classes, the church was a new, counter-society that relativized all of these social markers and declared their powers to be invalid, since valid social markers could be located only in the authority of Jesus, and he had left them with only one social marker—water baptism in his Name. Systematic and organized violence simply does not happen without an obvious political benefit for those who propagate the persecution. Just as Jesus was killed by the ruling establishment of Israel and a Roman governor because he threatened to tear down their structures of power and replace them with his own, the followers of Jesus were killed by Israel and Rome because they represented the fulfillment of that threat.

What does all this mean for the church today? Simply put, we must self-consciously seek to live as those who belong to a new society, one which has done away with the stratification and biases of the old pagan world and live as though the only significant socially distinguishing mark we receive is the mark that is given with water and pronounced in the name of the Father, Son and Holy Spirit. Practically, this means that when rich men come into a church, they should not be given authority or made elders, deacons, or members of a ruling council simply because of worldly power or wealth, but only as they demonstrate Christ-like servant leadership demanded by the teaching of Scripture.

Impartiality in our churches means that pastors should welcome each new visitor and potential member with equal eagerness and without even a hint of a mental calculation of their potential yearly tithe. The decisions of the church leaders ought not to be based on whether a rich man will take his money elsewhere. Giving dignity to the poor means striving to create a church environment that does not have recognizably separate white and blue-collar conversation circles and dinner parties, but ones that are mixed with both kinds of people. All of this must be manifest in our services, especially at the Lord's Table. The Corinthian churches were guilty of something strikingly similar to what is described here by James when they segregated the congregation into rich and poor during communion (1 Cor. 11: 17-22).

When Christians live in this way, we do so not for some American ideal of "democracy," but because of a mature understanding of the social implications of the gospel of our Lord, and an eager desire for the coming of his kingdom—one that is not distinguished by the money or power of its members, but by the love and authority of its king.

By naming those poor people whom God has chosen as "heirs of the kingdom," James is again invoking *royal* language for God's people. It is a major theme of James's epistle that those who follow Christ can endure suffering with joy because this is the process God uses to make them mature and to prepare them to rule with Christ, as was always his intention for mankind. We would do well to remember Paul's words, "The Spirit himself bears witness with our spirit that we are children of God, and if children, then heirs—heirs of God and fellow heirs with Christ, provided we suffer with him in order that we may also be glorified with him" (Rom. 8:16-17). From Jacob to Joseph, Moses, and David, this has always been God's way with this people—to bring them through suffering so that he may glorify them.

James has used a bit of wordplay in these verses, as he writes that God has chosen the poor of the world to be "rich in faith." This contrasts with the oppressors of the church in verses 6 and 7, who are also rich, but rich only in wealth and power, but not in the currency that makes one an heir in the kingdom of God. By juxtaposing these different kinds of riches, James is subtly reminding his readers again that they must not be stained by the world, but rather should place a greater value on the riches of faith than the riches of material wealth as they follow Christ and put away partiality from their communities.

When James writes in verse 5 that those who are chosen by God will be "heirs of the kingdom, which he has promised to those who love him," he is repeating nearly word for word the same phrase in 1:12, where he writes, "Blessed is the man who remains steadfast under trial, for when he has stood the test he will receive the crown of life, which God has promised to those who love him." Because those who love God will receive the crown of the life, they will also rule as heirs of God's kingdom. We are mistaken if we convince ourselves that this crown or this kingdom is exclusively heavenly or otherworldly. For the Bible never commends practices that are designed to escape from the material world. Rather, beginning with Genesis and ending in Revelation, we read the story of the creation, fall, and renewal of this very physical, very real world.

If the kingdom and crown of life that James promises will be given to those who love God mean anything, then they mean something that has to do with the earth on which we live. Through his church, and by the authority of his Son, God is building a kingdom of men and women who are marked by their death and resurrection in the waters of baptism and acknowledge no king but King Jesus. The members of this kingdom are committed to the created goodness of physical reality as well as the fact that all of it belongs fundamentally and exclusively to Jesus. This is the kingdom that James promises will be given to those who love God, and this promise, and others like it, is at the center of our deepest hopes and joys as followers of Jesus. Indeed, we who are being made mature through the endurance of trials suffer not for the sake of building "character" as though such a thing were significant in and of itself, but rather so that we may more fully participate in the best and most beautiful story of redemption—so that we may rule with Christ in the kingdom which is the destination and locus of the fulfillment and completion of every inch of creation.

James's words about God's kingdom here and elsewhere in his epistle will keep us from distorting and warping his exhortation to be made mature. For if we are made mature only for our own sake and are not being made mature in order to rule with Christ (which means, of course, to serve with and according to Christ's example) then we will collapse in our superiority and self-importance. Those who follow Jesus are not like the Stoics of Greece, who attempted to be conformed to their own definition of maturity so that they could remain separate from the immature. Rather, we are called into maturity so that we might selflessly serve and lay down our lives for those who have not yet been conformed into the image of Jesus. This is the pattern that Christ has set for us, and it is his pattern that we must hold onto as heirs of the kingdom.

## For the Love of God

Another question that immediately presents itself to us when we read verse 5 is what it means to love God, since it is those who love God to whom he has promised a share of his kingdom. Looking back to 1:12, James describes "the man who remains steadfast under trial" as the one who loves God and will receive the crown of life from him. To put this another way, we might say that James defines love for God as remaining faithfully obedient to his commands (that is, holding to the pattern of Jesus's life) even under trials and sufferings. This definition of love for God is very similar to the way that Jesus describes love in John 14:23, where, in response to Judas's question, Jesus says, "If anyone loves me, he will keep my word, and my Father will love him, and we will come to him and make our home with him."

From a certain perspective, we might say that James's epistle is about correctly understanding what it means to love and be loved by God. Again and again, James refers to his readers as "beloved" (James 1:16, 19; 2:5). But what does it mean, for James, to be loved by God? It certainly does not mean that his readers can expect lives of ease and safety, at least in worldly terms. Rather, those who are loved by God are confronted with the paradoxically easy yoke of Jesus and kept safe in the will of God (who cares exponentially more for his children than he does for the sparrows, Matt. 10:31). Those loved by God are brought into the difficult and unpredictable process of being shaped into the image of Jesus through discipline and suffering sovereignly portioned out by our Father God himself.

In short, for James, being loved by God means that we will inevitably be drawn into suffering and trials so that through our joyful obedience, by our holding to the pattern of Jesus's life, we will be shaped and matured into our place in God's design, made into someone able to fully participate in God's story for mankind and the world. This definition of love should remind us of the words of the writer of Hebrews, who exhorts his readers to embrace God's discipline and the suffering in their lives, reminding them that "the Lord disciplines the one he loves, and chastises every son whom he receives…if you are left without discipline, in which we have all participated, then you are illegitimate children and not sons" (Heb. 12:6, 8).

James's definition of what it means to love and to be loved by God is significantly different than modern conceptions of those terms. Where modern American evangelicalism defines love for God as an inward affection of the heart, James describes love for God as steadfast obedience during suffering and trials. Of course, this definition includes, but is never simply defined by, an inward affection for God himself. Unfortunately, it is often too easy for modern Christians to reduce God's love for them as his protection and care for their lives and his guarantee of their salvation in the next life. But James invites us to understand God's love to also include his goal of maturity for his children through his fatherly discipline which he properly understands to follow the biblical pattern of kingship preceded by suffering (as in the lives of Jacob, Joseph, Moses, David, etc.).

As we read of James's biblical understanding of the Christian life, we ought also to reconsider and repent of the unbiblical and worldly ways we have begun to imagine the practice and enjoyment of the love of God. What James demands from us is a fundamental shift in the meaning of love itself and this should shape both how we think of our relationship with God, his love for us, as well as how our own love is expressed as husbands, wives, parents, and children. When Christian parents hesitate to discipline their children because of their "love" for them, it is a reflection not simply of their misunderstanding of the proper role of parents in the lives of children, but also a misunderstanding of the manner in which their heavenly Father loves them (Heb. 12:3-17). Love without discipline is a love that exists only for itself and its own beauty, while godly love, paired with discipline and including the goal of maturity of the one who is loved, is a love that exists for others, and ultimately for the sake of the world.

## Dishonoring the Poor Man

James confronts his readers with a striking rebuke: "But you have dishonored the poor man!" (James 2:6). His harsh assessment of the conduct of his readers stands in strong contrast to God's opinion of the poor in verse 5, and James intends for his readers to understand and repent of this incongruity. But who is this poor man, and how has he been dishonored? On one level, the poor man is simply the man dressed in shabby clothes who has been dishonored by lack of love shown to him by the assembly. But, on another level, it is also likely that the poor man is Jesus himself.

James is intimately familiar with the teachings of Jesus regarding the poor, and it may be that he intends to subtly remind his readers of Jesus's parable of the sheep and the goats where Jesus makes the astonishing claim that the righteous are to be blessed and the wicked punished because Jesus himself is the poor man who is the recipient of their care or neglect (Matt. 25:31-46). The possibility that Jesus is the poor man in James 2:6 is supported by the fact that in the next sentence James condemns the rich for blaspheming the honorable name by which his readers are called, which is of course the name of Jesus (2:7). James is criticizing his readers for dishonoring Christ in their discrimination of the poor in the same way that the rich have dishonored the name of Christ in their blasphemy and persecution of the church.

The irony here is palpable. James is pointing out to his readers that in their treatment of the poor and their partiality toward the rich, they have become oppressors in much the same way that they have been oppressed. This is another way of saying that when God's people show partiality in their communities, they have become stained by the world by embracing and submitting to its ways and have in turn neglected the wisdom and ways of God. This contrast will be highlighted by James in James 4. This is not the path of maturity, and it is not consistent with the example of Jesus, and so it must be rejected. Just as Jesus honored the poor, and is himself to be honored, the people of God must honor and serve the poor man, especially since Jesus has given them his word that "as you did it to the least of these my brothers, you did it to me" (Matt. 25:40).

Once again, we see that love for Jesus is demonstrated not only in internal affection but also in the practical and concrete way we as Christian communities treat the poor and needy in our midst and in our communities. James calls the people of God to imitate God in their treatment of others (2:5), to be mature as he is mature not only in their submission to suffering and discipline, but also in their love and service for all of humanity.

## Political Footsies

James concludes this section by exposing the worldly political motives of his readers in their partiality toward the rich. "Are not the rich the ones who oppress you, the ones who drag you into court?" The identity of the rich in verses 2-3 is now clear. The "gold ring" and the "illustrious clothing" are marks of authority. The signet ring and the robe of office. These rich men who have been favored in the assembly of the church have been generously waited on and served hand and foot not simply out of Christian charity (since if this had been the case, the poor man would have been served in like manner), but rather in the hope that they will sympathize with the followers of Jesus and put an end to their persecution.

In his rhetorical question, James exposes the heart of the manner and implicitly forces his readers to consider their motives. Will the followers of Jesus play the political game according to the rules of the world, where power is a thing which can be manipulated and traded in exchange for fealty and service, or will they boldly confess and practice the politic of Christ, which proclaims that all power and authority rests in the one who has been proclaimed to be the son of God—and thus empowers those who bend the knee to this greater king to treat all of his subjects with equal deference and honor?

What James is pointing out to these brothers is that the rich are already set against them, and they will not change their ways simply because of the feeble attempts of the followers of Christ to curry their favor. Rather, the rich men, as representatives of the church's Jewish oppressors, oppose Jesus's disciples because they oppose Jesus himself. They engage in violent persecution of the church not simply because the Christians refuse to curry their favor but because those who follow Jesus and confess him to be Christ and Lord are the firstfruits of a new and intrinsically threatening world order which is being ushered in through their faithful lives of service and suffering.

Indeed, the overriding message of these verses is that the church of Jesus cannot have it both ways—their public confession of the Lordship of Christ requires that they treat all men impartially, since they believe all power and authority is in Jesus himself. The way in which we treat the poor and needy in our midst and communities reveals not only whether we personally are selfish or lazy, but also the extent to which we as the people of God fully confess and proclaim the lordship of Jesus. When Christians seek to ingratiate themselves with their enemies, hoping to gain influence and power, it is not merely an offense against our democratic sensibilities, but rather a radical betrayal of our allegiance to the one who claims to be the Lord of all things.

James adds to his indictment of the rich by questioning his readers again, "Are they not the ones who blaspheme the honorable name by which you were called?" (2:8). In his accusations, James has reserved the worst of the crimes of these rich oppressors for last. Not only have these rich and powerful men opposed the church with violence and unjust lawsuits, but they have publicly and shamelessly blasphemed the honorable name by which these followers of Jesus have been called—which is, of course, the name of Jesus himself.

As we have already seen, one of the primary concerns of James's epistle is ethical speech, and he has already focused closely on the mature man's wise use of his tongue in 1:19 and 1:26. Now in 2:7, James returns to the topic of speech ethics, this time leveling a critique against the enemies of God who use their tongues in the same manner of their father, the serpent, who whispered lies and blasphemy in the ear of Eve in the garden of Eden. Remember, the mature follower of Jesus is called to bridle his tongue and be slow to speak. And one cannot set aside these constraints even when the worst kind of blasphemy is directed against the Christians' Lord. As their rich oppressors loosely spew evil threats and profane the name of Christ, James calls his church to respond with quiet trust in the vindication of God rather than issuing angry condemnations or engaging in heated arguments. Again, worldly wisdom, which prizes the power of ridicule, mockery, and curses to subvert and upset the authority of one's enemies is rejected in favor of a bridled tongue and a determination to follow in the way of Jesus, who mutely faced his enemies and humbly endured their evil and foolish words.

We also see in verse 7 that James reminds his readers not only that their rich enemies blaspheme the name of Jesus, but that it is the name of Jesus by which they have been called, both in their public identification with Christ as well as in their baptism into the name of the Father, Son and Holy Spirit. Perhaps a more literal translation would make the baptismal reference clearer. The oppressors blaspheme "the honorable name which was invoked over you." By admonishing them to remember that they have been baptized into and thus marked with the name of Christ, James reemphasizes his point in 2:1, exhorting his readers to hold to the faithful life of Jesus, goading them with the reality that their baptism is not simply an external mark, but a sign of a shift in their total being. For once the name of Jesus is pronounced over us in our baptisms, we belong to a new master and have new responsibilities—we are no longer able to simply live as we please but are now beholden to another.

Like the Hebrew slave who would ask his master to pierce his ear as a sign of his new allegiance (Exod. 21:6), baptism for the Christian is a physical and public marker of our devotion and submission to King Jesus, and in these verses James exhorts his readers to remember the meaning of their baptism, and the responsibility they now have to live according to their king's teachings and his own faithful life-pattern and thus reject all partiality from their personal and communal lives. In 2:1, James simply exhorted his readers to follow in the path of Jesus in treating all in their midst with equality, but now in verse 7, he gives the grounds for his exhortation—the fact that they have been baptized and marked with the name of Jesus.

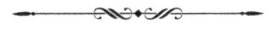

## Living Like Kings

*James 2:8-9*

⁸If you really fulfill the royal law according to the Scripture, "You shall love your neighbor as yourself," you are doing well. ⁹But if you show partiality, you are committing sin and are convicted by the law as transgressors.

What comes to mind when we think about what it means to "live like a king"? I suspect that for most of us our first thoughts are about the ease, luxury, and power so often associated with royalty. But that only confirms that our minds have been stained by worldly, unbiblical conceptions of kingship.

James now identifies the root command violated by the church of Jesus Christ when they show partiality in their fawning treatment of their rich oppressors at the expense of the poor—Jesus's command to love our neighbors as ourselves. As James says, if only the church would follow this "royal law" of love in its community life, they would in fact hold onto the pattern of the faithfulness of Jesus. This self-giving love of others is what characterized Jesus's royal service. The problem with the behavior of the church to whom James writes is not only their sycophantic behavior toward the rich, but the fact that they do not treat the poor with the same deference and generosity. James makes an important point here, as he calls the followers of Jesus to treat each person in their assemblies and communities with love that is marked by service and sacrifice regardless of their race, social class or any other identifying factor that the world deems important.

James calls the church to a love that generously gives without heed to what benefit may be gained in return. This is a rejection of the worldly assumption that power is accumulated by savvy back-scratching, or that service and charity are only tokens to be spent in exchange for future considerations from those whom we put in our debt by our good works. Instead, the love that James commends begins with the confession that all power and authority is truly and only located in Jesus himself, and it is this commitment that sets his followers free to love without condition and to serve without hidden motivation. It is only when the church confesses that Jesus is our glorious Lord (cf. 2:1) that she can love her neighbor as herself. To love as Jesus loves is to confess his royal kingship fulfills the law.

In James's reiteration of the love command we also begin to glimpse why the community of those who followed Jesus were targeted for persecution by the reigning political Jewish and

Roman authorities. Worldly political power is predicated upon the assumption that everyone within the authority structure will play by the same rules and accept the present governmental arrangement as both self-evident and comprehensive. But if, within a political structure characterized by tightly defined social classes, power games, and complex and hidden motives for every act of charity and loyalty, a community were to arise that rejected partiality toward the "powerful" in its shared life, and intentionally loved others without regard to personal gain, then the very existence of such a community would be a public repudiation of the most fundamental assumption of worldly political structures. This kind of community would be a renunciation of the politics of favoring some men because they able to guarantee safety and comfort.

The existence of the community of men and women who followed Jesus and adhered to his command to love without distinction was something like the political equivalent of the little boy who cried out that the emperor had no clothes. The faithful speech and behavior of the church community exposed that the self-assumed power of the emperor and the ruling class was fundamentally illusionary and based upon nothing other that the pleasure of Jesus Christ. Add to this the fact that these early Christians refused to be intimidated or shamed by the worst kinds of violence and torture against them because they believed that Jesus, their king, had conquered death in his resurrection from the dead, and that they themselves would be raised, body and soul, from the grave. This community was more than just an anomaly, a quirky social club with odd private beliefs, or even a new "religion." Rather, the church became a virus in the bloodstream of the Roman Empire that was immune to any antibody used against them.

For in declining to curry the favor of the rich and powerful and refusing to buckle at any threat of death and violence, the followers of Jesus broke the power of both the carrot and the stick that every human empire has always used to sustain its own existence. As James calls these churches to reject partiality in every aspect of its community life and embrace Jesus's command to love one's neighbor as one's self, he is not only calling them into compliance with Christ's summary of the law. He is also dressing them with the weapons of the Spirit, the armaments of Jesus, and bequeathing to them a way of life that when coupled with a willingness to suffer joyfully and die in hope of God's vindication would empower them for participation in bringing about the destruction and resurrection of the greatest and most ruthless empire this world has ever seen, from the ashes of which would rise western Christendom.

The law of self-giving love in this verse is identified by James as the "royal" law or instruction. Given that the purpose of this epistle may be summarized as an exhortation to its readers to suffer trials joyfully so that they will be made mature, fulfilling Jesus's instruction is the way for Christians to fulfill their kingly vocation. Like other apostolic epistles, James is calling these disciples to live and act and love as those who are being conformed to the image of Christ and rule with him (Eph. 2:6; Rom. 5:17; 2 Tim. 12:12; Rev. 5:10).

James is addressing his readers as inhabitants of the kingdom of God, for the Greek word *basilikos* translated here as "royal" (James 2:8) is a close derivative of the Greek word *basileia*, translated in verse 5 as the "kingdom" for which God has chosen the poor of the world to be heirs. These disciples already belong to this kingdom, and James calls them thus to live as kings—as royal rulers who are defined not, like worldly kings, by their careful maintenance of their own power and comfort, but rather by their generous and sacrificial service to others. Of course, this is the biblical definition of kingship, as demonstrated by many royal figures in the Hebrew Scriptures (e.g., Joseph, Boaz, David, and Solomon).

When James says that his readers are to "fulfill" the royal law of love, the Greek verb that he uses is *telew* (τελεω). This is the verbal form of the noun *telios*, which is used in 1:4 to describe the goal of the steadfast suffering process that God brings his people through, which is their maturity and completeness. In effect,

James is claiming that the maturity to which his readers are called to will be demonstrated by their mature fulfillment of the royal law of loving their neighbor as themselves. This is an extremely significant point, for what we as Christians believe to be the mark of maturity and completion in our churches will in large part determine the culture that is created by our shared worship, life, and mission together.

It is a constant temptation for modern churches to define maturity in any number of different areas where they deem themselves to be exemplary—whether liturgical faithfulness and beauty, doctrinal purity, racial integration, attention to social justice and the poor, rigorous Christian education, deep and insightful teaching, effectiveness of outreach to unbelievers, or any other good thing. But in these verses, James gives the ultimate standard of maturity for the church of Jesus Christ—sacrificial and intentional love.

For if our congregations are characterized by pure doctrine, strong teaching, and rigorous education but we do not live as a community of love and charity toward each other as well as the world around us, we have not met James's standard of maturity in our assemblies, and those areas of worship and Christian practice in which we excel may easily become avenues by which we measure ourselves against other churches and falsely congratulate ourselves on our faux maturity. Before we are churches of mature doctrine, worship and mission, we are called to be one thing only—churches of impartial, brave and costly love, and it is this love for which our Lord will speak into our ears those sweet words: "well done, my good and faithful servant."

It is because of the central importance of the royal love command that James can say in 2:9, "but if you show partiality, you are committing sin and are convicted by the law as transgressors." For, as clearly demonstrated by Jesus's parable of the Good Samaritan in Luke 10, it is when we show partiality that we fail to keep the love command in our lives and in our communities. For each of us, there are people whom we love as ourselves— our family and friends, those who are like us in race, social class and intelligence. But the true test of Jesus's command to love our neighbor as ourselves comes when we face the temptation to pick and choose whom we deem to be our neighbors. When we treat as neighbors only those who love us already, we are, as Jesus puts it, living only as pagans and tax collectors.

> You have heard that it was said, "You shall love your neighbor and hate your enemy." But I say to you, Love your enemies and pray for those who persecute you, so that you may be sons of your Father who is in heaven. For he makes his sun rise on the evil and on the good, and sends rain on the just and on the unjust. For if you love those who love you, what reward do you have? Do not even the tax collectors do the same? And if you greet only your brothers, what more are you doing than others? Do not even the Gentiles do the same? You therefore must be mature, as your heavenly Father is mature (Matt. 5:43-48).

But the radical demand of the parable of the good Samaritan and the love command of Jesus is that we treat as neighbors anyone God brings into our lives—whether rich or poor, beautiful or ugly, friend or enemy, black or white, we are called to love without distinction or bias. Simply put, when we love impartially, we are the mature keepers of Jesus's love command, and when we show partiality in our love toward those we favor for one reason or another, we do not keep his command. And since the command to love our neighbors as ourselves is one half of Jesus's summary of the entire biblical law, our partiality (and consequent violation of the love command) betrays our transgression of the whole law.

What does the accusation of being a "transgressor of the law" mean (2:9, 11)? On the one hand, we may say with confidence that to be a transgressor of the law means that we are rebels against God, and stand in need of justification through our trust in the life, death and resurrection of Jesus. But if we read James's teaching on law and transgression with only an eye toward the evangelistic usefulness of his words, we will miss a significant portion of the implications of his instruction on this topic.

The role of the law throughout the Biblical narrative of reality is far more extensive than simply setting a comprehensive hurdle at which mankind is bound to stumble and fall and thus realize their need of forgiveness and salvation. Indeed, while the law of God certainly identifies those who live under its instructions as helpless sinners, it is also God's tender and Fatherly instruction to those people he has brought into his kingdom. After all, Yahweh gave the Israelites the decalogue to show them how to live as those that had been redeemed from Egypt by his mercy and power (Exod. 20:1-2). The law was Yahweh's gift to his people. For the follower of Jesus, the law is not only a reminder of his need for Christ, but also a picture of the life fully lived in accordance to God's vision for the world and humanity. In other words, to be a keeper of the law, in Biblical terms, does not mean earning one's own salvation. Rather, it means to live as a man or woman who has been made fully mature in Christ.

Remember, James addresses "the twelve tribes of the dispersion," which we understand to be the Jewish followers of Jesus who have been driven from their homes by the violent persecution of their countrymen, and the purpose of his epistle is to guide these fugitives through their suffering in joy and steadfastness so that they will be made mature and rule with Christ. We ought not restrict the implications of James's teaching on the law in this section of his epistle to merely a discussion on the depravity of mankind. Rather, we ought to do our best to cooperate with the whole shape of the epistle and see also how James's teaching might help us learn as we seek to maintain the faithful example of our Lord Jesus and follow him in the path of maturity and fullness.

With this lens of maturity in our minds, let's look again at James's words. When the followers of Jesus fulfill his royal law by loving their neighbor as themselves, they are living as mature members of his kingdom, and ruling with Jesus by serving the world. As James points out in verse 9, however, when the church shows partiality in its love and service of others, favoring one over another based upon the anticipated benefit their preference will bring, they have sinned and are transgressors of the law, and have revealed themselves to have fallen short of the maturity and completeness that God longs for in his people.

To show partiality in our love of others is to fail to love as God loves, for he shows no discrimination in his treatment of humanity. As such, partiality in our communities, and especially our church assemblies, is a betrayal of our status as the image bearers of God and a failure to understand and live out the implications of our redemption into the kingdom of God. By pointing out the failure of his church to follow completely the commands of Jesus, James's intention is not to simply alert them to their sin, but rather to exhort and encourage his flock as they seek more and more to hold to faithfulness of the Lord Jesus Christ, the glory and goal of their suffering and obedience.

## THE MARK OF MATURITY

*James 2:10-13*

> [10]For whoever keeps the whole law but fails in one point has become accountable for all of it. [11]For he who said, "Do not commit adultery," also said, "Do not murder." If you do not commit adultery but do murder, you have become a transgressor of the law. [12]So speak and so act as those who are to be judged under the law of liberty. [13]For judgment is without mercy to one who has shown no mercy. Mercy triumphs over judgment.

Now James brings home his point from verse 9. If the church fails to selflessly love all who come into their communities, regardless of their wealth, race, or any other identifying marker, she has become guilty or accountable for the whole law. This is because the law of God is not a piecemeal ethical approach to human behavior, consisting primarily in a few central prohibitions that can be fulfilled merely by keeping ourselves from lying, cheating, or stealing. Rather, biblical law is a full-orbed vision of life that demands nothing less than total cooperation with its fundamental impulses and storied demands. To fail in one point of the law makes one accountable for it all, not because the law is an arbitrary list of dos and don'ts that will incur God's wrath if broken in the smallest way, but rather because the law is a cohesive and complete summary of life lived in accord with God's intention for humanity. To step outside of his will at any point (and especially at such a central point as love for others) is to fall short of God's vision for the world and to live in a way that is inevitably less than human.

But what does James mean when he talks about keeping "the whole law" (verse 10)? It is significant to note that the Greek word translated as "whole" is *holos* (ολο), which is closely related to the word *holoklaros* (ολοκληρος) used in 1:4b to describe the result of steadfastness in the midst of suffering for God's people ("that you may be made perfect and complete, lacking in nothing"). It is likely that, as in 1:25, that what James means here by keeping the "whole law" is not just someone that keeps every jot and tittle of the Torah, but someone who keeps the mature and perfect law, the law of liberty, the law that is summarized by Jesus when he says, "On these two commandments hang all the Law and the Prophets." What two?

> You shall love the Lord your God with all your heart and with all your soul and with all your mind. This is the great and first commandment. And a second is like it: You shall love your neighbor as yourself (Matt. 22:37-40).

If this is at least part of what James means by keeping the "whole" law, then it makes perfect sense why stumbling at one point would make a man accountable for all of it, for this is precisely what happens when we show partiality in our love for neighbor. That is, when showing partiality, we are keepers of the whole and mature law of love, except when confronted by those it is inconvenient or apparently not beneficial to serve and care for. But when we fail to show love toward even one person at the expense of another (i.e., "fail in one point"), we have done violence to the law of love at its most fundamental level. We have not simply neglected to keep the law of liberty perfectly, but we have misunderstood its basic purpose and primary demand upon our lives and are thus properly convicted as "transgressors of the law" (James 2:9).

Again, James's main purpose in verses 9-10 is not to establish that a man who sins in any small way is culpable for not obeying the entire law (though this is a legitimate application of these verses), but rather to convince his readers that impartiality in their keeping of the love commandment is of such central importance to their obedience to Jesus's law that failing to love any one person is a violation of the whole thrust of Jesus's ministry and life. Indeed, what James has done in effect is set up impartiality in love as a kind of ultimate test for the maturity of the followers of Jesus and the communities they together create.

Where modern Christians often judge spiritual maturity in terms of theological knowledge, doctrinal precision, heartfelt worship, or articulate descriptions of biblical themes, James poses this simple question to determine our mature keeping of the law of liberty: "How well do you love the least of these?" Unsurprisingly, this is the same question asked implicitly by Jesus in his parable of the Good Samaritan and explicitly in his parable of the Sheep and the Goats. Mature biblical religion, according to James and Jesus, is this: to suffer with joy the trials of life so that you will be made into the kind of man or woman who, with Christ, rules and takes dominion over all things by sacrificially loving and serving without distinction all those whom he brings into your life.

James then provides a hyperbolic example of how a follower of Jesus might also become a transgressor of the law by obeying him in one area and ignoring him in another. This is designed to demonstrate the severity of the sin of partiality for those who intend to keep the whole and mature law of God. "For he who said, 'Do not commit adultery,' also said, 'Do not murder.' If you do not commit adultery but do murder, you have become a transgressor of the law" (2:11). It is not likely that James merely brings up the fact that if a man is faithful to his wife and murders his brother, he is a transgressor of the law because he believes his church to be confused about the issue.

As we shall see, it is more than likely that some in the community to which James writes have indeed killed or sought to harm men in order alleviate the suffering of themselves and their families. Remember, at least some of the early Jewish converts included those who had been involved in the zealot movement, which accepted violence as an acceptable countermeasure against oppression. As we shall see James explicitly attacks zealotry in 3:13-18 and 4:1-10. Even so, the main thrust of this section of the letter focuses upon partiality in the community of the church, and we should seek to first understand this verse within that more dominant context.

That a murderer who honors his marriage vows is still a transgressor of the law appears to be a rhetorical device intended to point out the severity of the sin of partiality which exists in the church community to whom he writes. Because they have served and loved the rich over the poor to curry the favor of the powerful and alleviate their suffering by means of worldly political machinations, the readers of James's epistle have become just as much a transgressor of the law as the man who guards his eyes from the slightest hint of lust but also violently stabs his neighbor in an angry rage.

Though James's readers may believe themselves to be keepers of the mature and whole law of Jesus because of their faithfulness to his other commands, here he skewers them with the reality that they are just as much a group of deceived hypocrites as the maritally faithful murderer as long they continue to ignore the poor man in their assemblies. Of course, in pointing out the discrepancy between mortal violence and the keeping of the law of Jesus, he is also laying the foundation for the moment when he will more explicitly take up the apparent problem of murder and violence within the church in James 4.

We should also note here that the "he who said" in verse 11 is almost certainly Jesus rather than Moses, for several reasons. First, the fact that this whole section of James's letter centers on his intention that his readers hold to the faithfulness of the life of Jesus (2:1). Secondly, in this section James has already alluded to Jesus's summary of the law as loving your neighbor as yourself (2:8). Finally, the significant fact that the only two of the Ten Commandments expounded upon by Jesus in his Sermon on the Mount are "Do not murder," and "Do not commit adultery." Given the host of James's other allusions to the Sermon on the Mount, James is again reminding his readers of Jesus's teaching that they have received through the gospel writers.

Just as he has done throughout the epistle, James calls attention to the teaching and life of Jesus as the mature and whole law for his followers—not, of course, to be set against the law of the Old Testament, but rather properly understood as the fulfillment of the entire Old Testament law. Indeed, one could read the entire letter of James as an extended meditation on and contextual application of the life and teachings of Jesus to the struggles of the early church. For a letter that has been notoriously described as an "epistle of straw" due to its supposed lack of the gospel, James's contribution to the New Testament canon is chock full of wonder at and exhortation upon the basis of the life and teachings of Jesus—perhaps, with the exception of Hebrews, more so than any other New Testament epistle.

## Show Mercy

James sums up how the church should respond in their community life to his exhortations on impartiality in their love and service: "So speak and so act as those who are to be judged under the law of liberty" (v. 12). The immediate background for this command is verse 4, where James wrote that in their partiality, the church had become "judges with evil thoughts" because of the distinctions they had made within their community. Now James points out that though the church community has set themselves up to be judges by making distinctions between the rich and poor, they will be the ones who will be judged according to the law of liberty, which he has already summarized in verse 8 as, "You shall love your neighbor as yourself."

James does not appear to be criticizing the church for acting as a judge, but rather for the way she has used her power. Instead of judging as God, who impartially sends the rain and sun upon the good and wicked, the just and unjust, the church has resorted to superficial and worldly motives in the way she has ruled in Christ's kingdom. In judging between the rich and poor, the church has abused her authority, and now James reminds her that she herself is also under judgment. Though the church's authority and responsibility should not be underestimated, we who follow Christ must also remember that though we act as his representatives in this world, we are accountable also to his teachings and law, against which we will be judged. Again and again, the church has a responsibility to measure herself against the law of liberty and judge her own faithfulness to the instruction of Jesus. As James puts it in 1:25, we are to be a people that individually, as well as corporately, "looks into the mature law, the law of liberty, and perseveres."

After establishing that the church will itself be judged by the law of liberty, James now raises the stakes even higher in verse 13, implying that this judgment will be made based on the church's own actions, and how she uses her own authority, writing, "For judgment is without mercy to one who has shown no mercy."

In its warning that mercy will not given to those who themselves show no mercy, James's admonition echoes Jesus's parable of the unforgiving servant. In that parable (Matt. 18:21-35) Jesus responds to Peter's question of how many times he must forgive his brother by telling him a story of a man who was in enormous debt to a king and could not repay him. After the king ordered the man and his family to be sold into slavery, the man threw himself at the mercy of the king, who pitied him and forgave his debt. Immediately after this surprising turn of events, the same man found another servant who owed him a pittance and had him thrown in prison because he could not repay this small debt. When news of this reached the ears of the king, he angrily ordered the man to be brought back into his presence, and reversed his earlier decision, rescinding his forgiveness and commanding the man whose debt who had been forgiven to be given over to the torturers until his debt could be paid in full. And then, Jesus confronts Peter and his other disciples with these unsettling words: "So also my heavenly Father will do to every one of you, if you do not forgive your brother from the heart" (Matt. 18:35).

In the same way that Jesus warned his disciples that their sins will not be forgiven by God if they refuse to forgive the sins of others, James here alerts his readers that unless they show mercy toward others in love and service, no mercy will be shown to them when they are judged. What is the implication of this teaching of James and Jesus? Is it an attack on the gospel of grace? No. The teaching of James and Jesus is simply the biblical understanding that saving faith in Jesus is full-orbed, lived-out submission to his kingship demonstrated not merely by intellectual assent to the reality of his efficacious death and resurrection but also by a life that is marked by holding to his pattern of faithful obedience. In other words, the substance and character of our faith is not only found in our thoughts or our heart's affections, but also in our actions and words in real time and space. This will be made crystal clear in the next section of the letter (James 2:14-26).

Just as it is impossible to separate our souls from our bodies or our bodies from our souls, the way we live is no less a part of the content of our faith than what we profess with our lips and believe in our hearts. James is warning his readers that they must treat the issue of partiality in their assemblies with the utmost level of seriousness, because how they love and show mercy to others will impact the mercy and love they receive in judgment. Though it may frighten us at first to realize how significant our actions are in our reception of a merciful judgment from God, to have it any other way would effectively remove God's kingship from this world to a purely spiritual realm.

If Jesus were interested only in the affections of our hearts and not the physical obedience of our bodies, he would only be a great teacher, but he would not be the king of this present world. The consistent witness of Scripture, however, is that by virtue of his physical resurrection from the dead, Jesus has been proclaimed to be the Son of God—Messiah and Lord. This is the gospel we proclaim in his name, and to live and act as though our king cares only that we beg for his mercy and not whether we follow his laws in our life in his kingdom is to invite his wrath and judgment. If Jesus is truly king, then he is king of all of us, not only our heads and hearts, and he demands nothing less than full obedience. Outside of this lived obedience, our "faith" is no faith at all, and there is no salvation.

In the closing sentence of verse 13 James leaves his readers with this simple declaration and reminder: "Mercy triumphs over judgment." Echoing with hope and throbbing with promise, these words describe the fundamental commitment that James exhorts his readers to embrace. For holding to the pattern of the faithfulness of Jesus means, for all of us, that we must dare to believe and act as though mercy will indeed triumph over judgment. That serving the poor without distinction is not a waste of resources and time but a way of life that will result in blessing. That guarding our tongues and meekly enduring the violent persecution of our enemies and foreswearing our own violence against them will result in triumphant vindication, not meaningless annihilation. That patient suffering and quiet acceptance of God's discipline in our lives will lead not to insignificance but maturity and our establishment as rulers with Christ. That, in the end, it is not those who live by the sword and the accumulation of worldly power and wealth, but rather those who turn the other cheek and offer their enemies only love, not vengeance, who will inherit the earth. This is the promise of mercy. This is the fundamental call of the Christian life—to embrace the hope of mercy and cling to the promise that the judgment to come will vindicate the wisdom of a life of peace and generosity as we advance and proclaim the kingdom of Jesus through deeds of love and reject the idolatry of worldly power and put away all violence and evil.

## Summary & Reflections

After hearing James in 2:1-13 there can be little doubt regarding the significance of James's understanding of the importance of rejecting partiality in our communities as we seek to follow Jesus, especially when such preferential treatment is designed to secure influence with the enemies of the Church. Clearly, as we show impartial love and service toward all whom God sends into our lives, we imitate God in his care for all men, keep the royal law of love, demonstrate our faith in Jesus, and also show our fundamental commitment to the reality that mercy triumphs over judgment. But what does it really mean in the modern world to follow the commands of James in our personal lives as well as our congregations?

At the very least, James's commands mean that our congregations ought to be places where all outsiders are welcomed without distinction and without regard for their wealth or poverty. Realistically, this means that we must work toward cultivating churches that welcome men, women, and families from a broad range of socioeconomic backgrounds and income levels. Clearly, James calls us to treat each of these people with equal affection, enthusiasm, and hospitality. Though James explicitly describes the question of where outsiders will sit in the assembly, the principle of impartiality is easily extended to all kinds of hospitality we might show to those who come into our churches.

Perhaps a hypothetical scenario will help us get at the heart of these issues. For whom are we more likely to rearrange our Sunday afternoon plans and spontaneously invite over for a meal after church—the new, well-dressed family who arrive at church in their luxury SUV, or the shabby husband and harried wife, with their unruly collection of poorly dressed and badly-behaved children, who came ten minutes late and after the service quickly headed for the door, embarrassed by their appearance?

If, like most of us, your church is more likely to find time and space to show hospitality toward the rich family instead of the poor one, what does this reveal about our hidden motivations, our secret commitments to convenience, and our secret concern to love mostly only those who are likely to return our favors in kind? At the least, we can be sure that our preference for the rich and attractive betrays a significant way in which we have failed to hold to the faithfulness of Jesus, stumbled in keeping the law of love, and failed to show mercy in our judgment. James's teaching in James 2 ought to convict us that to favor the rich even in subtle ways in our congregations and personal relationships shows our lack of faith in Jesus, and rejection of his way of life. This, of course, does not mean that we ignore the rich and favor the poor, but rather we show equal eagerness in our hospitality toward all who enter our assemblies.

Of course, the implications of James's exhortations in this section run much deeper than simply how our churches treat the rich and poor, for to follow in the pattern of Jesus and live in submission to James's words in the second chapter of his epistle require Christians and the communities they inhabit to keep fully the royal law of love, which demands nothing less than full impartiality in our love, service, and attention to all people that God brings into our lives.

Consider how a congressman or mayor might be treated if he appeared in a pew on a Sunday morning. Would he be surrounded by church members eager to shake his hand and make him welcome? Though our churches do not suffer from the same kind of persecution as first century Christians, still we are tempted by the allure of political power, and the chance to influence those who wield the keys of the government. But if the manner of reception a congressman might receive in our churches were to vary widely from the attention paid to a lowly and easily ignored working-class man, then, according to James's words, we will have become, as a community, judges with evil thoughts and transgressors of the law. For to make distinctions between those in our assemblies based upon our perception of their political power or ability to further our social agenda is a fundamental denial of the church's real politic—her gathered and repeated assertion that Jesus is Lord, and all true power is his. Because Jesus is King, we are free to love without calculation or hidden motivation, because we pay homage to no lord but the one who is risen from the dead and ascended to the right hand of God the Father.

The fact that Jesus is both Lord and Christ (2:1) and the consequent demand for impartiality in our communities ought to have the effect of erasing not only wealth and power from our considerations, but indeed, all worldly distinguishing characteristics. In some of our churches distinctions are made because of race or color, and subtle discrimination keeps certain people from full community participation and sharing in the leadership of our assemblies. This must not be so, or Jesus is not Lord, and we are transgressors of his law. In some of our churches, dress and appearance are of the utmost importance, and we judge so quickly and instinctively that we mistake vain piety for spiritual superiority and forget that we also will be judged under the law of liberty, and that judgment will be delivered based on the mercy we show toward our fellow bearers of the image of God.

Though James's exhortations in this section are primarily addressed to "brothers" as leaders of the church as a community and thus directed toward their communal behavior and treatment of outsiders, there is no reason we cannot also apply his teaching to our conduct as individuals. James's basic command to "show no partiality as you hold to the faithfulness of our Lord Jesus Christ" also has significant implications for our personal attitudes, words, and actions toward others. For each of us is constantly confronted with the instinctive urge to prejudge every person we encounter based on their race, general appearance, type of dress, or manner of speaking, and to make distinctions and deal differently with people based upon our assumptions. While James is of course not pretending that we will be supernaturally "colorblind" or unaware of the differences that exist between different kinds of people, he does require that those who follow Jesus will adopt a stance of love and service toward every person we encounter, regardless of that person's social stature or willingness and ability to return the favor.

In his letter to the Galatians, Paul confirms James's point that it is because of God's impartiality (and our imitation of that impartiality) that we must not fall into the trap of currying favor with the powerful by making distinctions. While recounting to the Galatians the history of his ministry, Paul describes the council of Jerusalem, when he went up to the leaders of the church to defend his ministry and the uncircumcision of some of his followers. Paul explains, "From those who seemed influential (who they were makes no difference to me; God shows no partiality)—those, I say, who seemed influential added nothing to me" (Gal. 2:6). Though he spoke before the leaders of the church of Jerusalem (that is, those who seemed influential), Paul, who understood that God shows no partiality, also resisted the urge to tailor his message to fit the wishes of the powerful. Rather, he spoke with the courage of a man who believes that he serves the one who possesses all power in heaven and earth—Jesus, the Lord and Christ.

It may be easy for some readers to hustle through this section of James 2:1-13 in order to get to the "more significant" discussion of the relationship between faith and works in 2:14-26. Besides the fact that this earlier section forms an essential background and context for the more famous part of James 2, to dismiss the importance of James's exhortation in 2:1 to show no partiality and the supporting arguments given for that command in 2:2-13 is to misunderstand the centrality of impartiality to the Gospel message itself.

Because we live in a society that still bears the vestiges of a Christian foundation, the radical nature of James's commands in this passage have lost some of their edge. In the pagan world into which the gospel of Jesus Christ was spoken, the assertion that all men (and women) were equal in the sight of God and thus ought to be treated with equal deference was an absurdly bold claim. Though our society still has a long way to go before truly enacting James's commands, the role of the church is to lead in maturity, embodying a community of impartiality that has rejected power politics in all its shared life, and together has embraced the lordship of Christ.

It is important to see that what James is requiring from us in these verses is something far more radical than the democratic egalitarianism of modern Western society. While our contemporary sensibilities prohibit any explicit public favoritism based on external appearance, the reality is that our culture is still informally segmented and separated into a subtle social pecking order. On some level we all subscribe to this and participate in it. Each of us intuitively knows "our type" of people, and this more or less determines with whom we interact most comfortably. Those who are higher in our society's order can expect to be treated well by those below them and may return the favor with assistance or friendship. Though formal partiality is frowned upon and often prohibited by law, informal partiality is accepted and even expected.

In contrast, James's words require us to remove ourselves from this petty system of power plays and forbid us to withhold love from anyone because of our perception that they will be unable to return our generosity or further our pursuit of our own peace and security. The reason we can act bravely in this way toward those God has brought into our lives is because of the lordship of Christ, which James affirms in the beginning of this section of verses. Because Christ protects us, we have no reason to protect ourselves by appeasing the powerful and ignoring the weak. Because Christ is Lord, we are secure, and delivered from the anxiety of maintaining our comfort and safety. We will never be able to follow James and untangle ourselves from the web of power politics either corporately or personally without trust in Jesus's kingship that is built up by our corporate worship and embodied in our impartial and generous love.

7

# Deliverance & Vindication

*...an hour is coming when all who are in the tombs will hear his voice and come out, those who have done good to the resurrection of life, and those who have done evil to the resurrection of judgment*
– John 5:28, 29

### James 2:14-26

[14]What good is it, my brothers, if someone says he has faith but does not have works? Can that faith save him? [15]If a brother or sister is poorly clothed and lacking in daily food, [16]and one of you says to them, "Go in peace, be warmed and filled," without giving them the things needed for the body, what good is that? [17]So also faith by itself, if it does not have works, is dead.

[18]But someone will say, "You have faith and I have works." Show me your faith apart from your works, and I will show you my faith by my works. [19]You have faith that God is one; you do well. Even the demons have faith—and shudder! [20]Do you want to be shown, you foolish person, that faith apart from works is useless? [21]Was not Abraham our father justified by works when he offered up his son Isaac on the altar? [22]You see that faith was active along with his works, and faith was completed by his works; [23]and the Scripture was fulfilled that says, "Abraham put faith in God, and it was counted to him as righteousness"—and he was called a friend of God. [24]You see that a person is justified by works and not by faith alone. [25]And in the same way was not also Rahab the prostitute justified by

works when she received the messengers and sent them out by another way? ²⁶For as the body apart from the spirit is dead, so also faith apart from works is dead.

A few preliminary notes about the end of James 2 are in order if we are going to understand its function in this epistle. It may be way too easy for modern Christians to read James's exposition of living faith as if he is addressing questions common in modern debates about the doctrine of "justification." Did James just drop into his epistle a section on "how to get to heaven"? Of course, there is some very significant help here when it comes to questions about the doctrines of salvation, faith, and justification. I'll address that later, mostly in the "reflections" section.

But we would be violating the important contextual matrix necessary for understanding James's strong language here if we simply jumped to answer questions that present themselves so readily to contemporary theologians. It is all too easy for us to see words related to "justification" and dump into those words our "doctrine of justification."²³ But the presence of the word "justified" does not necessarily mean that James will be answering all the questions we may have about the *doctrine* of "justification," especially given the long and complex history of the controversy.

In addition to this, another crucial contextual mistake would be to read James and think that he is writing about the dispute and the questions that the apostle Paul deals with in his epistles regarding justification. The evidence suggests that James's epistle was written a decade or more *before* Paul begins his ministry to the Gentiles. Questions about the status of the Gentiles in the Christian community and the need for the observance of "the works of the law," especially circumcision, are not addressed by James. The "works" James commends here are works of mercy (v. 15), obedient sacrifice (v. 21), and courageous rescue of those

---

23 See Vern Poythress, *Symphonic Theology* (Grand Rapids: Zondervan, 1987), especially chapter 7, maxim #2: "No term in the Bible is equal to a technical term of systematic theology."

in danger (v. 25). James does not say anything about sabbath keeping, circumcision, food laws, and other observances that set the Jews apart from the Gentiles. Reading James 2:14-26 as some sort of polemic against Paul's "faith alone" will get us nowhere and will cause us to miss James's larger concerns.

Remember, James is writing to "brothers" that are leading displaced, victimized Christian communities. They are being oppressed by zealous adversaries and certain brothers are being tempted to mimic those adversaries with angry rhetoric designed to stir up resentment and to vindicate/justify themselves before God and their enemies. When James begins this section with a reference to someone who "says" he has faith (v. 14) and then throughout his argument contrasts what people "say" with how they act or behave, this is consistent with James's argument against the dangerous speech being propounded by the leaders (3:1-12). This kind of "faith"—heated speechmaking designed to inflame people against their enemies—will not save/deliver any of them (2:14). Loud-mouthed leaders that *talk* about faith but give no evidence in their lives of *works* of mercy and obedience are fools (v. 20), and they should not expect justification/vindication from God (vv. 21-24). As he has warned them already, they should be "slow to speak, slow to anger, for the anger of man does not produce the righteousness of God" (1:19).

Provocative talk about faith will not bring them the vindication and deliverance they are looking for. It may seem counterintuitive to them, but what will save/deliver them will be wise, merciful, loving behavior within their communities. They need to grow up. As we have noted all along up to this point in the epistle, these trials are designed by God to produce maturity (1:4). In 2:13, James again confronted his readers with the reality that they must grow up into maturity in their lives, "for judgment is without mercy to one who has shown no mercy." If these brothers refuse consistently to allow the example of Jesus to act as a guide for their own lives and actions, then they will not experience salvation/deliverance from their enemies, but rather receive the Lord's judgment without mercy.

They are, of course, looking for rescue/deliverance (Greek: σωζω) rather than judgment. They need a faith that can liberate them (2:14). In the context of their exile, they desire that which "is able to deliver their lives" (1:21). Therefore, the "salvation" and "justification" held out here by James to these banished, oppressed believers is so much more than just a procedure to secure access to heaven after death. They are expecting God to vindicate and rescue their lives in the present. Since all of this is about faith and trust in God, knowing his gracious acceptance produces fruit in both the present and the future. So in this section, James explains why this threat of judgment (2:13) against those who do not conform to Christ's pattern in their lives is real and valid—because it is only by a worked out and lived faith that they will be vindicated, called "friends of God," and be rescued/saved by God from their dire situation. As the apostle Paul will say later to Timothy, "godliness is of value in every way, as it holds promise for the present life and also for the life to come" (1 Tim. 4:8).

### James 2:14

><sup>14</sup>What good is it, my brothers, if someone says he has faith but does not have works? Can that faith save him?

After asserting in the previous verses that his readers should speak and act mercifully because "judgment is without mercy to the one who has shown no mercy," James now anticipates and attacks the objection that a person's bare faith in Jesus with or without merciful obedience of his commands will ward off his judgment, and James launches his attack by telling another small parable, just as he did in 2:2-3. James asks his readers to imagine a brother or sister who has come to them without sufficient clothing and little or no food. How will the follower of Christ respond to such a person? If our response is simply to bless ("Go in peace") and pray for them ("be warm and filled") without actually giving them clothing or food, then what good is that? James's implication is that, in this case, words alone are useless—it is action that is required. He then goes on to explain the parable to his readers: "So also, faith by itself, if it does not have works, is dead." In the terms of the parable, the verbal profession of caring for the person in need ("Go in peace, be warm…") is what it means to have faith, and to physically provide food and clothing for the needy brother or sister is to have works. Just as it is no good simply to bless and pray for those in need without doing something, so a profession of faith that is not matched by faithful actions is useless, empty, and dead.

While it is tempting to isolate this section of James's epistle and read it out of context of the rest of his letter, it is important to note that James is not saying anything here that he has not already taught. For example, in 1:3 we find that our faith is to be tested—that is, our verbal profession of trust in Jesus will be challenged and strengthened in order to produce steadfastness. Clearly, this means that our faith will be tried in the everyday circumstances of life, and that we will be forced to demonstrate with our actions that we truly believe what we say with our mouths. In 1:22 James commanded his readers to "be doers of the word, and not hearers only," exhorting his readers to live out their professed faith, and not be content only to read and meditate on the word, but also to act in obedience to it. And in 1:26-27, James instructs his flock to bridle their tongues and "visit orphans and widows in their distress."

Rather than extracting James 2:14-26 from its original setting and reading it simply as a systematic theological discussion of the relationship of faith and works in our justification, we must be careful to first read James's words in this section in his pastoral context. The goal of James's words in 2:14-26 is the same as his teaching throughout the epistle: to exhort his readers to endure their trials with joy in God's care for them and steadfastness in their obedience to his law, so that they will be complete and mature, conformed fully to the image and life pattern of Jesus—

his patient suffering and rejection of worldly wisdom, and his unassailable trust in his future vindication by the power of the only true God.

Specifically, in 2:14-26, James is exhorting that his readers follow Jesus in rejecting partiality and fully keeping the royal law of love (that is, following Jesus into maturity), but is concerned that some of his readers believe that their faithful speechmaking will guarantee their merciful judgment, regardless of whether their faith shows itself in their lives (thus rejecting James's desire that they participate in God's plan for their maturity and completeness). In the face of this apparent objection, James harshly condemns this heresy for what it is—a denial of the Lordship of Jesus and a rebellion against the integrity and promises of God. As we shall see, in his rejection of the salvific power of a bare verbal confession and his commendation of a lively saving faith in God's people, James stands shoulder to shoulder with the consistent teaching of the entire Bible: the Hebrew prophets, the apostle Paul, and most importantly, Jesus himself.

With a firm understanding of the immediate context of James's teaching in 2:14-26, let's now return and examine his words in more detail. In 2:14, James writes, "What good is it, my brothers, if someone says he has faith but does not have works? Can that faith save him?" The good that James describes here is not generic or abstract—rather, given that the preceding verse is concerned with God's judgment, we can only assume that "good" in verse 14 refers to the ability to provide protection from their enemies. "What good will it do?" is perhaps a better translation. The "good" these brothers are looking for, remember, is "the righteousness of God." Unfortunately, they believe that wordy, bombastic expressions of "faith" will bring them the "good" they hope for.

But like a ship built with a leaking hull, this kind of faith is no good in the storms they are experiencing. The merely verbalized faith that James exposes here turns out to be worthless in bringing about the justice they desire. What are these works this faith lacks? Again, the broader context provides us with a clear answer: they are mercy (v. 13), love of neighbor (v. 8), and care for the poor (vv. 2-4). But James will also go on to cite Abraham as an example of sacrificial obedience in the face of inexplicable circumstances (v. 21). Then, too, there's Rahab and her protection of the spies from the Canaanite officials (v. 25). James cites these two examples of living faith because of their direct relevance to the banished churches real-life trials—losing children to the violence of their persecutors and having to be wise as serpents when dealing with their enemies. However dreadful such situations were these are "works" they would have resonated with.

While there is no direct allusion to Jesus's words here, his teaching and parable of the wise and foolish man in Matthew 7:21-27 stands directly behind James's assertion that faith without works is unable to save any man. There, at the end of his Sermon of the Mount, Jesus concludes his teaching by claiming that it is not those who listen and confess him as Lord who will be saved, but rather those who listen, confess and obey. As Jesus says,

> Not everyone who says to me, "Lord, Lord," will enter the kingdom of heaven, but the one who does the will of my Father who is in heaven…Everyone then who hears these words of mine and does them will be like a wise man who built his house on the rock. And the rain fell, and the floods came, and the winds blew and beat on that house, but it did not fall, because it had been founded on the rock. And everyone who hears these words of mine and does not do them will be like a foolish man who built his house on the sand. And the rain fell, and the floods came, and the winds blew and beat against that house, and it fell, and great was the fall of it (Matt. 7:21, 24-27).

Jesus required that in order for his followers to receive his salvation they needed not only to assent to his lordship, but also to obey his commands. Just as a man who swears fealty to his king and does not live according to his laws does not have faith in his sovereign, so the man who verbally acknowledges Jesus as his Savior and Lord but refuses to live according to his teaching and example does not truly trust in him, and his "faith" is worthless. Indeed, the one who falsely confesses his faith and does not live out its demands is the worst kind of traitor and rebel because he has deceived himself, his community, and his Master (like the man described in James 1:22).

The unstated assumption of the teaching of both James and Jesus is that there is no separation between having faith in something and acting according to that faith. For example, a soldier may have faith or trust in his commanding officer, but unless he acts in obedience to his commands, that faith is useless and will not result in his physical salvation when threatened by an enemy. Does this mean he is saved by his actions? Of course not, for he would not know how to act or even survive without his faith in his general. But without action, his faith is worthless and will lead only to his destruction.

Everyday we engage in countless acts of faith that we match with our actions. For example, we have faith that drinking water and eating food will hydrate and provide the necessary nourishment for our bodies. But without actually eating and drinking, our assent to these principles (that is, our faith) is useless. In the same way, James and Jesus teach that faith in the kingship of Jesus means nothing, and will not result in our salvation, unless it is actually lived out.

We confess that we are saved by faith in Jesus alone. But if our faith is only pious words and no obedience, then it will not save us—for saving faith is a faith that is revealed in obedience, a faith that is tested and tried and perseveres. This is not only the teaching of James and Jesus, but also Paul, who writes in Galatians 5:6, "For in Christ Jesus neither circumcision nor uncircumcision counts for anything, but only faith working through love." As J. Gresham Machen comments in his *Notes on Galatians*, "What Paul means by faith...is not a mere intellectual assent to certain propositions, but an attitude of the entire man by which the whole life is entrusted to Christ...The faith about which Paul has been speaking is not the idle faith which James condemns, but a faith that works. It works itself out through love. And what love is Paul explains in the whole last division of Galatians. It is not mere emotion, but the actual fulfilling of the whole moral law."[24]

In his biting comment in James 2:14b, "Can that faith [without works] save him?" James tips his hand that there is indeed a faith that does save—not a faith without works, but a faith that is full and vibrant. Thus Paul and James's teaching is the same—we are saved by faith alone, and not works, but the faith that leads to our salvation from the judgment of God (James 2:13) is a faith that works through love.

## Faith Working Through love

*James 2:15-17*

> [15]If a brother or sister is poorly clothed and lacking in daily food, [16]and one of you says to them, "Go in peace, be warmed and filled," without giving them the things needed for the body, what good is that? [17]So also faith by itself, if it does not have works, is dead.

What is lacking when one merely talks about faith is now revealed. It is the work of love, the act of "giving...the things needed for the body" to those who are in need. Here James tells another parable, just as in James 2:2 where he told the story of the "poor man in shabby clothing" who entered the assembly of believers. This time he describes "a brother or sister [who] is poorly clothed and lacking daily food" and presumably comes to a Christian for help. What this needy person requires is not pious words and prayers, but rather, actual physical assistance.

It is tempting to read the reaction of the deceived disciple in James's parable, ("Go in peace, be warm and filled...") as simply a description of callousness to the poor. This is our modern

---

24 J. Gresham Machen, *Notes on Galatians* (Philipsburg, NJ: Presbyterian and Reformed Publishing Co., 1972), 220-221.

temptation, for in our relative wealth, the acts of charity to which we are called do not require great physical or financial sacrifice on our part, but rather simply a heart of mercy that expresses itself in personal contact with the poor. Remember the life situation of the church to which James originally writes. Having been scattered from their homes in Jerusalem, they are now almost certainly trapped themselves in poverty, forced to begin their lives anew in strange cities, and without the support of their families or the resources of their accumulated possessions. It is quite likely that the readers of James's epistle would have been tempted to stop short of blessing the poor with food and clothing not because of callousness but rather a calculated fear that sharing their limited resources with the poor who came to them for help would threaten their own livelihood and security.

When we consider the reluctance of James's readers to care for the poor was likely based less on their own callousness and more upon their desire for self-preservation, we begin to understand the radical nature of the faith to which James is calling his readers. To have a faith that works does not mean simply to be a kind person who volunteers at the local soup kitchen once a month (although it certainly may include that). Rather, the faith which will save and the mercy which will avert judgment is a total life commitment to the ways of Jesus—a lived trust in his lordship that is expressed in treating the poor no different from the rich regardless of the political protection the rich offer (2:1-4), and sharing your last piece of bread with the hungry man who knocks on your door even though you have no assurance your own family will have bread for the next day (2:15-17).

To treat the poor with mercy is not simply to act as a "good person" (as these acts of charity are often conceived of in our culture) but also a dramatic political affirmation of the kingship of Jesus, whose lordship enables us to give up our lives and possessions for others. When we give away our hard-earned money or spend a day normally free from labor serving the physical needs of others, we subvert the prevailing assumptions of our narcissistic culture and proclaim that our master is not money but God.

It is for this reason that there is such a close connection between faith and works — not primarily because our works "prove" the vitality of our faith, but because a true faith in Jesus's kingship proclaims his kingship in action. When we invite the poor man to our table we demonstrate "I believe in Jesus." When we spend a Saturday fixing a widow's leaky roof we exhibit "Jesus is king." When we distribute blankets to the homeless on a cold winter night we reveal "Jesus is risen from the dead." The trouble with the mere verbal profession of faith in verse 14 is not that it is only articulated, but that it is not fully articulated — that is, that verbal profession of faith in Jesus has not been demonstrated in our lives.

It is for this reason that it is absurd to think that James is somehow teaching "works righteousness" or that we can earn our righteousness before God with our charity. All the works that James describes in James 2 are not simply works borne out of our faith, but they are themselves bodily articulations of our faith. Like the sacraments of Baptism and Lord's Supper, our acts of love are embodiments of faith. This is why James can write that Abraham's "faith was completed by his works" (2:22) — because mature faith in Jesus must be expressed not only with our lips but also our lives. Or, to return again to the words of Paul, our works of charity are simply and most fundamentally our "faith working through love" (Gal. 5:6).

James writes, "If a brother or sister is poorly clothed and lacking in daily food, and one of you says to them, 'Go in peace, be warmed and filled,' without giving them the things needed for the body, what good is that?" In reading this, it may be helpful to consider the link between James's instruction and the Lord's Prayer. In teaching his disciples to pray to their Father, Jesus did not neglect to command us to pray, "Give us this day our daily bread" (Matt. 6:11). Reflecting on these words, James is now criticizing his readers for their lack of provision of this bread to their brothers and sisters. Essentially, the rhetorical thrust of James's story is to call his readers to enact in their communities the reality of the Lord's Prayer—and that this enactment is not a superfluous addition to a heart affection for Jesus, but that it is the natural expression of true faith and trust in the kingship of Jesus.

Two implications flow from this connection between the prayer of Jesus and the words of James. First, there is no separation between the kingdom of God and physicality — Jesus is not Lord only of our hearts or spirits, but his kingdom is physically established in real time and space. If Jesus is not king of this material and physical world — king over our country, city, and neighborhood—then he is not king at all. To act and live as though Jesus is concerned only with the affections of our hearts and does not demand physical obedience to his law is not only to fail to understand true faith, but it is also to engage in rebellion against our risen Lord. Second, as the disciples of Jesus, we have a necessary part in the fulfillment of his prayer. Just as God fed the Israelites with manna in the wilderness, we are called to act on behalf of God for those who come into our lives with hungry bellies and weary bodies. In sharing our daily bread, we follow the disciples who distributed the loaves and fish to the crowd—feeding the hungry with bread provided by our king (Matt. 15:13-21).

James completes his explanation of why faith without works is unable to save. "So also faith by itself, if it does not have works, is dead" (James 2:17). Just as a blessing and prayer for the provision of a person in need without action on their behalf is useless, so also a profession of faith without acting out the implications of that profession (i.e., living in obedience to the demands of the one you have professed trust in and fealty to) is dead. Looking back to verse 14, we see that a faith that lacks lived-out action is dead in the sense that it will not save in the judgment to come, the time when we will be judged by Jesus according to the mercy we have shown toward others (vv. 12-13).

One perspective of understanding why faith without works is "dead" may be found by reflecting on the teaching of Jesus in the parable of the sower. In that parable, some seed was scattered on rocky ground where they sprang up quickly because of the lack of soil, but then withered under the scorching heat of the sun. Jesus explained his parable to his disciples thus, "As for what was sown on rocky ground, this is the one who hears the word and immediately receives it with joy, yet he has no root in himself, but endures for a while, and when tribulation or persecution arises on account of the word, immediately he falls away" (Matt. 13:20-22). From our study of the epistle of James, we have seen that God's intention for his children is that their initial faith develop and grow (through steadfast obedience and joy through suffering) into a mature and complete faith—one that is tested and tried and is lived out in service for others. The seed that was scattered on the rocky ground is like those who articulate faith in Jesus with their words, but never mature in that faith so that it becomes lived out not only in their speech before men, but also in their works. Like the Exodus generation of Israelites who professed faith in Yahweh but failed to mature in their trust of him and were left dead in the wilderness, a faith that does not mature in the manner that God has designed will whither and die. A faith without works will not endure and it will not lead to salvation—in the heat of God's judgment it is like a rootless sprout in the full heat of the noonday sun.

## Demonic Faith

*James 2:18*

[18]But someone will say, "You have faith and I have works." Show me your faith apart from your works, and I will show you my faith by my works.

James responds to the anticipated objection that faith and works are separable and can exist apart from each other—to the person who proclaims, "You have faith and I have works." It is impossible to know exactly why James feels the need to respond to this argument, but it is most likely that because the church to whom he writes struggles to treat the rich and poor without distinction (2:1-7) and is guilty of ignoring the needs of the hungry and homeless (2:15-16). James fears that this disconnect between their professed faith and their actions is due to a stunted theological understanding of the necessity of not only faith but also faithful works in Christ's disciples. James's interlocutor is attempting not only to *distinguish* between faith and works (which must be done when engaging in systematic theological discussions) but also to *separate* them from one another—to assert that faith with or without works is able to save.

In response, James offers this challenge: "Show me your faith apart from your works." This, of course, is impossible, for we cannot show someone our words, or the inner commitment of our hearts, except by our actions. James's point is to expose the ridiculousness of the position of the man who believes faith in Jesus and obedience to his commands are separable. Just as the unrepentant, adulterous husband who exclaims to his wife, "I have love, and you have faithfulness," is a fool and hypocrite, so also is the Christian who claims to have saving faith while living a consistently disobedient life. For marital love is inseparable from marital faithfulness, just as faith in Jesus is inseparable from doing the works of Jesus. Like an acorn that does not grow into an oak, or a child that does not become a man, faith without works is a contradiction in terms, a logical impossibility. Either faith will show itself in works, or it is dead.

James goes on to complete his argument: "And I will show you my faith by my works." In this statement, the apostle reveals his understanding of the organic and essential connection between belief and action, mere talk and bodily obedience. Obviously James is not talking about works that are meritorious in themselves—for his works spring from his faith. To introduce "merit" into this discussion would be to sidetrack the thrust of James's argument. He is not talking about earning God's favor or doing enough good works to please God and to warrant eternal life. His seemingly ridiculous hypothetical is designed to take down the loud-mouthed brother who talks incessantly about faith and what it means but shows no real interest in the needy, hurting community he is called to lead. He calls others to acts of angry zealotry, but he himself is not willing to make the difficult sacrifices (v. 21) or risk his life to rescue others (v. 25).

The heart of James's claim in James 2 is that if these brothers believe that their public talk of faith will usher in their deliverance and vindication before God and men, they are mistaken. Rather, James confronts them with the reality that the hour is coming when all men will be called upon to show their faith not by their words, but by their works. And so he encourages both his readers as well as us to live daily in light of the approaching judgment—not in the ungodly fear of man, as though we must reform ourselves and do a certain number of good deeds in order to ward off the judgment of Jesus, but rather look forward to our judgment in Spirit-filled hope, confident in our king's promise that if we acknowledge him as lord and work out our faith through love in obedience to his commands, we will receive his protection, vindication, and resurrection on the day of judgment.

Indeed, it is the consistent teaching of Scripture that Jesus will judge all men according to their works. John tells us that Jesus himself taught his disciples that the Father has given him "the authority to exercise judgment," and "an hour is coming when all who are in the tombs will hear his voice and come out, those who have done good to the resurrection of life, and those who have done evil to the resurrection of judgment" (John 5:27-29). Every New Testament text that references the Last Day reveals that judgment will be rendered by the Lord according to how people have behaved (Matt. 16:27; 25:31-46; Rom. 2:16; 2 Cor. 5:10; Rev. 20:12; 22:12).

James emphasizes the severity and danger of Jesus's judgment, but we must remember that the one who will judge us is also the one who, while pronouncing destruction and judgment on his enemies, pauses also to say to any who will submit in faith to his kingship: "Come to me, all who labor and are heavy laden, and I will give you rest. Take my yoke upon you, and learn from me, for I am gentle and lowly in heart, and you will find rest for your souls. For my yoke is easy, and my burden is light" (Matt. 12:28-30).

Those who follow Jesus and sometimes doubt the veracity of their internal commitment to him, or even doubt at times the reality of God himself, would do well to note the test that James sets for the reality of faith. For he does not say to his disciples, "I will show you my faith by the steadiness of my internal affections for God." Nor does he say, "I will show you my faith by the consistency of my will to believe in the claims of Jesus." Rather, he says simply, "I will show you my faith by my works." When we understand our good works rightly and see them not as a basis for vainglory or pride before men or God but rather as the fruit which springs forth from our lives and demonstrates our connection to the true vine, they become tethers of hope and confidence for the one who is weak in his faith and doubts the love of God.

For in the moment of struggle and temptation to believe that we do not truly belong to our Father or are not truly united to his Son, we need only look at the works of love and service that mark our lives. Just as baptism publicly marks us as the sons and daughters of God, so also our works of love publicly mark the vitality of our trust in him. In the end, James's assertion that "I will show you my faith by works" is only a restatement of Jesus's declaration to his disciples that, "By this all people will know that you are my disciples, if you have love for one another" (John 13:35), with the understanding that "all people" refers not only to the watching world, but also to the community of believers in which we worship and live, and also even to inner chambers of our own doubting hearts.

## James 2:19

<sup>19</sup>You have faith that God is one; you do well. Even the demons have faith—and shudder!

James continues his attack against the person who would separate faith from works with these words: "You believe that God is one; you do well. Even the demons believe—and shudder!" James refers to the core tenet of faith for true followers of Yahweh— Moses's words to all of Israel, "Hear O Israel, Yahweh our God, Yahweh is one" (Deut. 6:4). In their simple verbal articulation of faith in God, James says his readers do well. But in itself, this kind of verbal faith is not enough. For even the demons have this kind of faith in God, and it does no good. Indeed, it only assures them of their doom, for their works show them to be set in rebellion against God. Indeed, when Jesus went to the country of the Gadarenes and was met by two demon-possessed men, they cried out to him, "What have you to do with us, O Son of God?" (Matt. 8:29). Confronted with Jesus, these demons confessed that he was truly the Son of God, but their belief was not a saving faith—rather it led only to their destruction. In the same way, bare intellectual faith in the Lordship of Jesus or his salvific death and resurrection will do no good unless this faith is also expressed in the works of repentance.

Although it seems awkward to us to talk about the demon's having "faith," it helps to see that James is using the same word throughout this section—not two different terms: one for "faith" and one for "belief." The verb "to have faith" or "to trust" (πιστευω) and the related noun "faith" (πιστις) are used over a dozen times in this section. They are translated differently in some verses, which might lead to some confusion for the English reader. James is not distinguishing between the workless faith of James 2:17 and bare intellectual belief in verse 19. Rather, his point is that both are the same. Faith without works will no more rescue us than the confession of the demons at Gadarenes saved them from their fate when they were confronted with the judgment of Jesus (Matt. 8:28-34). Again, James reminds his readers of the uselessness of a bare faith that is not worked out through love. What is needed for true followers of Jesus is a faith that goes beyond the faith of demons—not merely a verbal confession of the Lordship of Jesus but also a life that is lived according to his commands, lived as though he is truly both Lord and Judge.

If we really want to get the shock value of verses 18-19 in something close to the original Greek, it should be read like this: "Show me your faith apart from your works, and I'll show you my faith by my works. You have faith that God is one, you do well—even the demons have that kind of faith." And what is more, the demons do something that you don't do, you foolish man—they shudder. They understand that their works will earn them eternal destruction, and they're terrified. But you, apparently, just willy-nilly, make a confession about the oneness of God's being, a propositional, theological statement, but it doesn't make an impact in your life at all. At least the demons shudder, but you don't seem to be moved, changed at all by your profession of faith.

But perhaps there is more here than meets the eye. The confession that God is one (Deut. 6:4) has always been among the Jews a declaration of the universality of the "kingdom of God," an acknowledgement of God as sole ruler.

> And Yahweh will become king over all the earth; on that day the Lord will be one and his Name one (Zech. 14:9).

Given the context of this letter, the dangerous temptations that are being set before the dissident believers, and the bad example of the Jewish zealots, it is likely that the announcement that "God is one" is a reference to the very highly charged public statements that James is contrasting with genuine faith. In other words, these zealous brothers think that their loud pronouncement of the oneness of God is all that is needed to rally their people for action and fight back against their pursuers. But James says that in the absence of mercy, kindness, and sacrificial obedience this kind of talk is not a living faith in the Lord, but a demonic distortion of Christian living.

## Justified by Works and Not by Faith Alone

*James 2:20-24*

> [20]Do you want to be shown, you foolish person, that faith apart from works is useless? [21]Was not Abraham our father justified by works when he offered up his son Isaac on the altar? [22]You see that faith was active along with his works, and faith was completed by his works; [23]and the Scripture was fulfilled that says, "Abraham believed God, and it was counted to him as righteousness"—and he was called a friend of God. [24]You see that a man is justified by works and not by faith alone.

For almost a decade I served on the examinations committee of our presbytery. The members of the committee were charged with administering written and oral exams to men applying for ordination in our churches. At some point in most oral exams, I would ask the ordinand a simple question. Please evaluate the following statement: "You see that a man is justified by works and not by faith alone." Almost every one of them would immediately react passionately, making sure the committee knew they believed the statement was false and dangerous. I would then ask where they thought I got that statement. Some would suggest some Roman Catholic book or catechism. When I told them it was a verbatim quotation from the apostle James's epistle some were shocked, but most of the time we were able to have a healthy discussion about the truth of James's declaration.

James continues to argue against the person who believes that faith and works can be separated from one another and exist independently. As James notes, this person is "foolish," and this judgment is related to his earlier warning to the "double-minded, unstable" man of 1:8 (who asks for wisdom, but is unwilling to live according to wisdom's demands), as well as the one who hears the word only but does not do it, and is thus deceived (1:22). Much like the rhetoric of Psalm 1, James here sets before his readers alternative visions of life, commending the way of the righteous while warning against the path of the wicked. Naming this person a "fool" is not only a rhetorical tactic designed to impugn the character of James's opponents. Rather, by describing the person who speaks eloquently of his faith but refuses to act in accordance with the demands of his professed fealty to Jesus as a "fool," James exercises the name-giving power of Adam (Gen. 2:19-20) and evokes the background of the Hebrew Scriptures regarding the "fool."

Like Solomon, James delineates the path of the wise and the fool and commends to his readers the way of wisdom, knowledge, and integrity instead of foolishness, self-deception, and inconsistency. One of the primary concerns in the Proverbs of Solomon is wise speech, and one of the main characteristics of the fool is his babbling tongue. As Solomon puts it, "The tongue of the wise commends knowledge, but the mouths of fools pour out folly" (Prov. 15:2). It is because of this tendency to wag their tongues that James has named his opponents as "fools." For they freely confess their faith ("God is one" and "Go in peace, be warm and filled...") but do not match this belief with their actions. Like the fool of Solomon's Proverbs, the man who would separate faith and works from one another is a man who believes that wisdom and integrity are found in simply saying the right words. The fool's tongue runs freely, but he does not follow up his works with actions. For James, just as for Solomon, this man is a "fool" and his "mouth is his ruin, and his lips are a snare to his soul" (Prov. 18:7).

We are also told that "faith apart from works is *useless*." (James 2:20). Useless for what? Once again, James is examining the usefulness of faith in the context of their exile and suffering—this kind of faith is useless because it cannot deliver (1:21; 2:14), for it has not been expressed in acts of mercy, and thus the man with this kind of empty faith should not expect to himself receive mercy in judgment (2:13). Indeed, if we connect this with James 3, this kind of foolish talk will never accomplish what these leaders want (3:9-12), especially "the harvest of righteousness" they long for (3:18; 1:20).

James begins to show the foolish man why faith apart from works is useless by reflecting upon the story of Abraham. "Was not Abraham our father justified by his works when he offered up his son Isaac on the altar?" (v. 21). The story to which James refers is found in Genesis 22.

> God tested Abraham... He said, "Take your son, your only son Isaac, whom you love, and go to the land of Moriah, and offer him there as a burnt offering on one of the mountains of which I shall tell you" (Gen. 22:1-2).

According to the text, Abraham did not hesitate in his obedience to God's command. The next morning, he rose and cut wood for the sacrifice, journeying with his son toward Moriah. Three days later, Abraham bound his son and placed him on the altar, only to be halted by the words of an angel of Yahweh. As the writer of Hebrews tells us, Abraham's actions were the physical expression of his faith in God. "By faith Abraham, when he was tested, offered up Isaac…he considered that God was able even to raise [Isaac] from the dead, from which, figuratively speaking, he did receive him back" (Heb. 11:17, 19).

Though James says that "Abraham was justified by his works," we know from the context of this passage that James is not considering Abraham's works apart from his faith. Indeed, James 2 has been a meditation on the impossibility of separating one from the other. In other words, just as James expects us to understand that true faith works itself out through love, so also our works justify us when they are the expression of faith in Jesus.

James does not mean that we are justified by works in the sense that our works merit favor before God and *earn* our salvation, but rather that we are justified by faith working through love. Though Abraham professed faith in God, when God commanded him to sacrifice his son Isaac, his faith was forced out from the realm of mere intellectual assent. If Abraham had not obeyed God's command, his faith would have been useless, and it would not have saved him. But Abraham was not a foolish man, and he understood that to have faith in God meant not only to believe that God would keep his promises to him, but also to act in a way that was consistent with that belief. So Abraham not only professed his belief that God would bring his only son back from the dead, he also raised the knife to spill the lifeblood from his bound son. And because Abraham's faith was expressed in his works, he was saved.

James explains it like this, "You see that faith was active along with his works, and faith was completed by his works; and the Scripture was fulfilled that says 'Abraham believed God, and it was counted to him as righteousness'—and he was called a friend of God" (vv. 22-23). Here James makes explicit that Abraham was not justified by his works before God in a meritorious sense, but rather by his faith working through love. Literally, the Greek of 22a reads, "You see that faith was working with his works." What is highlighted here is that works are not something we add to our faith that make it "true" (as though the two could be separated) but that genuine faith works.

When James writes that Abraham's "faith was completed by his works," he uses the passive form of the Greek verb τελειοω, and we may also translate his words as "Abraham's faith was matured by his works." This is a significant point, for we see here the importance of reading 2:14-26 in the context of James's entire epistle (see also 3:2). For as we have noted throughout this commentary, the necessity of our faith being *matured* by our works is not a new theme for James—indeed, it is merely a restatement and expansion of his declaration in 1:3-4 that the "testing of [our] faith produces steadfastness," (i.e., it requires our faith to work itself out through love) and when we remain steadfast and joyful in the midst of trials, we become "mature and complete, lacking in nothing."

This picture of faith being made mature through works is consistent with our own everyday experience. When our children first begin to profess their faith in simple and childlike ways—for example, saying, "I love Jesus," we are delighted and humbled by their trust in God. But we also expect that as they grow up in the world, their faith will also grow up and become mature—that they will obey their parents, that they will confess their sins, that they will more and more seek to live out their trust in Jesus in concrete and real ways. If their faith remains only a simple profession and is not expressed in works of love and obedience, then they will not mature, and they will remain children in their faith even as their bodies and minds grow. This is not God's will for his children, and James's point is that this kind of immature and undeveloped faith will not save us.

Of course, what is true for our covenant children is also true for adult converts to the Christian faith. When an adult confesses his faith in Jesus for the first time and is baptized, his faith is also immature. If he does not grow into maturity of faith by living in obedience and love, by confessing his sins and receiving forgiveness, by submitting to the teaching and discipline of the church, by feeding on Christ in Word and Sacrament, he is not cooperating with God's will for his life and therefore should not have any confidence that his faith will save him. Indeed, if we were to create a one sentence interpretive summary of the entire message of the book of James, it might be simply: "Do not remain children in your faith."

Understanding how Abraham's faith was properly matured by his works helps us to see why it is that a faith without works will not save us in the final judgment. God's plan for humanity has always been for men and women, created in his image, to grow into maturity and rule over creation. Though Adam and Eve did not remain steadfast in their trial with the serpent and grow into maturity, God's plan for humanity did not change. He created a new humanity in Noah and then Abraham, growing them into maturity through trials and suffering, through death and resurrection. Finally, the time came for Jesus to fully enact God's plan for humanity. And so Jesus was born—not only to live a perfect life and die a sacrificial death in order to appease the justice of God, but also to grow in wisdom and stature—to remain steadfast and be made mature where Adam failed.

Jesus was drawn into the wilderness to do battle with the serpent and resist the temptation to attain kingship without suffering (precisely the point at which Adam stumbled). After pushing aside Satan's offer of kingship, Jesus gained his crown God's way by living as a suffering king for his people—healing the sick and feeding the hungry, wandering as a homeless and poor stranger, steadfastly enduring the persecution of his enemies and the rejection of those who should have welcomed him. Finally, when he had learned maturity by his obedience (Heb. 5:8), Jesus faced his most intense trial—the desertion of his apostles, the conspiracy of Israel and Rome against him, the physical torment of his executioners, and finally, the excruciating pain of the worst kind of death ever devised by the most brutal of all the world's empires.

Even in the midst of his suffering and death, Jesus again had to resist the temptation of Satan and the path of Adam by refusing to call upon the armies of heaven to deliver him from death. For in the wisdom and plan of God, there is only one true path to kingship and maturity—and Jesus embraced the will of his Father completely, dying on the cross as an accused insurrectionist. Three days later, the earth shook, the stone rolled away, and the firstborn of God's new humanity stepped out of the grave. Forty days later, the fully mature king, in his glorified, yet still physical body ascended to his throne and sat down to begin his rule. This was how God's plan for humanity was fulfilled in the person of Jesus, and the normative pattern for all who would also be sons and daughters of God was displayed.

Now, when we put on Christ at our baptisms, we are united to the mature and complete Son of God. But this union is not merely mystical or abstract or spiritual. For Jesus speaks to us in his Word. He forgives our sins and teaches us to pray in his name. We chew on his body and drink his blood. And his life becomes our life. We also minister to the sick and feed the hungry. We also suffer the hardships of this life and the persecution of God's enemies and resist the temptation of Satan. We embrace death itself (whether violent or natural) with steadfastness and faith in the power and love of God. And we wait now, groaning for the resurrection of the dead, for the renewal of all things, for the day when we will be fully mature and glorified and human.

This is the way of salvation. This is the plan of God for the world. And when James says that faith without works cannot save, this is shorthand for saying "Unless you live as Jesus lived, unless you suffer as he suffered, unless you serve as he served, unless you die as he died, you will not be made mature." Every step we take on the pathway of Jesus is made by faith, but steps must be taken, and our faith must be made mature by works. Without maturation, our faith is useless and dead, and there is no salvation for those whose faith does not work through love.

James does not arbitrarily choose the story of Abraham in his explanation of the role of faith and works in the life of the believer. For Abraham is "the father of us all" (Rom. 4:16), and his example of faith is paradigmatic for us as his sons and daughters. Like Abraham, our trust in God must find expression in how we live our lives. Just as Abraham believed the word of God (Gen. 15:6), so we are also called to trust in Jesus. But just as it was not sufficient for Abraham to lay hold of the promises of God by simply saying "I believe," but also had to express his belief in obedience to God's command to sacrifice Isaac, so we also are called not only to confess our faith in Jesus but also to walk in radical obedience.

In this way, like Abraham, our faith is matured by our works, and we will be protected, shown mercy, and saved in the day of the judgment of the world by the world's one true king. For to be "in Christ" means far more than to mouth our trust in Jesus as our Lord, but rather to live as though he really is king and to act as though we really will stand before him in judgment. But we do not live in fear, as though our Lord and Judge is malicious or deceptive, as though our faith expressed in works will be rejected and discarded. To live in light of the judgment of Jesus is to live confidently by faith, like Abraham, who believed and lived as though God rewards those who seek him and when confronted with the death of his son put his faith in God's power to raise the dead to life. For Jesus is not only our judge, he is also our shepherd. And since we are his sheep, he promises, "no one will snatch [us] out of his hand" (John 10:28).

We should not miss that in choosing the story of Abraham, James has his readers' situation in mind. In Genesis 22:1, the author of Genesis says that God "tested" Abraham by commanding him to sacrifice Isaac. In this way, God brought a trial into Abraham's life so that he would be tested and, in his steadfastness, his faith would be matured in his works. Though there is not an exact correlation between the experience of Abraham and the experience of the exiled church, this is very similar to how James describes the experience of the church to whom he writes in the first verses of his epistle (James 1:2-18).

Like Abraham, these exiled, persecuted disciples are experiencing trials that threaten their own safety and security as well as that of their families. And this is a test (James 1:3) that requires them to remain steadfast in their faith so that they will be made mature and complete—true sons of God. It is not a stretch to think that many of the believers in these exiled communities had lost sons, husbands, and family members at the hands of their Jewish inquisitors. Stephen was someone's son (Acts 7). Paul, just one of the perpetrators of violence against the Way, was "breathing threats and murder," and himself tells of many tortured and even executed because of their faith in Jesus (Acts 22:4; 26:9-11). Many of these exiled Christians would have had to exercise the same confident faith as Abraham did. They would have to trust God's promise that he would raise their family members who suffered as victims of their oppressors' deadly zealotry.

James reminds us of the story of Abraham to encourage us in our tests. By reflecting on the trials of our father Abraham we see the history of the faithfulness of God and his ways with his people. Therefore, our perspective on our own tests is broadened and we come to understand that tests and trials are the normative pattern of the Christian life—and our trials are not a demonstration that God is evil or malicious, but rather that he is truly our father (Heb. 12:7).

James says that Abraham's faith was matured by his works, "and the Scripture was fulfilled that says, 'Abraham believed God, and it was counted to him as righteousness'—and he was called a friend of God" (James 2:23). The passage that James quotes is Genesis 15:6, where, after Yahweh declared to Abraham that his offspring would be as many as the stars in the sky, the writer of Genesis tells us, "[Abram] believed Yahweh, and he counted it to him as righteousness." This is the normal pattern for the Christian life—our articulation of faith in Jesus is counted to us as righteousness (that is, our covenant loyalty), but our verbal faith must be fulfilled in steadfastness and obedience in our daily lives. Of course, this does not mean our works merit righteousness or earn our salvation. But, under the Fatherly hand of God, through the power of the Holy Spirit, and by virtue of our union with Jesus, we are called to grow into the obedience of faith, and God's declaration of our righteousness is fulfilled in our lives.

This process of maturity and fulfillment should not be dreaded or feared. Rather, we ought to understand that the maturity that God desires for us is like a father's desire for his son to mature and grow into a man. Just as we as fathers and mothers long for our children to grow up and live as faithful and mature men and women, and train them up so that they will do so, so our heavenly Father trains and matures us. And if we, as sinners, know to give good gifts to our children, then we can trust that our heavenly Father will also give to us the gifts of maturity and wisdom.

> For everyone who asks receives, and the one who seeks finds, and to the one who knocks it will be opened. Or which one of you, if his son asks him for bread, will give him a stone? Or if he asks for a fish, will give him a serpent? If you then, who are evil, know how to give good gifts to your children, how much more will your Father who is in heaven give good things to those who ask him! (Matt. 7:9-11).

James also notes that through his obedience and maturity, Abraham was called "a friend of God," a designation he draws from Isaiah 41:8 and 2 Chronicles 20:7. Though in the Hebrew Scriptures, only Moses (Exod. 33:11) and Abraham are directly called the friends of God, Jesus gives a fuller exposition on this theme.

Speaking to his disciples, Jesus says,

> This is my commandment, that you love one another as I have loved you. Greater love has no one than this, that someone lay down his life for his friends. You are my friends if you do what I command you. No longer do I call you servants, for the servant does not know what his master is doing; but I have called you friends, for all that I have heard from my Father I have made known to you (John 15:13-15).

This concept of friendship is important for James—later in his letter he will challenge his readers to reject friendship with the world (James 4:4). Here he shows us through the story of Abraham what it means to be God's friend—to live in obedience to his commands, to not only confess our love for him, but also to do what he says.

More than this, becoming a "friend of God" means being elevated to a place of honor in the Lord's court. Remember, Abraham was the first man to be called a "prophet" in Scripture (Gen. 20:7). That designation is given to him by God so that the tyrant Abimelech would know that Abraham could intercede for him and restore his family. Prophets in the Bible are not simply errand boys. They are not merely charged with delivering messages from God. They are elevated to positions of counsel in God's court. They are members of his privy council, so to speak. They have God's ear. When they advise God, he graciously listens and incorporates their wisdom into his plans. In other words, just as Hushai was a "friend" of King David, a trusted counselor, so also are prophets called "friends of God" (2 Sam. 15:37).

If the brothers reading this epistle would take the time to reflect on the implications of James's reference to obedient Abraham as a "friend of God," they might just find encouragement in their present difficulties. If they would behave like Abraham and not just talk about God's justice, then they would be elevated as "friends" of God and given a privileged place to advise the Lord about their present circumstances. James will make this explicit at the end of his epistle when he holds before them the "example of suffering and patience" displayed by the prophets (James 5:10). But especially righteous Elijah whose prayers were able to bring both drought and rain (5:16-18). This is what these brothers could be as "friends of God."

## Rahab's Righteous Deception

*James 2:25-26*

²⁵And in the same way was not also Rahab the prostitute justified by works when she received the messengers and sent them out by another way? ²⁶For as the body apart from the spirit is dead, so also faith apart from works is dead.

After reflecting upon the story of Abraham in Genesis 22, James now shifts to a consideration of the description of Rahab in Joshua 2. In that narrative, we see that Rahab confesses her faith in Yahweh in Joshua 2:8-13 ("Yahweh your God, he is God in the heavens above and on the earth beneath") and then acts out her faith by receiving the messengers of Joshua and protecting them by sending them out of her window through the city wall so that they could report back to their leader without being captured by the king of Jericho. Later, in Joshua 6, we find that the family of Rahab was protected in the destruction and judgment of Jericho because she acted in faith.

Rahab was justified by her works—it was not simply her profession of faith in Yahweh which won her protection and deliverance from judgment, but also her action (that is, her work) in protecting the messengers of Joshua. Without her action, Rahab's profession of faith would have been worthless and would not have resulted in her deliverance. But because she not only confessed Yahweh as God, but also feared him and acted as though he was truly God (even though this meant risking the wrath of Jericho's king), Rahab was delivered.

We may be confident that James cites the story of Rahab intentionally, because there is something in her life and actions that is particularly instructive for his readers. First, we may note that James explicitly says that Rahab's faith is of the same kind as that of Abraham (2:25, "And in the same was not also Rahab the prostitute justified..."). This is significant for several reasons, perhaps most importantly because Rahab was not an Israelite or a blood-line descendant of Abraham.

Though the church at the time of James's letter was most likely nearly exclusively ethnically Jewish, James is anticipating a time when the Gentiles will flood into the church, and here implicitly declares that it is not the "proper" bloodline which leads to our justification, but rather confessing our faith in the Lord and living that faith out in our lives. Thereby James protects his Jewish readers from ethnic pride and opens the doors for Gentiles to understand that, like Rahab, it is not their ancestry that counts, but their demonstrated faith in Jesus.

We should also note that the particular work for which Rahab is commended in this passage is her hospitality toward and protection of the followers of Yahweh from persecution and death, ignoring even the edict of her king to do so (and thus risking her own death). The readers of James's epistle are in much the same situation as Rahab. Because of the persecution of the Jews, the followers of Jesus are faced with a choice—cooperate with their earthly rulers and deliver their friends up for conviction or risk the wrath of their rulers and their own deaths by protecting each other from the evil men who seek their lives. By showing hospitality and protection to their fellow Christians, James's readers follow in the path of Rahab and confess Jesus as Lord not only with their lips but also in their lives, even at great cost.

The political implications of James's words should not go unnoticed. He is encouraging his readers to join in peaceful subversive and dissident activity that is in rebellion against the directives of the Jewish authorities. And James's command to act in this politically subversive way is based squarely on the conviction that it is not the Jews or the Romans who truly rule his flock, but rather Jesus himself. This "deceptive" tactic is often commended in Scripture when God's people are troubled by tyrannical political leaders. For example, Abraham's wife has to deceive both Pharaoh and Abimelech because of their twisted designs for her. In both cases Abraham is blessed by God and the evil ruler is rebuked (Gen. 12 & 20). These two incidents are proleptic exoduses. In Exodus 2 the faithful midwives are blessed by Yahweh for deceiving Pharaoh and saving the male Israelite babies. Examples of righteous deception by God's people in Scripture could be multiplied. James's reference to Rahab is a reminder to these exiled people that "faith working through love" has many ways of presenting opportunities in their situation. Even the apostle Paul will later have to be stealthily helped out the back window of a house in Damascus when the Jews are seeking to arrest him (Acts 9:23-25). Helping wanted Christians to escape clandestinely from their pursuers is a righteous act, evidence of a living faith.[25]

It is because of the Lordship of Jesus that his followers are ultimately traitors to the apostate Jewish authorities in that the interest of the state is never the final interest or rule of those who have bent the knee to Jesus. Even those of us who live in "free" states and have no obvious conflict of interest between the command of the state and the command of Jesus must reserve within us the commitment to betray our nation if our Lord

---

[25] For more on the biblical justification for deception of ungodly tyrants see James B. Jordan, *Primeval Saints: Studies in the Patriarchs of Genesis* (Moscow, ID: Canon Press, 2001), chapters 5 & 7. Also see James B. Jordan, "Rebellion, Tyranny, and Dominion in the Book of Genesis," in *The Tactics of Christian Resistance*, ed. by Gary North (Tyler, TX: Geneva Press, 1983), 38-79.

demands it of us. We may be patriots, but never blindly, for there is only one true king in this world, and our loyalty to him cannot be compromised.

James concludes his argument by writing, "For as the body apart from the spirit is dead, so also faith apart from works is dead" (James 2:26). This is a clear echo of verse 17, and structurally frames James's three demonstrations of the significance of faith working through love—the demons, who have faith but no works and are condemned, and Abraham and Rahab, who have both faith and works and are justified. Here James gives a final and vivid image of what it means for faith to exist without with works—it is like a body whose spirit has departed and is dead. The backdrop for this judgment is Genesis 2:7, where God forms Adam's body out of the dust and then breathes life into him so that he became a living creature. In death, this spirit-body connection is severed, and the body dies, though the spirit lives on.

This image of the faith without works being like the body without the spirit teaches us several important concepts of the significance of works. First, we see it is necessary for faith to be completed and perfected by works, just as James previously argued in verse 22. Without works, faith is incomplete, just as the body of Adam was incomplete before God breathed into his nostrils. The natural completion of faith is through good works. If a man has faith, but no works, he has yet to truly be a participant in the new creation, and his immature faith cries out for completion in works of obedience.

We also see that faith without works is not truly alive, just as Adam's body lay lifeless on the ground before God breathed into him. This is a significant point, because often theologians argue that good works in the life of the believer merely *testify* to the vitality or liveliness of his faith. But this is not quite what James is saying. The image he uses in verse 26 implies that works are actually *part* of the vitality of faith. That is, good works do not simply *prove* that our faith is true, but they are a *necessary component* of a true faith—they are part of the process that makes our faith alive, just as the spirit does not simply testify to the life of the body, but it is itself part of that life. Good works are not merely the natural consequence of a living faith (as though faith could be living apart from works), but they are organically connected to faith in such a way that the union of the two leads to life.

Significantly, this gives a renewed dignity to our works of obedience as we lead lives of trust in Jesus. For no longer is faith "the only thing that matters"—our works are equally essential and equally important. As Paul puts it in Romans 1:5, it is the "obedience of faith" that is our lively response to the gospel. Not faith alone, and not works alone, but the organic union of faith and works is the obedience of faith that our Risen Lord demands. Certainly, "by grace you have been saved through faith," (Eph. 2:8), but the mere faith through which we are saved does not exist apart from works of repentance and obedience.

Finally, in James's image of faith without works being like the body without a spirit, we see another significant truth about the nature of faith and works. Just as we boldly confess that our faith is a gift from God, and not from ourselves, we also confess that our works are equally gifts from our Father, and do not ultimately spring from our own effort or merit. For Adam's body lay lifeless on the ground until God breathed his spirit into his body. And in the same way, our works are the gift and result of God's work in our lives, as he breathes obedience and love into our lifeless bodies. Our works are his works, so that there is no place for us to boast in our merit, but only to delight in the graciousness and free love of our Father. "For we are his [God's] workmanship, created in Christ Jesus for good works, which God prepared beforehand, so that we should walk in them" (Eph. 2:10).

## Summary & Reflections

In this section James engages in an extended discussion and explanation of his assertion in James 2:13, "judgment is without mercy to the one who has shown no mercy. Mercy triumphs over judgment." Jesus will show no mercy to the one that himself does not show mercy in his life toward others because a profession of faith in Jesus without abiding in the life pattern of Jesus is worthless, and that kind of faith will not save. After all, even the demons have faith that Jesus is God's son, but their faith will not save them, for they do not respond in the obedience of faith to his commands. After showing the necessity of works in the life of faith of two Old Testament saints, James concludes his argument by asserting in the strongest possible terms that faith without works is useless—like a body without spirit, this kind of faith is dead.

Why does James argue in such strong terms for the necessity of works in the life of faith? There are at least three reasons. First, so that his readers will be vindicated in the judgment of Jesus, and they will be saved—so that mercy will triumph over judgment in their lives. Fearing that some in his congregation are separating faith and works in such a way that they have come to believe that their faith can be vital and salvific without working itself through love, James confronts this misunderstanding of the gospel by emphasizing the reality that true and living faith is always expressed in acts of obedience—and that a profession of faith in Jesus without following his commands will not lead to salvation, but to death.

We would do well to pause and remember that every time the Final Judgment is presented to us in the New Testament, it always involves a judgment of works.

> Do not marvel at this, for an hour is coming when all who are in the tombs will hear his voice and come out, those who have done good to the resurrection of life, and those who have done evil to the resurrection of judgment (John 5:28-29).

> When the Son of Man comes in his glory, and all the angels with him, then he will sit on his glorious throne.... The King will say to those on his right, "Come, you who are blessed by my Father, inherit the kingdom prepared for you from the foundation of the world. For I was hungry and you gave me food, I was thirsty and you gave me drink... (Matt. 25:31-46).

> For we must all appear before the judgment seat of Christ, so that each one may receive what is due for what he has done in the body, whether good or evil (2 Cor. 5:10).

> Then I saw a great white throne and him who was seated on it. From his presence earth and sky fled away, and no place was found for them. And I saw the dead, great and small, standing before the throne, and books were opened. Then another book was opened, which is the book of life. And the dead were judged by what was written in the books, according to what they had done (Rev. 20:11-12).

This should give some Christian leaders pause, especially when so many people have been taught that entrance into heaven will be determined by a theological exam at the gate. Too many people believe their admission into heavenly glory will depend on what they say, how they answer certain questions when they appear before the Lord. "Why should I let you into my heaven?" If we can just articulate the correct answer, then we will be admitted. The way these evangelistic stories are told everything apparently depends on what we say. If we can articulate the doctrine of justification by faith alone or of salvation by grace alone, everything will be okay. But is that true? Does James or the rest of the Bible give us any hope that our judgment by God will be all about the accuracy of our confession of faith? If someone says they have faith but does not have works, can *that* faith save him?

What James is teaching us is that "God has appointed a day, wherein He will judge the world, in righteousness, by Jesus Christ, to whom all power and judgment is given of the Father. In which day, not only the apostate angels shall be judged, but likewise all persons that have lived upon earth shall appear before the tribunal of Christ, to give an account of their thoughts, words, and deeds; and to receive according to what they have done in the body, whether good or evil" (Westminster Confession of Faith, 33.1). In this sense, we who follow Jesus are justified by our works and not faith alone—because, on the last day, it is not simply our verbalization and explanation of our faith in Jesus that will save us, but a life lived in obedience to his commands.

The second reason James focuses so closely on the importance of works for those who profess faith in Jesus is found in the overall purpose of James's epistle. He writes this pastoral letter to encourage his readers to "Count it all joy, my brothers, when you meet trials of various kinds, for you know that the testing of your faith produces steadfastness. And let steadfastness have its full effect, that you may be mature and complete, lacking in nothing" (James 1:2-4). Simply put, the purpose of James's letter is to encourage his flock to remain joyful and steadfast in the midst of trials and suffering, knowing that in their steadfastness, they are being made mature in Christ.

But part of remaining steadfast means to walk in obedience to the commands of Jesus by imitating his life of patient suffering and merciful service. By working out their faith through love, those who follow Christ are made mature and grow more and more into the image of God's son. James alludes to this reality when he writes that when Abraham obeyed God by offering Isaac as a sacrifice, "[his] faith was active along with his works, and faith was completed [or matured] by his works" (James 2:22). The purpose of James's epistle is to encourage his readers to grow into the maturity that God desires for them. And the route to maturity is found in obedience to Jesus's commands, in a faith that works in love.

But James commends the importance of works in the Christian life not only because they are part of the process of maturity, but also because works of obedience and mercy are the purpose of our maturity in Christ. In other words, God does not desire the maturity of his children simply so that they will grow into adults for their own sake, but also so that they will rule with Christ over his creation. And the mature ruling that we are called to is not a self-absorbed maintenance of power or comfort but rather life-giving service for the world.

Biblically speaking, to rule with Christ means to embody Jesus's prophetic declaration that, "Whoever would be great among you must be your servant, and whoever would be first among you must be your slave, even as the Son of Man came not to be served but to serve, and to give his life as a ransom for many" (Matt. 20:26-28). This pattern is found not only in the life of Jesus, but also in all the saints of the biblical story—Joseph and Boaz, David and Solomon, Paul and Peter—these men acted as kings and rulers of God's people as they laid down their own lives for the sake of God's people, as they joined Jesus in taking up their crosses so that other might live. It is just this "wisdom" that seems so topsy-turvy to embattled, exiled Christians. It is counterintuitive. Apparently for these brothers, serving one another simply cannot be as effective as rallying the oppressed to fight back against their enemies. As we shall see in James 3 and 4, cursing and making speeches inflaming the community to "fight back" are, in the minds of these brothers, so much more effective.

In summary, James emphasizes the significance of works in the life of the believer for at least three reasons—so that we will receive mercy in the judgment of Jesus even as we have shown mercy toward others, so that we will remain steadfast in the midst of suffering by continuing in obedience to the words of our master and be made mature, and finally so that we may join with Christ in the exercise of his dominion and authority, ruling with him over all things by offering our lives as a sacrifice of love.

Martin Luther once famously remarked in his introduction to the Letter of James that, "James is truly an epistle of straw...it has nothing of the nature of the Gospel about it." Though Luther removed this comment from later editions of his introduction, it still expresses the discomfort many modern Protestants feel when they read the words of James, and in particular the conclusion of James 2:24, "You see that a person is justified by works and not by faith alone" But why did Luther start off with such a strong reaction against the book of James, and especially this passage? Why do we sometimes share his visceral reaction to James's strong emphasis on the importance of works?

Much of Luther's reaction to the letter of James is tied to his particular historical context. Luther spent most of his life combating the late-medieval, Roman Catholic view that one who believes in Jesus earns their salvation by works. In practice, this meant that we earn God's favor by living in obedience to his commands. If we do enough good works, we can draw down God's love and favor. If we add up enough works, then those works will counterbalance our sins, our unrighteousness, and God will analyze our *lives* and declare us righteous—because we will have merited his favor. Luther correctly saw this understanding of salvation as a flagrant violation of the biblical gospel. And he rightly attacked and corrected the false gospel of the late medieval Roman church by proclaiming the reality that it is by faith that we are saved. It is our trust and belief in the promises of Jesus that will save us.

But as the heirs of Luther, the sons of the Reformation, we also need to hear James's teaching that if our faith is merely intellectual assent to propositional truth, then we are in trouble. Indeed, if we think somehow that because we have a mental act that we call faith, and no change of life, no actions, no works, but somehow, we're saved, we have missed one of the basic messages of Scripture. Even Luther, in his later life, emphasized the necessity of good works, because he began to see that bare faith was not a sufficient response to the Gospel.

When we're sick, when we have a disease, it manifests itself in various ways, with many different symptoms. When we have the flu, we not only have a stuffed-up nose, but we also have a headache. And we might also be dizzy and weak. And what we see in the New Testament is that Jesus and Paul and James and all the other writers of the New Testament are analyzing the pathology of Israel's sickness. And there are various ways to characterize that sickness. Because of Israel's unbelief, their faithlessness manifested itself in a certain way for Paul, in that they would not receive the Gentiles as full members of the new Christian community. And so Paul addresses that problem in most of his letters. His polemic against "the works of the law" is directed against those who taught that obedience to the Israel-specific regulations of the Torah (circumcision, sabbaths, food laws, etc.) was necessary for Gentiles to become full members of the Christian community.

But James also has another equally valid perspective on Israel's sin, her problem, her sickness. James's perspective dovetails and works together with what Paul says, but in the end it is a bit different. Interestingly enough, James's analysis, his diagnosis that one of the problems with the early church is their belief that mere intellectual assent fulfills God's requirement for faith in the gospel fits very well with what Protestant Christians sometimes struggle with.

This struggle to properly understand the nature of faith was a common problem for Israel. Often in her history, she got to the place where she became proud, and she thought that because she confessed certain doctrinal truths about God, then she was safe. So now, James brings these new Jewish Christians back to the biblical truth that faith without being lived out is dead. In the Hebrew Scriptures, it was not sufficient for Israel to confess that Yahweh was one without living in covenantally faithful ways, and so now the followers of Jesus cannot confess him as Lord without living in obedience to his commands. In both the Old and New Testaments, a faith that remains inside our heads will not save us. Neither will a faith that is primarily bombastically proclaimed in one's speech or one's internet presence.

Martin Luther's misunderstanding of James and the continued evangelical reluctance to deal squarely with the implications of this passage reveal something deeply significant about how we have misunderstood the full Gospel of Jesus. There is no contradiction in the teaching of James with the rest of Scripture. If we are uncomfortable with the explanation he gives of the relationship between faith and works, what might this reveals about our own hearts and separation of faith and life? Rather than explain away his words because they do not fit with our prior theological commitments, perhaps we need to listen a bit more carefully to what James has said.

Ultimately, the words of James in this passage are a difficult challenge. His teaching confronts us with the reality that Jesus is Lord not only in our words or even in the internal commitments of our hearts, but also of our entire lives. But James's challenge, that "faith without works is dead" is also the challenge of Jesus, and ultimately of all of God's Word. It is a wonderful and necessary thing to recite with our lips belief in Jesus's death and resurrection, but as we live out the obedience of faith we embody this faith in our actions and materially confess our belief in Jesus. Like James, we show our faith by our works and truly exercise the faith that through which, by grace, we are saved.

Finally, for Christian dissidents living in cultural exile, who are tempted to believe that the most effective way of deliverance for an embattled community is verbal combat against the enemy, this section of James's letter would argue otherwise. Can we be rescued/saved from our trials and suffering by talking, writing, lecturing, etc. about our faith? Can *that* faith save us? Will we be vindicated before God and men because of the theological accuracy of our words and speeches? Is the internet the ultimate place to do spiritual warfare? Perhaps we should take a closer look at the kinds of works James identifies as leading to deliverance and vindication. These include caring for brothers and sisters who lack clothing and food (v. 15), sacrificial obedience when tested (v. 21), and even risky, loving action to help those that need protection from danger (v. 25). These are exactly the kinds of "works" needed in times of marginalization and persecution. To the "worldly" mind, these acts seem impotent and ineffective. But the believer understands that these works will result in "a harvest of righteousness" (3:12-18).

8

# THE POTENT POWER OF THE TONGUE

> *I wish to pour the water of patience into the strong wine of revolutionary excitement, so that my contemporaries may not waste their time in feverish and fruitless efforts*
> – Eugen Rosenstock-Huessy[26]

*James 3:1-18*

¹Not many of you should become teachers, my brothers, for you know that we who teach will be judged with greater strictness. ²For we all stumble in many ways. And if anyone does not stumble in what he says, he is a mature man, able also to bridle the whole body. ³If we put bits into the mouths of horses so that they obey us, we guide their whole bodies as well. ⁴Look at the ships also: though they are so large and are driven by strong winds, they are guided by a very small rudder wherever the will of the pilot directs. ⁵So also the tongue is a small member, yet it boasts of great things. How great a forest is set ablaze by such a small fire! ⁶And the tongue is a fire, a world of unrighteousness. The tongue is set among our members, staining the whole body, setting on fire the entire course of life, and set on fire by hell. ⁷For every kind of beast and bird, of reptile and sea creature, can be tamed and has been tamed by mankind, ⁸but no human being can tame the tongue. It is a restless evil, full of deadly poison. ⁹With

---

26 Eugen Rosenstock-Huessy, *Out of the Revolution: Autobiography of Western Man* (Providence, RI: Berg, 1993; reprint), 13.

> it we bless our Lord and Father, and with it we curse people who are made in the likeness of God. ¹⁰From the same mouth come blessing and cursing. My brothers, these things ought not to be so. ¹¹Does a spring pour forth from the same opening both fresh and salt water? ¹²Can a fig tree, my brothers, bear olives, or a grapevine produce figs? Neither can a salt pond yield fresh water.
>
> ¹³Who is wise and understanding among you? By his good conduct let him show his works in the meekness of wisdom. ¹⁴But if you have bitter jealousy and selfish ambition in your hearts, do not boast and be false to the truth. ¹⁵This is not the wisdom that comes down from above, but is earthly, unspiritual, demonic. ¹⁶For where jealousy and selfish ambition exist, there will be disorder and every vile practice. ¹⁷But the wisdom from above is first pure, then peaceable, gentle, open to reason, full of mercy and good fruits, impartial and sincere. ¹⁸And a harvest of righteousness is sown in peace by those who make peace.

After explaining to his readers the reality that Jesus will judge them based on their works (James 2), and it is not simply their verbal profession of faith in Jesus that will save them, James now comes to one of the main concerns in this letter: the power of speech in the Christian community. James's emphasis on speech in James 3 fits well with the overall theme of his epistle, which is to exhort early Jewish converts to persevere in the midst of their trials and suffering so that they will be made mature and be prepared to rule with Christ (James 1:2-4, 12, 17-18). Throughout the Scriptures, God's people rule with him by speaking righteously, and here in James 3, James outlines what it will mean for these early Christian disciples to grow in maturity and take their place in Jesus's kingdom—mature and righteous speech.

We are now at the center of the book. If we recognize the chiastic structure of the letter, then everything moves toward and then away from James 3.

A. 1:2-8 - Trials, faith, steadfastness
  B. 1:9-27 - Suffering, Patience, Piety
    C. 2:1-7 – The Rich and "the Poor Man"
      D. 2:8-13 - Love, Liberty, & Mercy
        E. 2:14-26 - Justification & works
          **F. 3:1-12 - The Teacher's Tongue**
        E' 3:13-18 - Wisdom & works
      D' 4:1-12 – Enmity, Adultery, & Pride
    C' 4:13-5:6 – The Rich & "the Righteous One"
  B' 5:7-18 - Suffering, Patience, & Fruit
A' 5:19-21 - Wandering, sin, death

Why does James place such a high emphasis on the power of the tongue? In the words of Martin Luther, "The church is a mouth house, not a pen house." To put it another way, the church community is primarily a place where spoken words are exchanged, and not principally a community where documents are written and exchanged. For those most familiar with the Protestant church tradition, this may not seem like an obvious statement. But consider: What is it that we do when enter the church on Sunday morning? We greet our friends and visitors. We shake hands and engage in speech, participate in little conversations until service begins. And in the worship service, we again exchange words. The pastor speaks to the congregation, and the people respond. God speaks and we respond. We sing, pray, engage in responsive readings, hear the Word of God read aloud, and listen to the Scriptures expounded and applied to us. Speaking and listening dominate the Christian worship service.[27]

This exchange of words constitutes the life of the church. The exchange of words between God and man, and between man and man, all of us, one with another, this is foundational

---

[27] For a fuller explanation of the centrality of the Word in Christian worship see Jeffrey J. Meyers, *The Lord's Service: The Grace of Covenant Renewal Worship* (Moscow, ID: Canon Press, 2003).

for the health of the church. Indeed, words spoken and words heard and received constitute what it means to have a personal relationship with anyone. If there are no words, then there is no personal relationship. For at the heart of every normal personal relationship is the exchange of words. Even if there are exceptional circumstances, because one of the members of the relationship can't speak or can't hear, there's other kinds of communication that must take place. And the formal relationship between God and man, which the Bible calls a "covenant," is grounded in words of promise and command. There are rituals to be sure, but a covenant is grounded in the words of the parties.

For relationships cannot be based simply on physical contact. We know this in marriage—sexual contact in marriage, although good and necessary, is nothing without the exchange of words. Physical intimacy is only meaningful if the husband and wife talk to one another, communicate, love, and honor one another with their words. In the same way, when the church comes together for worship it is not a unified body, a true community just because people are sitting in the same location at the same time. The church itself is in its essence a community of words, and we personally are a part of that community to the extent that we exchange words with one another. Indeed, though it runs counter to much of American spirituality, the primary way that we are to receive the word of God is by hearing it read to us, by hearing it explained to us, and reciting it together with the rest of the church. The primary way we are to receive the word of God is not by receiving it individually—for no community is formed when we read the Bible by ourselves. True Christian community is formed when we hear the word read publicly, and when we speak the word to one another. If it is true that words constitute personal relationships, then words have enormous power in the Christian church.

The church is a mouth and ear house, and words make or break the life of the church. Words bring people together and guide people in the way of truth. But words also have the power to do lasting harm. They have the power to divide and fracture the people of God, the power to destroy. This is the theme of James's teaching here in the first part of James 3. The potent power of the tongue must not be underestimated. Remember that the purpose of James's epistle is to bring his readers into maturity, both individually and corporately. In James 2, James has focused on the significance of maturity in the actions of the church community, exhorting them to match their pious words with a life lived in obedience to Jesus. But now, lest anyone get the idea that maturity is found simply in acting in accordance with the commands of Jesus, that somehow what we say is unimportant, James focuses on the necessity of speaking righteously for true maturity.

The biblical connection between words and ruling (the purpose for which the church is being made mature) goes back as far as the story of creation. God, ruling over the world, spoke all things into being by the power of his Word. Then Adam, as the pinnacle of God's word-creation, rules in God's image by speaking the names of each animal, thus also speaking new things into being by the power of his word. After also speaking to the Woman her own name, Adam then fails to rule over the garden by remaining silent while listening to the deceitful words of the serpent. Instead of speaking words of rebuke to the tempter or words of support to his wife, Adam mutely allows his wife to be deceived by the serpent. Instead of ruling over creation as he was intended, Adam fails.

The story of the rest of the Bible is a mending of what was torn by Adam's silence in the garden. Slowly, God trains up humanity and teaches him to rule over creation by speaking. We see this, for example, in the blessings and curses of Israel's patriarchs. In the words they pronounce over their children for good and ill they exercise righteous authority. When Noah was sinned against by his son Ham, he responds by ruling with his words, speaking a new reality into being, "Cursed be Canaan [Ham]; a servant of servants shall he be to his brothers…blessed be Yahweh the God of Shem; and let Canaan be his servant. May God enlarge Japheth, and let him dwell in the tents of Shem, and let Canaan be his servant" (Gen. 9:25-27).

When the Old Testament patriarchs issue blessing and curses, their words change reality—they upset the order of things and create new paradigms. When Isaac blesses Jacob instead of Esau, his words cannot be taken back or unspoken (Gen. 27:37). His blessing is not simply well wishing or an old man's sentiment, as we often think of words today. Instead, Isaac rules by the power of his word. And though Jacob is forced to flee for his life because of his brother's wrath, he still bears his father's blessing, which is fleshed out in the rest of his life. Indeed, Esau's anger against Jacob makes sense only in a world where words really do matter—where men rule in the world by the power of their speech.

This pattern of ruling by speaking is seen in Israel's kingship. Israel's greatest kings, David and his son Solomon, ruled primarily through their words. By composing, singing, and writing the bulk of the songbook of the Bible, David faithfully ruled over the people of God. By both speaking to them and giving the people words to speak and sing in their own worship of God, David acted as a righteous king to Israel. In the same way, Solomon ruled over his people by speaking words of wisdom, by teaching Israel the manner in which they ought to follow the Lord, and describing for them the way of life.

Of course, this pattern of ruling through speech is seen most unmistakably in the life of Jesus. The bulk of Jesus's earthly ministry was spent speaking to disciples and to the people of Israel. With his words, Jesus spoke into reality a new order—a new law, and a new people. And the people "were astonished at his teaching, for his word possessed authority" (Luke 4:32). And when Jesus was raised from the dead, he stood before his disciples and spoke these words to them:

> All authority in heaven and on earth has been given to me. Go therefore and make disciples of all nations, baptizing them in the name of the Father and of the Son and of the Holy Spirit, teaching them to observe all that I have commanded you (Matt. 28:18-20).

Because of the authority given to him by his Father, Jesus spoke to the apostles and commanded them to speak his words for him—to baptize (that is, speak the name of Jesus over men and women) and teach (that is, speak the words of Jesus to the baptized) all of humanity. The great commission of Jesus is nothing less than an order to his followers to rule over the earth by speaking into existence a new reality—the kingdom of God.

On the day of Pentecost, Jesus's command to the apostles to rule in his name by speaking his words began to come to fruition, as *tongues* of fire descended upon them, and the Holy Spirit filled them, and they began to *speak*. The fiery-tongued Peter spoke first, and with his words, prophetic judgment was announced for the unbelieving Jews and the new humanity of the church was called into being (Acts 2). As many of the Jews who had gathered on that day heard his words and repented, they then had the name of Jesus spoken over them when they were baptized by the apostles. In this way the church, the mouth-house spoken into existence by Jesus and his apostles, was born. And in the same way she endures today as the words of Jesus continue to be spoken as we baptize and teach all that he has commanded us.

Most of us will know the children's song chanted back and forth in the playgrounds of our youth that goes like this: "Sticks and stones may break my bones, but words will never hurt me." Implicit in these lines is the modern and Western assumption of the primacy of material things. In our modern world, talk is cheap, and it seems as if only those with physical power and wealth have real power and authority. But these assumptions could not be farther from the Bible's understanding of these things. In the Scriptures, words matter—for it is when men speak that they most closely image God's manner of ruling. Though our actions are important as well, righteous speech is a significant and necessary component of our fulfillment of God's command to take dominion over every living thing that moves on the earth.

Perhaps now we can see more clearly the reason James chooses to address the topic of speech ethics in chapter 3 of his epistle. In James 2:14-26, James confronted his readers who erroneously believed that using pious words without a matching integrity in their actions would lead to their vindication and right standing before God. In response, James argued that there ought to be a correspondence between words and action, such that the Christian who professes to have faith in Jesus must live out that faith in his life. Without mature integrity in one's actions, words are useless. But James has anticipated that some of his readers may commit the error of believing that because of his arguments in 2:14-26, it is simply actions that matter, and not words. For them words are simply tools for leaders to move and inspire others to action. James combats this error in James 3, arguing for the power of speech in the life of the Christian community, and the necessity for integrity in our words. In James's understanding, the mature man is one who both speaks and acts in obedience to Jesus—not placing one over the other but holding both as important and essential for true righteousness. James calls these exiled brothers into maturity in their speech so that they will rightly rule over creation, serving their fellow image-bearers not only with actions of mercy but also words of love and blessing.

He begins his exhortation in James 3 by reminding his readers that they will be judged on the basis of their words (3:1-2), and then explaining the significance of mature speech for individual and corporate righteousness (3:3-5). Following this introduction, James goes on to warn his readers of the dangers of immature and wicked speech, and the great suffering these kinds of words can bring in a community (3:6-12). Finally, he closes this chapter with an exhortation on the blessing of a righteous and mature tongue (3:13-18).

## Every Careless Word

*James 3:1-2*

¹Not many of you should become teachers, my brothers, for you know that we who teach will be judged with greater strictness. ²For we all stumble in many ways. And if anyone does not stumble in what he says, he is a mature man, able also to bridle the whole body.

James begins his teaching on the tongue with a pointed warning: those who would publicly teach and instruct God's people ought to be careful as they consider God's call on their lives, for teachers in the church will be judged by the Lord with a higher strictness for their words. Though this principle may seem to cut against the grain of our egalitarian culture, James's words obviously fit with the teaching of Scripture, as well our theology of the Word.

As Jesus himself says to Peter, "The servant who knew his master's will but did not get ready or act according to his will, will receive a severe beating. But the one who did not know, and did what deserved a beating, will receive a light beating. Everyone to whom much was given, of him much will be required, and from him to whom they entrusted much, they will demand the more" (Luke 12:47-48). This principle of a more severe judgment for those in authority is also taught in the Westminster standards. In response to Question 151 in the Larger Catechism—*What are the aggravations that make some sins more heinous than others?*— the answer given is, "Sins receive their aggravations…[in part] from the persons offending if they be of riper age, greater experience or grace, eminent for profession, gifts, place, office, guides to others, and whose examples is likely to be followed by others." In other words, some sins are more heinous than others when they are committed by persons in authority.

This warning should not be missed, either for young men who desire to be pastors or for old men who have shepherded God's people for many years. Though it is easy to first apply this passage to other, more prominent teachers who abuse the power that has been given to them, judgment must begin with our own hearts and lives. James's teaching here should cause us to take a sober and careful look at our own ministries, to see if we are being faithful as we feed the lambs that Jesus himself has given us. The basic warning here is simple: those who follow Jesus must not accept positions of leadership that require maturity with which they have not been blessed.

The judgment that James refers to in 3:1 surely includes the final judgment promised by Jesus (John 5:25-29) but would not exclude historical judgments as well. James's words here are linked to his warning in 2:12-13 that "judgment is without mercy to one who has shown no mercy." A theme that ties together chapters 2 and 3 of James's epistle might be summarized in this way: "Grow into maturity, so that you and your people will be rescued when God comes in judgment." In James 2, James focused on the impotence of mere talk, stressing the necessity of maturity in our *actions* if we expect vindication and deliverance. Now in James 3, he considers the significance of maturity for "brothers" who, by means of their speech, are leading their local assemblies.

It is also worth noting that writing into a context where Christians are already being persecuted for the political threat they posed to their contemporary authorities (a threat summarized well in Stephen's final words to his Jewish interrogators: "Behold, I see the heavens opened and the Son of Man standing at the right hand of God," Acts 7:56), James does not minimize the political implications of their membership in the body of Christ and urges them to embrace "spiritual" piety instead of "earthly" works. Indeed, if anything, James responds to the political persecution of the church by emphasizing the very things which cause them to be a political threat to the world's rulers (steadfastness in the midst of persecution, refusal to participate in the world's value systems, showing no partiality in their interaction with other men) and assuring them of the eventual triumph of the church over its enemies, a victory which Jesus will accomplish for them soon (James 5:8).

Though James's warning in 3:1 that those who teach will be judged with a greater strictness is most certainly first directed toward those who hold public teaching roles in the church the application of this passage is not limited to those who are ordained teachers. For all of us who are a part of the body of Christ teach and instruct others in various ways.

For example, parents constantly are using their tongues to instruct their children, and are, in a sense, teachers. There are also those who are not parents themselves, but participate in the training of covenant children: schoolteachers, Sunday School teachers, sports coaches, youth leaders, music instructors, even babysitters and older brothers and sisters. All of these men and women are teachers, who are constantly involved with instructing others in the body of Christ. James's warning regarding the seriousness of teaching and instruction for the Christian is applicable to them as well.

But there are also times of informal instruction that we engage in without even realizing how our words may be influencing others. Consider all the conversations that happen in the foyer of the church or the fellowship hall after the worship service on Sunday morning. One person describes a struggle in his life or asks for advice, and another person gives it. Or one person expresses an opinion about God or the Bible or politics or education and another person corrects or confirms it. This is a kind of teaching. When we engage in this kind of informal instruction with friends or neighbors or even strangers, we must also carefully heed James's warning about the significance of teaching and the necessity of maturity in our words when we instruct others. And of course, these kind of "instructive conversations" don't only take place in the foyer of the church. They also happen on the couches at Starbucks, around the dinner table at home or at a restaurant, in the break room at the office, and on the phone. More and more, they are also happening on the internet, either through email, or on a blog. Everyone who speaks and writes with the aim of instructing others in these different contexts is acting as a teacher and finds him or herself squarely in the realm of application for James's warning.

Therefore, James's warning here is for all of us, not just for pastors and elders. What is the main thrust of James's warning here? That careful deliberation should precede our instruction of others. No matter how informal or casual, or what the context is, when we open our mouths to teach others with our words, we must be careful and wise. We must consider the soundness of what we are about to say. Do we really have knowledge of the subject we are about to comment on? If we are making an assertion about another person, do we really have authority to comment on their lives? Or are we simply spreading hearsay and gossip and disguising it as instruction?

According to James, the main reason we need to be exceedingly careful and wise in our formal and informal instruction of others is because we are the subjects of a righteous Lord who will bring into judgment everything we say. As Jesus himself has promised us, "The good person out of his good treasure brings forth good, and the evil person out of his evil treasure brings forth evil. I tell you, on the day of judgment people will give account for every careless word they speak, for by your words you will be justified, and by your words you will be condemned" (Matt. 12:35-37), and also "Nothing is covered up that will not be revealed or hidden that will not be known. Therefore, whatever you have said in the dark shall be heard in the light, and what you have whispered in private rooms shall be proclaimed on the housetops" (Luke 12:2-3). If our Lord has promised to do something, then it will come to pass. And he has certainly promised that there will be a day when every word that has escaped from our lips will be judged publicly by him before all the world.

But how often do we remember Jesus is our Judge when we speak? How often do we consider the warnings of Jesus regarding judgment before we open our mouths to speak a careless word? How often do we pause to fear the Last Judgment before we express our opinion on a topic that we really know nothing about, or criticize another person's character? How often does the Day of Judgment enter our minds when we send an email to a friend or to a discussion list, or comment on someone's blog post? How many of us, honestly, regularly, before we open our mouths to speak, think to ourselves, "I will be judged one day, for what I say in this moment"? But whatever is whispered and spoken in the back rooms, will be, as Jesus says, shouted from the housetops. What we say on the phone may be repeated for all to hear one day. When was the last time we stopped ourselves from saying something, and just for a moment we weighed what we were about to say, knowing that our words will be evaluated by our Lord?

James's teaching in this chapter should also cause us to consider carefully the following question: Do we really fear the Lord's judgment? Or do we instead hope, deep down, that there won't be a judgment day? Do we hope that what Jesus promises in the Gospels regarding the last judgment, and what James teaches here about the inevitability of judgment is simply an exaggeration to get people to behave? Is Jesus like the father that promises punishment to his children as threat to force them to obey, but has no intention of following through on his word? If so, then Jesus is not king, and all authority on heaven and earth has not truly been given to him. When we neglect to fear our Lord's judgment, we are not merely careless, but we are also rebels against the lordship of Christ. We live as though he is not really Lord of all things, as though he desperately promises punishment but has no ability or intention to follow through on his schemes.

Therefore, James's promise that those who teach will be judged with a harsher strictness should cause us to fear. Remember, this epistle is all about mature wisdom. And mature wisdom begins, according to Proverbs, with proper fear. "The fear of Yahweh is the beginning of knowledge; fools despise wisdom and instruction" (Prov. 1:7). Healthy fear should motivate us, as the children of God, to be careful when we speak, and to consider the ways in which we instruct others that we have never really viewed as significant or important. It should cause us to live as wise and mature men and women, men and women who do not habitually open their mouths and let careless words slip out.

But though we fear the last judgment, we do not fear as those with no hope. For we know that to be righteous is not to be sinless. We know that as we participate in the life of the body of Christ, his Spirit is at work in us, shaping and molding our hearts and minds and bodies so that we are made mature, holy and blameless before him. For, as Paul writes, "He who began a good work in you will bring it to completion at the day Jesus Christ" (Phil. 1:6). Our Father has called us to himself, and he will not neglect to bring us to maturity before we stand in judgment before the world's true king. This is the meaning of Paul's words to the Philippians, and it is a sweet and essential promise for us to cling to as we anticipate the Day of Judgment.

And finally, we do not dread our Lord's judgment without hope because we know, in the end, that "mercy triumphs over judgment" (James 2:13b). The man who will judge us is also the one who causes us to lie down in green pastures, who restores our soul, protects us from all danger, anoints our heads with oil, prepares a feast for us, and whose mercy and loving-kindness will follow us all the days of our lives. Jesus is the king of the world, and he will surely judge all men. But for those who have been baptized and called by his name, who have eaten his body and drank his blood and who are a part of his bride, he is our shepherd king and rest-giver. Of course, we fear the judgment day—but we also confidently hope for that day when we will be finally and publicly vindicated as the sons and daughters of God.

James adds this comment: "For we all stumble in many ways. And if anyone does not stumble in what he says, he is a mature man, able also to bridle the whole body" (3:2). James's assertion that we all indeed stumble should give us assurance that he is not advocating perfection. The full maturity that James calls his readers to has not been attained but for one man, and it is because of our union to him and his life, death, and resurrection that we may be assured of our own future maturity. James goes on to tie full maturity to righteous speech, asserting that anyone who does not stumble or sin in what he says is a "mature" (*teleios*) man. Here James builds on a theme he began in chapter 1 of his letter, where he instructed his readers to "be quick to hear, slow to speak, slow to anger" (1:19), and denied that a man who "does not bridle his tongue" (1:26) could be called truly religious. In the latter part of 3:2, James explains this connection between righteous speech. If the mature man is able to bridle his tongue, he is "able also to bridle the whole body." As the tongue of a teacher goes, so goes the whole body/community of believers. The manner in which leaders speak will either hinder or empower the well-being of the church community. Such is the power of the tongue.

## The Tongue & the Body

*James 3:3-5*

> ³If we put bits into the mouths of horses so that they obey us, we guide their whole bodies as well. ⁴Look at the ships also: though they are so large and are driven by strong winds, they are guided by a very small rudder wherever the will of the pilot directs. ⁵So also the tongue is a small member, yet it boasts of great things.

The power of the tongue is now explained through various analogies drawn from everyday life. He first compares the tongue to a bit in the mouth of a horse. When a man puts a bit in the mouth of a horse, he knows that whichever way he pulls on the reins is the direction in which the horse will be compelled to go. Just like a horse, the church community is led by a mouth, and the whole body is guided by the direction that tongue points. In the same way, a ship is buffeted by strong winds and driven this way and that, and seems to be completely at the mercy of the wind, but in reality, it is constantly guided by the will of the pilot, who controls the tiny rudder and thus directs the ship in the manner he wishes. Just like ships, communities sometimes also appear to be driven this way and that by the powerful storms and the winds of fate and chance. But, the direction of a community is often controlled, for better or worse, by a very small rudder, that is the tongue of an influential leader.

James concludes this section with these words, "So also the tongue is a small member, yet it boasts of great things." Like the bit and the rudder, the tongue is small and seemingly powerless, but in fact it is mighty and powerful, boasting of its exploits. James's meaning here can be easily understood and summarized:

the tongue, though small, is potent—and when the tongue is bridled, the whole body is bridled and made mature, but when the tongue is set loose, the whole body is led into sin and foolish behavior.

James's teaching fits well with the image of humanity that is painted in the biblical narrative. Man's first kingly task is to rule in God's image by naming all creatures. After speaking wisely he is rewarded with the most beautiful creature he can imagine. Later, when Adam foolishly silences his tongue in the face of the serpent's tempting words, he is led into sin and rebellion. And his tongue leads him further downward when, confronted by God, he refuses to repent of his sin and instead slyly uses his words to cast blame on his wife and the serpent. By first not speaking at all when his bride was being tempted with the seductive words of the serpent and then in the presence of Yahweh when he speaks foolishly, Adam fails his body, his wife, with whom he has been made one flesh.

Just as Adam was directed by his tongue, so our lives are directed by words. We live in a world created by the very Word of God, and there is no use fighting against the pattern he has set in place or pretending it doesn't exist. The only way in which we will be able to temper the potency of the tongue is if we reconcile ourselves to its power. There is nothing corrupt or sinful or appalling about the life-giving and life-taking power of words—indeed, just the opposite—this is the way in which God created man to live and mature.

The point of James's teaching on the power of the tongue is not to instruct his readers to rebel against that power (i.e., to reduce the tongue's power over their lives), but rather to recognize and submit to it. They should use their words for blessing and mercy and peace, so that they will not stumble in what they say and be made mature, and so that their words will bear fruit in the community, "a harvest of righteousness" (James 3:2, 13-18). Just as a ship will never be fully a ship unless it accepts and cooperates with the rudder which directs it, and as a horse will constantly be frustrated and powerless unless he accepts the guiding power of the bit in his mouth, so also each man and woman who follows Jesus will never grow into maturity unless they acknowledge the power of the tongue, and then live daily in light of that reality.

With this in mind, read again the words of James regarding the horse, "If we put bits in the mouths of horses so that they obey us, we guide their whole bodies as well." In comparison to the size and weight of a full-grown horse, the bit put into his mouth by his rider was a tiny and insubstantial piece of metal. And yet, as James says, through this tiny piece of metal, the great and powerful animal is tamed and used by men. The relationship between the bit and the horse is not a reality easily discerned by someone unfamiliar with the mechanics of horse riding. Indeed, an ignorant man faced with the sight of a soldier on horseback would have been amazed at the way the enormous beast acted in compliance with the wishes of his (by comparison) small and weak rider. The relationship between the bit and the horse is fundamentally a mystery to the uninitiated, a matter of wisdom that can be gained only by submission to patient instruction.

Also consider the staggering absurdity of the power of the rudder over a ship. In the ancient world, ships were large and powerful, and just like horses, they were essential modes of transport and commerce as well as powerful military weapons. And, just like horses, their mighty strength was directed by a tiny piece of wood, turned this way and that by a man whose strength and size was dwarfed by the ship that he controlled. Just as the way a bit controls the mighty power of a horse, so also the relationship between a rudder and a ship is a great mystery to the ignorant. This is not self-evident knowledge that can be gained simply by watching a ship glide across the ocean. The power of the bit and the power of rudder are complex and mysterious, and wisdom is needed to understand their importance.

In the same way, the power of the tongue is not obvious to the ignorant. The relationship between the tongue and the body that James describes will only be understood by the wise. What James is calling his original readers to (and us with them) is a new way of seeing the world. Instead of living in ignorance, watching men live their lives without any understanding of why some grow to maturity and others remain foolish, James opens our eyes to the inner workings of humanity. He reveals the power and determinative function of the tongue of the teacher over the righteousness and maturity of everyone in the church. The instruction that James gives regarding the power of the tongue is difficult for us to understand and truly believe. It runs counter to everything we see with our eyes, which tell us that men and women are fundamentally self-directed actors, and words are relatively insignificant and immaterial. But James's instruction is true wisdom, and it is God's gift to his sons and daughters, if only they will steadfastly receive it (James 1:5-8).

> The words of a man's mouth are deep waters;
> the fountain of wisdom is a bubbling brook (Prov. 15:4).

The fundamental application of James's teaching in this chapter regarding the power of the tongue is to accept his wisdom and to reconcile ourselves to the power of our words in the communities in which we serve—our marriages, families, neighborhoods, schools, but especially the ecclesiastical community. Remembering the words of James in the first chapter of his letter, we must seek to be "one who looks into the [mature] law, the law of liberty, and perseveres, being no hearer who forgets but a doer who acts" (James 1:25). This is our appropriate response to our new understanding of the significance of the relationship between our tongues and the people we serve. This simply means that, as wise leaders, we need to train our tongues to speak righteously, for as we train our tongues in obedience to God's law, so also will the body of Christ be edified and grow. As we mature as leaders, being conformed more and more to the image of Jesus, our speech will mature so as to guide and direct the church well. With this broad application in mind, let's now consider some ways we may seek to train our tongue to speak righteous words.

**1.** *Regular participation in vibrant and responsive corporate worship.* Though we gather on Sunday mornings to praise God simply because he is glorious and worthy of our adoration, our worship also has the effect of training our tongues to speak righteously. When we sing songs of praise to God, we are trained to confess his glory with our lips. When we confess our sins together with the rest of God's people, we are trained to speak in humility and reject pride. When we recite the historic creeds of the church, we train our tongues to speak words that are true, good, and beautiful. As we discussed earlier, the church is a mouth house, not a pen house. And when we live in the mouth house that is the church, obediently speaking words of praise, confession, and belief in the company of our brothers and sisters in Christ, our tongues are trained in righteousness and God works to mature us by his Spirit.[28]

**2.** *Learning to sing, chant, and speak the psalms. The psalms are the corporate worship book of God's people.* Their primary purpose is not for theological exposition or as a source of pithy quotes to put on our walls. The psalms are given to us by God to teach his children how to speak the language of righteousness and peace, the language God expects to hear when we draw near to him. Too often Scripture memorization and recitation has been presented as the way in which we accumulate knowledge and are prepared to give an answer for our hope. While there is an element of truth to this, the primary reason we ought to learn to sing, chant, and speak the words of the psalms is so that our tongues will be tamed, and our words will be righteous. As we sing and pray the words of the psalms we will be grown into the image of God, made mature, and learn to reign with him.

**3.** *Praying for our friends, God's enemies, and the world.* Of course, we offer our prayers to God because we believe our prayers impact the world around us and bring about God's will on earth, just as it is in heaven. But we also must learn to pray because our prayers

---

[28] For more on the benefits of corporate worship, see Meyers, *The Lord's Service*.

will also change us personally. As we pray the prayers of Scripture (the Psalms), the prayer that Jesus taught us, and the historic prayers of the church, and our own extemporaneous prayers, our tongues are trained to speak words of blessing and mercy. It is not just the world that God promises to change through our prayers, but also our own tongues and thus our mind, heart, and bodies.

## To Bless or To Curse?

*James 3:5b-12*

⁵ᵇHow great a forest is set ablaze by such a small fire! ⁶And the tongue is a fire, a world of unrighteousness. The tongue is set among our members, staining the whole body, setting on fire the entire course of life, and set on fire by hell. ⁷For every kind of beast and bird, of reptile and sea creature, can be tamed and has been tamed by mankind, ⁸but no human being can tame the tongue. It is a restless evil, full of deadly poison. ⁹With it we bless our Lord and Father, and with it we curse people who are made in the likeness of God. ¹⁰From the same mouth come blessing and cursing. My brothers, these things ought not to be so. ¹¹Does a spring pour forth from the same opening both fresh and salt water? ¹²Can a fig tree, my brothers, bear olives, or a grapevine produce figs? Neither can a salt pond yield fresh water.

Here James undoubtedly intends to communicate the terrifyingly destructive power of the tongue, which is compared to a small fire with the power to set ablaze an entire forest. To fully understand the dramatic nature of this metaphor ("the tongue is a fire") we need to do our best to step into the context of the ancient world that James addresses. In ancient cities, houses were built on top of one another, and were usually built of wooden materials without masonry. Without the modern fire prevention techniques that protect our own neighborhoods, the smallest house fire could quickly spread and destroy large swaths of a city, as demonstrated by the Great Fire of Rome in A.D. 64. As when he compared the tongue to a bit in the mouth of a horse and a rudder on a ship, in likening the tongue to a fire which quickly spreads, James emphasizes the tiny size of the tongue in contrast to the destruction it can cause. A tiny flame can destroy a city.

Remember earlier that James warned his readers that a mark of true religion is "to keep oneself unstained by the world." Now in 3:6 James argues that the tongue is not only a fire, but also a "world of unrighteousness" that when set loose among the members, "stains the whole body." By repeating the words "world" and "stain" James wants his readers to understand that one of the primary ways they become stained by the world is through unrighteous and worldly speech. Though our first inclination may be to identify using profanity and obscenities as the way the tongue is a "world of unrighteousness," it is far more likely that James's warning here is directed primarily against the danger of worldly speech patterns corrupting the life of the church. Gossip and slander and all other kinds of malicious and manipulative speech are a far greater threat to the peace of the church than any "dirty word." For James, true religion expresses itself in speech that is founded in the "meekness of wisdom" (3:13) and "full of mercy and good fruits, impartial and sincere" (3:17). When the community of God's people rejects worldly patterns of speech and embraces the speech ethics that James proscribes, our communal life embodies the rule of Jesus on earth.

In verse 6, James begins to apply the danger of the unrighteous tongue to the corporate situation of the church. Just as a man's body is directed by his tongue, so also the life of the church is primarily defined by the speech of its members. When the speech of the members of the church is in submission to the lordship of Jesus, blessing and peace ensue. Conversely, when the tongue burns as a fire, it is a "world of unrighteousness" and stains the whole body of the church, setting on fire the entire course of its life, spreading the flames of hell. James's warning here should be taken soberly, for it is not only our own individual judgment on the Last Day that is at stake when we open our mouths, but the vitality of the whole people of God of which we are a part. If nothing else will bridle our tongues, then love for our neighbor ought to do so.

James's intention in these statements is to force the community he addresses to reckon with the power of the tongue, to encourage "the brothers" to know when to speak and when to be silent, and to consider the content of the communication. He echoes the clear teaching of Scripture. As Solomon writes, "a word fittingly spoken is like apples of gold in settings of silver" (Prov. 25:11). Before we speak, do we reckon with the Day of Judgment, do we reckon with power that our words will have in the community of Christ? In some ways, this text does not need to be analyzed. It simply needs to be heard and sink into our hearts. So that we'll remember it when we're about to say something stupid and foolish, harmful, and destructive, so that before we curse someone else to our friend or tear down a brother or a sister in Christ and bring division in the body of Christ to exalt ourselves, and to make ourselves look good, we'll pause to consider the power of our words.

James continues to describe the destructive and powerful nature of the tongue: "For every kind of beast and bird, of reptile and sea creature, can be tamed and has been tamed by mankind, but no human being can tame the tongue. It is a restless evil, full of deadly poison" (James 3:7-8). It is interesting to note that, according to Genesis 2:19-20, the initial way mankind tamed every beast and bird, reptile, and sea creature was by his tongue, by giving them their names and asserting his dominion over them. Ironically, that which man uses to tame the beasts and exercise god-like rule over creation is itself untamable. Since the beginning of all things, words have been at the root of man's glory but also at the root of his rebellion against God. It is for this reason that the prophets described the Last Adam, Jesus, as one who bridles his own tongue, who speaks only words of blessing and righteousness.

The prophet Isaiah portrays the Messiah as one who will bridle his tongue in the midst of suffering and will not stumble in his speech, despite the violence and injustice done against him:

"He was oppressed, and he was afflicted, yet he opened not his mouth; like a lamb that is led to the slaughter, and like a sheep that before its shearers is silent, so he opened not his mouth" (Isa. 53:7). The point of calling attention to Jesus's control of his tongue in the face of torture and oppression is not to encourage a stoic approach to suffering in his followers. Rather it is to underscore the way in which Jesus succeeded where Adam failed—by taming his tongue and not stumbling in what he said, Jesus is the "mature man, able also to bridle his whole body" (James 3:2). Of course, the body that Jesus bridles is not only his own physical body, but also his one-flesh bride, the Church. Because Jesus does not stumble in what he says, he is able to bridle the people of God by speaking words of instruction, forgiveness, commission, and blessing to his body.

And as the mature Son of God, Jesus is also able to speak these words to his body: "For as the rain and the snow come down from heaven and do not return there but water the earth, making it bring forth and sprout, giving seed to the sower and bread to the eater, so shall my word be that goes out from my mouth; it shall not return to me empty, but it shall accomplish that which I purpose, and shall succeed in the thing for which I sent it" (Isa. 55:10-11). As the mature Adam, Jesus truly rules over all things by the word of his mouth, fulfilling the dominion mandate originally given to mankind (Gen. 1:28). As those who are united to Jesus, we now rule with him, embodying his kingdom on earth in our speech. As the shalom of Jesus spreads throughout all the world, his rule is realized to an ever-greater degree in the faithful and righteous life of the church. And this righteous life is rooted in righteous speech, according to the pattern of creation and the pattern of Jesus's own life. When we as the people of God speak words of blessing and peace, when we bridle our tongues in the manner of Jesus, we are not only avoiding sin in our lives, but we are also bringing to earth the kingdom and rule of Jesus—enacting, as it were, the words of Jesus's prayer that his Father's will would be done on earth as it is in heaven. Jesus was sent by his Father to earth to succeed where the first Adam failed, to grow up the human race into maturity, and an essential part of Jesus's maturity was the taming of his tongue.

James points out the incongruity of a Christian's tongue being used for unrighteousness, "With [our tongues] we bless our Lord and Father, and with it we curse people who are made in the likeness of God. From the same mouth come blessing and cursing. My brothers, these things ought not to be so" (James 3:9-10). One possible scenario that James seems to imagine is a church that is publicly pious, blessing God loudly before others, but then cursing one another behind the scenes, tearing each other apart with divisive gossip and slander. But given the context of persecution into which this letter was written, it may be more likely that James is confronting brothers in the church for blessing God during Lord's Day worship, and then out of the same mouth publicly cursing their oppressors.

Angry speech and cursing are a natural human reaction to violence and persecution, and ancient society was no exception to that rule. Even today when someone threatens our comfort or dignity, we easily lash out against them. Considering that the lives, families, and vocations of James's readers were under threat when he penned these words to them, the temptation to bitterly curse their oppressors must have been overwhelming. And yet, James refuses to condone this type of speech, even under some of the worst imaginable conditions. Indeed, James condemns this kind of cursing, citing it as a prime example of the evil and poison of which the tongue is capable (3:8).

Why does James condemn so strongly the cursing of other human beings, even when the men receiving curses are the initiators of great evil? First, because every human being is "made in the likeness of God" (3:9). On the sixth day of the creation week, God said, "Let us make man in our image, after our likeness," and the writer of Genesis 1 records, "So God created man in his own image, in the image of God he created them, male and female he created them. And God blessed them" (Gen 1:27-28a). In the very beginning, God created man and woman in his likeness, and he blessed them. Therefore, when the sons and daughters of God curse men and women who are made in his likeness, they subvert and rebel against the declaration of blessing that God has placed upon mankind and we take upon ourselves the prerogatives the Creator has over mankind. (We exercise judgment in a way that is reserved for God alone). James rebukes his readers for cursing other men not only because to do so reveals the anger of their own hearts, but also because to curse that which God has blessed is to set one's own self up in the place of God and to engage in rebellion against the creator and Lord of all things.

Second, when the followers of Jesus curse that which God has blessed they not only deny the initial blessing of God upon mankind in creation. They also deny and rebel against God's ongoing plan to bless all the earth. In Genesis 12:1-3, God calls Abraham to a new path of faith and obedience that will result in the enactment of God's original blessing of mankind in Genesis 1:28 with these words, "Go from your country…to the land I will show you. And I will make of you a great nation, and I will bless you and make your name great, so that you will be a blessing. I will bless those who bless you, and him who dishonors you I will curse, and in you all the families shall be blessed." In Genesis 22:17-18, after the faithful obedience of Abraham in offering his son Isaac, God reiterates his promise to bless all mankind through Abraham, saying, "I will surely bless you, and I will surely multiply your offspring as the stars of heaven and as the sand that is on the seashore. And your offspring shall possess the gate of his enemies, and in your offspring shall all the nations of the earth be blessed, because you have obeyed my voice."

As the church of Jesus, the true offspring of Abraham, we are both the benefactors of and participants in the promise of God to bless the nations of the earth. It is for this reason that Jesus instructs his followers, "Love your enemies, do good to those who hate you, bless those who curse you, pray for those who abuse you" (Luke 6:27-28). In the face of cursing and violence and all kinds of persecution, Jesus commands his church to bless their oppressors, for in doing so they maintain God's initial creational blessing of mankind, affirm his intention to bless all the nations of the earth, and enact his blessed promise for all men. When we bless those who oppress us, we take up our place in God's narrative of the world, living as the sons and daughters of Abraham, and our obedience becomes the instrument through which God blesses all the nations of the earth. Conversely, when those who follow Jesus curse men instead of blessing them, they hinder and fight against God's intention for the earth, and show their unbelief in his ability and promise to redeem and renew all things by our lack of obedience.

Often, Jesus's command to love our enemies has been understood as simply an instruction for Christians to be "nice" to those who work evil against them and therefore has resulted in a false meekness and passivity in the church that Jesus never intended. When James rebukes his readers for cursing the men who intend evil against them, he does not rebuke them for their intention to defend their families from destruction. Rather, he rebukes them for defending themselves using the same weapons as the men who are persecuting them. For when we participate in God's plan for the world, we are not left defenseless. Rather, we shall "possess the gates of [our] enemies" (Gen. 22:17b), a promise that is reaffirmed in Jesus's declaration to Peter that against his church, "the gates of hell shall not prevail" in Matthew 16:18b. When we bless our enemies instead of cursing them, we do not defend ourselves with the weapons of the world (thus remaining "unstained from the world," James 1:27) and yet we are not defenseless.

Third, when the church blesses those who intend evil against her, surprisingly, by her humble service and prayer, she heaps burning coals on the heads of her enemies and overcomes evil with good (Prov. 25:22; Rom. 12:20-21). For the enactment of God's plan for blessing the world can mean nothing other than judgment against those who oppose him and oppress his people—either in bowed knee and submission to Jesus, or in their just destruction at his hands. In the new earth, Jesus's promise to his saints that he will "wipe away every tear from their eyes"

(Rev. 21:4) is not simply a sentimental pledge that one day all the evil done against us will be forgotten, but it is a promise of justice intimately linked to his declaration that "for the cowardly, the faithless, the detestable…the murderers, the sexually immoral, sorcerers, idolaters and all liars, their portion will be in the lake that burns with fire and sulfur, which is the second death" (Rev. 21:8). In the judgment of Jesus, nothing is forgotten, and no act of violence or oppression done against God's people will be set aside. This is why he can give this mandate to his church: ". . . bless those who curse you, pray for those who abuse you" (Luke 6:28).

James's rebuke of his readers for cursing those who do evil against them is not a command to passively accept whatever evil is meted out to them. Rather, it is an affirmation that when we bless our enemies, we enact the promises of God for the world and hasten the day of his judgment against all his and our enemies. Our blessing of those who do us evil is not simply a sentimental refusal to wish for the destruction of any man or woman, no matter how wicked, but rather our blessing is a battering ram aimed against the gates of hell based squarely on the gospel announcement that Jesus is Lord of all men and he will one day bring his terrible vengeance crashing down on the heads of his enemies. James's rebuke to his readers is intended to cause them to put aside swords of iron and rise with the sword of Spirit, the only sure defense against all evil and wickedness.

Although it may seem counterintuitive, one powerful way in which we "bless" our enemies is by asking God to judge them. As was noted earlier, when God judges someone it may lead to the person's death and destruction. But God also saves *through* judgment. In fact, the Lord always saves through judgment. Praying that the Lord would judge our enemies is not to curse them, but to ask God to administer his promised justice either by removing them or converting them. There's a world of difference between *cursing* someone and *petitioning* God in prayer to judge them in righteousness. The Lord has given us models of such prayers in the Psalms. Unfortunately, these prayers for judgment against enemies are often classified as *imprecatory* Psalms. An "imprecation" is a curse. But nowhere in these Psalms are we given words to use for cursing. Rather, we are pleading with God to act. We are not spitting out curses against anyone. Consider a portion of Psalm 7:

> Oh, let the evil of the wicked come to an end,
> and my you establish the righteous—
> you who test the minds and hearts, O righteous God!

There are many other examples of this in the Psalter (e.g., Pss. 58, 109). When we bring these petitions to the Lord, it frees us from resentment and the temptation to exact our own retribution against those who have wronged us. For the recipients of James's circular letter, this is precisely the problem in their communities. Instead of petitioning God to act against their enemies and waiting patiently for him to act, the leaders are spewing curses and publicly inciting aggressive, violent action against their enemies (James 4:1-4).

The final reason that James rebukes his readers for cursing their enemies instead of blessing them is rooted in the necessity for integrity in the mature sons and daughters of God. As James writes, "From the same mouth come blessing and cursing. My brothers, these things ought not to be so. Does a spring pour forth from the same opening both fresh and salt water? Can a fig tree, my brothers, bear olives, or a grapevine produce figs? Neither can a salt pond yield fresh water" (James 3:10-12). Throughout James's epistle, to be truly mature means that his flock must "be doers of the word, and not hearers only" (James 1:22). Thus to be mature, it is not enough simply to bless God, unless that blessing is also extended to our communities and even our enemies. James's demand for integrity in the speech of his readers is part and parcel with his assertion that "faith apart from works is dead" (James 2:26), for when we bless God, we express our trust in him, and our works of love toward all men must match that professed trust.

Just as a fig tree does not bear olives, or a grapevine produce figs, nor a salt pond yield fresh water, a man or woman who is united to Jesus cannot engage in speech that is characterized by cursing and hatred toward those whom God has called him to bless. In the biblical paradigm James operates from, such a thing is unthinkable, just as it is nonsensical for a follower of Jesus to bless a brother or sister in need without providing them with the things their bodies need. To live without integrity, to bless God and curse men is to live without true faith, to be "a double-minded man, unstable in all his ways" (James 1:8). The maturity that God is working in his people demands consistency between belief and action, faith and works, and in these verses, James calls his readers to this integrity in their speech.

## Cultivating a Harvest of Righteousness

*James 3:13-18*

> [13]Who is wise and understanding among you? By his good conduct let him show his works in the meekness of wisdom. [14]But if you have bitter jealousy and selfish ambition in your hearts, do not boast and be false to the truth. [15]This is not the wisdom that comes down from above, but is earthly, unspiritual, demonic. [16]For where jealousy and selfish ambition exist, there will be disorder and every vile practice. [17]But the wisdom from above is first pure, then peaceable, gentle, open to reason, full of mercy and good fruits, impartial and sincere. [18]And a harvest of righteousness is sown in peace by those who make peace.

James now expands on the question of how his readers ought to respond to the violence of their persecutors. This paragraph reveals the depth of the problems in these exiled communities. But it also holds out hope for the justice they long for. He challenges his readers to identify themselves as "wise and understanding." It is not hard to imagine that the church that James writes to was populated with different factions and groups, each advocating a different manner of survival in the face of Jewish persecution, and each claiming to be wise and understanding. But James challenges the truly wise man with these words: "By his good conduct let him show his works in the meekness of wisdom."

Just as he connected abstract belief to concrete action in James 2 by proclaiming "faith apart from works is dead," James now challenges those who claim insight and knowledge to show their true character in the nature of the actions—works characterized by good conduct and meekness. In demanding that the supposed wisdom of those who would direct the path of God's people be expressed in actions, James moderates the rhetorical power of the tongue and undermines the influence of unrighteous speech issuing from mouths of blessing and cursing (3:9). By demanding that these men demonstrate their rhetorical "wisdom" in their actions, James hopes to guard the future of his church from domination by those who advise violence and political manipulation in the face of persecution.

In concluding this chapter James introduces the central question that faces his readers—how will they respond to the violence and persecution of their Jewish oppressors, and how will they participate in bringing about "the righteousness of God" in the world (1:20)? The path that James commends is clear: it is the path of meekness and peace. This is the second time James has commended "meekness" to his readers as a description of their posture toward the world, a way of living that participates with God's way of putting things to right in the world (cf. James 1:20-21). Since living in meekness is one of James's primary applications of what it means to remain joyfully steadfast in trials, it is worth pausing for a moment to consider in more detail what James means.

Of course, the most prominent backdrop for James's commendation to live "in the meekness of wisdom" is the words of Jesus in Matthew 5:5, where he declares, "Blessed are the meek, for they shall inherit the earth." According to Jesus, to live meekly is to be the recipient of his blessing and to own the promise of the future inheritance of the earth. The words of Jesus are rooted themselves in the promise of the Hebrew Scriptures. David himself prophesies boldly regarding the fate of the meek, "In just a little while, the wicked will be no more; though you look carefully at his place, he will not be there. But the meek shall inherit the land and delight themselves in abundant peace" (Ps. 37:10-11). Elsewhere the Messiah is portrayed as the one who will give justice to the meek (Isa. 11:4), and God promises to protect the meek from their enemies (Ps. 45:4; Isa. 29:19).

But what does it mean to truly live "in the meekness of wisdom"? Again, the Hebrew Scriptures come to our aid. Often, in our modern world, when we hear the word "meek" we instantly think of weakness or passivity. But in Numbers 12:3, Moses is described as "very meek, more than all the people who were on the face of the earth." This description of Moses comes at a time when he is being attacked by his siblings Aaron and Miriam because of his marriage to a Cushite woman, as well as their desire to share in his authority and prominence. What is striking about this story is that Moses does not defend himself overtly against Aaron and Miriam's threats and accusations. Rather, Yahweh deals with their wickedness by first rebuking them and then striking Miriam with leprosy for seven days, as a sign of public shame for her as well as Aaron. Moses was the leader of God's people, a prophet who spoke with God face to face. He stood toe to toe with the Pharaoh of Egypt, the most powerful nation on earth in his lifetime, before leading the people of Israel out of slavery. If, as the Bible tells us, Moses was the meekest man on the face of the earth, then something other than weakness and passivity must be at the core of what it means to be meek.

The story of Numbers 12 reveals that Moses is called "meek" because he trusted in God to defend him against the wicked instead of using his own power to protect himself. That posture is made more explicit in the description of the meek in Psalm 37. Though we cannot be certain of the circumstances of this Psalm, we know that it is written by David, and that he writes it in his old age (Ps. 37:25). After leading a life of trust in Yahweh to protect him from the wicked, David composes a Psalm to commend this same path of trust to Israel. Psalm 37 is a richly structured Psalm, and sets in contrast the wicked, who "will soon fade like the grass" (37:1) with those who trust in Yahweh, who will remain steadfast because of his protection. Repeated five times through the Psalm is the refrain "shall inherit the land," and given the nature of parallelism in the Psalms, the five different types of people who are said to inherit the land can be considered parallel descriptions of the wise man that trusts in Yahweh.

According to David in Psalm 37, those who "shall inherit the land" are "those who wait for Yahweh" (v. 9), "the meek" (v. 11), "those blessed by Yahweh" (v. 22), "the righteous" (v. 29), and those who "wait for Yahweh" (v. 34). Since all these descriptions are parallel with one another (that is, they describe the same kind of person from different angles, providing a fuller portrait of him), we see that one of the most prominent attributes of the meek person is that he is someone who waits on God for his vindication. Thus the meek are "still before Yahweh and wait patiently for him." They "refrain from anger and forsake wrath" and they join in the laughter of their God against the wicked who plot their demise. The meek know that "the wicked will perish, the enemies of Yahweh are like the glory of the pastures; they vanish—like smoke they vanish away" (vv. 7, 8, 13, 20).

Given this background, what does it mean for James to command his reader to "show his works in the meekness of wisdom"? It means that meekness requires maintaining one's trust in Jesus even in the midst of violence and evil, waiting patiently on God for both protection and vengeance against one's enemies, and delighting in the pleasure of God to deliver his chosen people. It was meekness that caused David himself to put aside vengeance against his oppressor Saul even though God delivered him into his hands on two occasions. It was meekness that caused David's descendant Hezekiah to cry out to the Lord in response to the threat of the Assyrians at his gate, trusting in the power of God to deliver his people instead of their military strength. It was meekness that caused Jesus to heal the ear of the High Priest's servant and tell his disciples to put up their swords. He went meekly to his death because of his trust in the resurrection and vindication of God.

Therefore, the meekness James calls his readers to in this chapter is not passive acceptance of the violence they have suffered and naive submission to the machinations of the wicked Jews who are set against them. Rather it is a bold and confident resolution not only to speak but also to act out the confession "Jesus is Lord" by patiently waiting for his judgment and vindication instead of taking matters into their own hands by conspiring against their oppressors.

But the behavior of at least some of these "brothers" is altogether opposed to this mature posture: "But if you have bitter jealousy and selfish ambition in your hearts, do not boast and be false to the truth" (James 3:14). When we read passages like these, as modern people, we are used to reading them through individualistic lenses. And so, when we see jealousy and ambition, we think of the inner pride of our hearts and quickly leap to the assumption that this is what James is warning his readers against in these verses. While there is certainly an aspect of pride and vainglory that James is seeking to curb, his full intentions here run much deeper. The word that is translated "jealousy" in this verse is the Greek word *zealos* (ζηϖλος) which is also used to refer to the various Jewish revolutionary movements during the years of A.D. 6-70. These insurrectionist cabals led to the destruction of Jerusalem and the Temple by Titus in A.D. 70. Though there were many different revolutionary groups during this time, they all shared the common belief and commitment that looked forward to the time when their God would defeat the Romans and would himself rule over them. They were willing to use any means necessary, including political manipulation and violence, to hasten the coming of that day.[29]

---

[29] For a detailed account of the history of zealotry among the Jews see Martin Hengel, *The Zealots* (Edinburgh: T&T Clark, 1989).

In addition, "selfish ambition" is here a translation of the Greek word *eritheia* (εριθεια), a word used throughout Greek classical literature, and Aristotle in particular, to describe specifically political ambition—the narrow, partisan zeal of those seeking power. What James is warning his readers against harboring in their hearts is not merely individualistic and petty jealousy, but also a corporate mentality of bitterness and political vengeance against their oppressors. Since the church to which James writes is made up of predominately Jewish converts, and this attitude of bringing about the righteousness of God (that is, the establishing of God's promises on earth) by means of aggressive political schemes had so come to dominate the Jewish mindset of the day, it is not surprising they would carry this same perspective on the relationship between their actions and the actions of God into their new submission to Jesus. Because the temptation is so strong to effect social change through violence and political machinations, James addresses this threat head on and rebukes his readers for responding to their persecution with the same tactics as their oppressors.

What violent and political temptations might these early Christians have been confronted with? We will investigate this further in our analysis of the next chapter. But notice that several of their temptations have been already made explicit in the earlier sections of James's letter: angry and divisive speech directed against the enemies (James 1:19-20), pandering to the rich and powerful in hopes of gaining their protection (1:27c-2:7), hurling curses and violent words against those that do them violence (3:6-10), and even, as we shall see, killing those who threaten them (4:2; cf. 2:11). As James writes in 3:15, though these kinds of actions by a persecuted minority might seem justifiable and even wise (and indeed, they are wise according to the pattern of this world), "This is not the wisdom that comes down from above, but is earthly, unspiritual, demonic" (3:15). Reacting with these kinds of violent and desperate measures to end the persecution and oppression has its own kind of wisdom—indeed, it is the tactic of nearly every abused minority in world history, and the basis for the kind of guerrilla warfare that is engaged in all over the world today by those who are outmanned and outgunned and unable to live at peace.

But James's point is that to live in this kind of violent and manipulative way is to embrace worldly wisdom and reject the wisdom of God. It is to follow the way of men ever since Cain's murder of Abel out in the field and to reject the path of Jesus. Instead of patiently accepting suffering as the God-appointed path to maturity, the wisdom of man impetuously grasps after maturity, seeking to short-circuit the process of patient obedience by which maturity is gained by returning violence for violence, malice for malice, curses with cursing. Like Adam and Eve who grasped for wisdom instead of waiting for God to give it to them, these early Christians are tempted to grasp for maturity on their own terms, through violence and scheming, instead of the way the Lord has set before them, the way of patience and joy during suffering (1:2-15). It is for this reason that "zealotry" and "political ambition" are described as "demonic." Because like Satan and his demons, to behave this way is to take the security and comfort that we want on our own terms, in our own way, without patiently accepting the discipline of our Father—just as Satan and his demons did in their rebellion.

James gives his community a test to determine if they are living according to the wisdom that comes from above or the wisdom that is earthly and demonic, if they are walking in the way of Cain or the way of Jesus as they pursue maturity and godliness: "For where zealotry and political ambition exist, there will be disorder and every vile practice" (v. 16). The Greek word translated here as "disorder" is *akatastasia* (ακαταστασια), a word that is fraught with political overtones, and is often translated into English as "insurrection." In Luke 21:9, Jesus uses *akatastasia* to describe the violent signs that would precede the destruction of the Temple. That prophetic word spoken by Jesus was fulfilled in the rebellion of the Jews against the Roman Empire—a rebellion that sought to bring about the righteousness of God in their world. That effort failed utterly because of the Jewish nation's rebellion against

Jesus and his church and resulted in the destruction of the Temple and much of the Jewish nation by the Romans. James instructs his readers to avoid the way of insurrection as they endure violence done against them. Though the apostasy of the Jews would eventually lead them to a series of violent revolts against the Romans, these new Christians should not be characterized by *akatastasia* if they are truly to mature into the image of the Son of God and receive the crown of life (James 1:12) and the vindication of Jesus.

In contrast to this earthly and demonic wisdom which leads to "disorder and every vile practice," "the wisdom from above is first pure, then peaceable, gentle, open to reason, full of mercy and good fruits, impartial and sincere" (3:17). James's list of positive attributes echoes Jesus's beatitudes. He commends purity, peacefulness and mercy. In addition, James challenges his readers to embrace gentleness and reason in contrast to violence and uncontrolled passion and reiterates the necessity of impartiality (cf. 2:1). Taken together, this list describes James's understanding of the character of the mature community that is conformed to the pattern of Jesus's life and teaching. In the face of violence and oppression, James's description of heavenly wisdom is counterintuitive—truly a new way of being human. In the eyes of the world, it is foolishness to respond with gentleness, peace, and mercy to those who threaten us; but according to James, and to Jesus, this kind of radical trust in God's vindication is true wisdom.

Earlier in his epistle, James chastened his readers that "the anger of man does not produce the righteousness of God" (1:20). Now at the end of his letter's third chapter, James describes the way of life that will produce the righteousness of God (that is, the putting-to-right of all things that God has promised). "And a harvest of righteousness is sown in peace by those who make peace" (v. 18). In contrast to the wisdom of their Jewish oppressors, who seek to bring about the righteousness of God through the violent persecution of those who follow Christ, James commands his readers to participate in God's plan for the renewal of all things by making peace.

What does making peace mean for James's readers in their context? Often when we read of working to make peace in our contemporary context, we understand a passive and detached pacifist interaction with the world. But James is not commanding his readers to simply do nothing in response to the evil and violence perpetrated against them. Reading back through his epistle, we find the kind of peacemaking that James desires for his readers is to bridle their tongues in the face of oppression (1:19), care for the poor and needy in their suffering (1:27b), reject worldly paradigms and wisdom (1:27c), resist partiality and political pandering to the wealthy (2:1-7), and bless their enemies instead of cursing them (3:10).

James commands his readers to make peace confidently because they are the recipients of the promise of Jesus to set all things to right. Though a life that follows the pattern of Jesus in response to persecution does not always appear to have much impact on the world, James promises that such a life is like a seed sown in the ground. For a long time nothing can be seen, but then one day a sprout appears, which grows into a mature plant and results in a harvest of righteousness. In commending his readers to embrace peacemaking instead of insurrection, James is asking them to live by faith, to act based on the reality of things unseen. To pursue peace is to reject the wisdom of this world, to put aside the false security of inflated rhetoric and violent power plays, and instead to hold fast to the power of the Spirit and wait patiently for the seed to grow into a tree, for the yeast to leaven the dough, for those who make peace to be openly proclaimed as the sons and daughters of God (Matt. 13:31-33).

## Summary & Reflections

In his epistle's third chapter, James continues to expand and explain themes that he has explored throughout his letter: the significance of future judgment for our present obedience to Jesus, the reality that our maturity is demonstrated and directed by the words of our mouths, and only through continuing to follow the way of Jesus will righteousness be enacted in the world. This question of how lasting change may be brought to the society and culture we find ourselves in is one of the primary questions of James's epistle and remains one of the most prominent questions in our world today—not only for Christians, but for all men and women who long for a better world.

In our contemporary culture, all kinds of different paths for societal change are regularly set before us. Every four years, we are promised by various presidential candidates that if only we will vote for them, change will be enacted in our society through their political leadership and ability to pass laws, raise or lower taxes, and provide leadership for our country. Others promise change through greater communication between disparate groups of society, better education, an increase in commerce, technological advances, or the promise of a new, globally connected, and wireless world. Christians are not immune to these ideal visions of change for society, and often seem to latch on to a political agenda or an educational system as the sure cure for a sick world. Increasingly, across the world, violence is also seen as a legitimate means for societal change and is a method that has been used effectively by all different types of groups to achieve the change they desire. Americans have just experienced (2020) a surge of political violence in our cities designed to address various real and imaginary injustices.

Indeed, one of the gifts of the church to the world is an indelible future orientation—a belief that history is not inherently static or cyclical, but that history is going someplace, and human beings really have the power and responsibility to affect its direction. Increasingly, the world is full of people who want to change things, who want to create a culture and society that is better for our children than it is for us. We want to better our cities, our states, and our nation. We're compelled to make things right, to rectify the wrongs, and bring about change for the better. This is one gift that the Christian faith has brought to the world.

For pagan civilizations and societies, history is cyclical or static.[30] Change was either bad or at least not going anywhere, and the future never held any hope, because it would always come back to where it had been. But for Christians, we know that this isn't true. We know that history moves and brings new realities, and God brings new things through us in history. That means if a government goes bad, we want to do something about it. And so Western civilization, where the church took root in past centuries, moved forward by "revolutions." Sometimes they were peaceful, sometimes violent, but each revolution brought with it change and vision for the future. Even the French revolution in the late 1700s, for all its professed devotion to atheism and reason, stripped of any connection with history, was only possible because it borrowed capital from the Christian vision for a well-ordered society. This is true for Marxism as well, which was always a parody for the Christian hope for the future. And so the story of the Christian history is one of change and progress and revolution. And this is true for us today as Christians experience cultural marginalization in America. But it is much worse in other parts of the world.[31]

---

30 Peter J. Leithart, *Deep Comedy: Trinity, Tragedy, & Hope in Western Literature* (Moscow, ID: Canon Press, 2006).

31 Rosenstock-Huessy, *Out of Revolution*, 23. "The present time is—for reasons to be explained in this book—bound to attempt an organization of future society by which the dynamite of revolution may be manipulated as persistently and consciously as contractors use real dynamite in building tunnels and roads."

Today many feel more passionate for change than other Christian communities have in the past. We all want to right the wrongs of our present-day society. And the question is, how can we bring about change? What does a biblical "revolution" look like? How does God bring about the promised kingdom of righteousness through us? How can we be his instruments, the means by which things are rectified? How can our children and grandchildren inherit something even better than what we have?

The answer to these questions is of course found in the Bible itself, and particularly in the New Testament, for those who followed Jesus after his resurrection and ascension were faced with a world that needed changing, that needed to be brought into subjugation to the rule of Christ. And in James's letter to these early disciples we find some of the answers to these questions. The early Christian disciples to whom James wrote all had passion to change their world—they knew the promises of Yahweh in the Hebrew Scriptures that the promised Messiah would bring in a righteous kingdom. They knew the prophecies of Isaiah 65 of the new heavens and new earth, and they knew that Jesus's resurrection from the dead meant that he would be the one to right all wrongs, that he would set things right, that he would renew the creation. They all looked for it. They all wanted it. They all knew that they themselves were the instruments for the promised change.

When the first disciples, the apostles, gathered around Jesus on his last day of earth before his ascension to heaven, the disciples ask, "Lord, will you at this time restore the kingdom to Israel?" And Jesus responded simply, "It is not for you to know the times or seasons that the Father has fixed by his own authority. But you will receive power when the Holy Spirit has come upon you, and you will be my witnesses in Jerusalem and in all Judea and Samaria, to the end of the earth" (Acts 1:6-7). This is how the book of Acts begins—with the disciples longing for all the promises of Jesus to be fulfilled before their eyes, and Jesus cautioning them to wait patiently for the timing of the Father. It is clear from the question they ask that the disciples didn't at that time understand either the nature of Jesus's kingdom or the way it would be established. Jesus himself would have to teach them. The Spirit would be poured out on them. They would enter the kingdom through many tribulations, as Paul would later explain to the new Christians at Lystra (Acts 14:22). Even so, it wasn't an easy lesson for the "firstfruits" apostolic church. For the kingdom would not come in an instant as they hoped, but slowly, through their obedience and suffering as the delegated ambassadors of Jesus in the world.

As the story of the establishment of Jesus's kingdom continues through the book of Acts, the revolution comes in a way that the disciples did not expect, that Rome did not expect, and in a way that the apostate Jews did not expect. The change brought by the rule of Jesus did not follow the normal pattern of revolution already established in their world. It did not happen through violence, or political power plays, or rhetorical persuasion to radical action. Rather, their revolution came through steadfastness in the face of persecution, through obedience, suffering and faith in the promises of Jesus. The apostles had to be cleansed and refined by fire. They had to have their minds stripped of all the pagan thinking regarding how to change the world. Through suffering they matured in their understanding of God's way of establishing his kingdom in the world. As the Spirit instructed them, they grew in the wisdom that comes from above. And thereby the revolution of Jesus's kingdom came into the world.

God's way of bringing change through the early church was, in many ways, profoundly counter-intuitive, and diametrically opposed to the way of Rome, and to Rome's imitator, the apostate Jewish nation. Almost immediately after the ascension of Jesus, after his declaration that all authority belongs to him, and that he will establish his kingdom throughout the entire earth, his disciples, the inheritors of that promise, are persecuted, hated, reviled. Their community is ostracized and marginalized. Christians were physically banished from the city of Jerusalem, the center of God's promises during the kingdom phrase of Israel's history, and sent out into the wilderness with no access to the institutions of power and influence. From the perspective of the disciples, they must have been asking, "What in the world is happening? This is not the way things are supposed to be. This is not what Jesus promised."

Imagine, if you can, the perplexity and the bewilderment of those early Christians experiencing suffering and persecution and apparent abandonment by God when they expected power and authority from their Messiah. And in that crisis time for the early disciples, they were soon faced with choice between two reactions to their persecution and marginalization. On the one hand, some argued that since Jesus had already given them all power and authority, it was their responsibility to seize it for themselves through angry rhetoric, political manipulation, and subversive violence. But the other viewpoint, the one argued for by the apostles and ultimately adopted by the church, urged patience and humility—that suffering was a prelude to glory and to victory—that the path to the resurrection and authority and power must also include the way of the cross.

This is the way of the wise which James commends. Wisdom is found in the way of mercy, obedience, and the joy of remaining steadfast during suffering. It is the way of tongue bridling, of caring for the poor and needy, of resisting partiality toward the rich in the hope of gaining their ear and power, of blessing your enemies instead of cursing, of patiently waiting for the kingdom to be established according to the timing and manner of God.

Even in our society today in America, things are bad, but things are not nearly as bad as they were for the early church. But we still have loud and angry voices, even from the Christian community. And we are tempted by the power struggles, the leveraging, the lobbying, and everything else the world says is necessary for real, lasting change. And there may be a place for some of those actions, some of that rhetoric, as a rear-guard action. But acting in these ways will never bring lasting change. Identify whatever evil we think is most characteristic of our society today, and ask how should it be changed? Should we pass a law? A constitutional amendment? Though laws and amendments are good, they will never bring the kind of change Jesus promises. Rather, his change will come only through works of meekness and wisdom. Not pious, fancy talk, but works.

How does Jesus change the world? How does Jesus advance his kingdom? The Jews expected him to come in riding on his warhorse, with a flashing sword. But he didn't do that. He comes in on a donkey, humble, meek, and confident in the favor of his Father. He submits to torture and persecution and suffering with steadfastness and joy. He gives himself for others. Therefore, he is highly exalted, and given a name that is above every name. Just as it is for Jesus, so also it is for us, his anointed ones. Surely, the way of Jesus is the way that we are to follow. Jesus came from above, from the father, and takes on our flesh, and he shows us the life of God. He shows us the humility of God. He shows us that the way of Father, Son and Holy Spirit is not the way of grasping and taking and anger and selfishness, but the way of giving and humility.

And where will the way of Jesus take us? It may be a place in the dungeon next to others waiting to be executed or tortured. What will that get us? It may mean that we will die. And how will that make things right? The answer is contained in the vivid picture James gives us at the end of this chapter. It will come as a harvest of righteousness. Fields of grain, bursting with flowers and fruit—the harvest, the fruits of righteousness bursting out all over the earth. But notice that the harvest of righteousness is sown in peace by peacemakers. Like a seed, we sow it, and it goes into the ground, and we may not immediately see the fruit of that action. We probably won't experience it, like Jesus himself, who was sown, who died, and was buried. And then he rose again. And so the new world comes into being, not in a moment, but over many lifetimes, many seeds, many acts of patience and obedience and meekness. It comes through Jesus's bride, through his sons and daughters, his disciples, who learn to act as Jesus acts. This is how God changes the world.

9

# Exposing the Contagion of Mimetic Violence

*What Christianity conquers is the pagan way of organizing the world*
– Rene Girard[32]

## James 4:1-17

[1]What causes quarrels and what causes fights among you? Is it not this, that your passions are at war within you? [2]You desire and do not have, so you murder. You covet and cannot obtain, so you fight and quarrel. You do not have, because you do not ask. [3]You ask and do not receive, because you ask wrongly, to spend it on your passions. [4]You adulterous people! Do you not know that friendship with the world is enmity with God? Therefore, whoever wishes to be a friend of the world makes himself an enemy of God. [5]Or do you suppose it is to no purpose that the Scripture says, "He yearns jealously over the spirit that he has made to dwell in us"? [6]But he gives more grace. Therefore, it says, "God opposes the proud, but gives grace to the humble." [7]Submit yourselves therefore to God. Resist the devil, and he will flee from you. [8]Draw near to God, and he will draw near to you. Cleanse your hands, you sinners, and purify your hearts, you double-minded. [9]Be wretched and

---

32 Rene Girard, *I See Satan Fall Like Lightning*, trans. James G. Williams (Maryknoll, New York: Orbis Books, 2001), 139.

mourn and weep. Let your laughter be turned to mourning and your joy to gloom. ¹⁰Humble yourselves before the Lord, and he will exalt you.

¹¹Do not speak evil against one another, brothers. The one who speaks against a brother or judges his brother, speaks evil against the law and judges the law. But if you judge the law, you are not a doer of the law but a judge. ¹²There is only one lawgiver and judge, he who is able to save and to destroy. But who are you to judge your neighbor?

¹³Come now, you who say, "Today or tomorrow we will go into such and such a town and spend a year there and trade and make a profit"— ¹⁴yet you do not know what tomorrow will bring. What is your life? For you are a mist that appears for a little time and then vanishes. ¹⁵Instead you ought to say, "If the Lord wills, we will live and do this or that." ¹⁶As it is, you boast in your arrogance. All such boasting is evil. ¹⁷So whoever knows the right thing to do and fails to do it, for him it is sin.

James concludes the third chapter of his epistle by exhorting his readers with these words: "A harvest of righteousness is sown in peace by those who make peace" (3:18). In other words, there is only one way in which those who follow Jesus will effectively establish his kingdom and bring about the making right of all things—by sowing and making peace. Of course, we need to understand that what James means by "peace" is fundamentally different than the way of living that word evokes in our modern context. James is not against every form of "violence" and in favor of peace for the same reasons as many of those who protest wars and oppression in twenty-first century America, for he does not oppose violence itself—after all, the epistle of James is full of references to violence and judgment.

Indeed, the judgment of Jesus is a deeply significant theme throughout James's letter. In 1:10, he warns that the "rich man" will "pass away" in the scorching heat of the sun. Later, in 2:13, James pointedly admonishes his readers to match their verbal articulations of faith with actions of obedience and conformity to the example of Jesus, because the judgment of the risen Son of God will be without mercy to the one who has shown no mercy. In 3:1, teachers are warned they will be "judged with greater strictness" on the last day, and in 4:12, James concludes his exhortation to his readers to repent of their commitment to worldly assumptions of power and live in peace with one another by reminding them that "there is only one lawgiver and judge, he who is able to save and to destroy." Finally, in 5:1-6, James engages in a long diatribe against the oppressors of the church, warning them that because of their wickedness and violence against the followers of Jesus, misery is coming against them, and judgment that will "eat their flesh like fire" (5:3b).

In the context of James's epistle, the promise of the coming righteous judgment of Jesus is what enables and compels the church to respond to the violence of their persecutors by sowing and making peace. The promised future of judgment by Jesus is the only reason that James can command his church to bridle their tongues instead of responding in anger to the injustices done against them, to resist anger and instead serve those in need. Without the promised imminent judgment, the pursuit of peace by the followers of Jesus would be foolish and meaningless. But because Jesus would judge the Jewish nation for their oppression of the church in A.D. 70, and because he will return to judge the world on the Last Day, the peacemaking of his followers is significant and will bear the fruits of righteousness in the new kingdom inaugurated by Jesus's ascension to rule the world. So the message of James's epistle is simply this: do not live as the world lives. Pursue neither violence nor power nor peace as the world pursues these things, but only as one who is subject of King Jesus, who will soon return to judge his domain, to save his people and destroy his enemies.

Now, in the fourth chapter of his epistle, James continues to explain in detail what it will mean for his readers to sow a harvest of righteousness in peace, and he considers why living in this way is so difficult for them. With what these Christian exiles were experiencing at the hands of their apostate Jewish enemies, the strong temptation to "fight back" was winning out among many of the leading brothers in their communities. A basic outline of the structure of James's argument in this section is as follows:

*From whence comes the sin of violence in your communities? (4:1a)*

Answer #1: From within your depraved hearts (4:1b-3)

Answer #2: From your imitation of and friendship with the world (4:4-5)

*What is the solution?*

Repentance and humility before God (4:6-10)

    A. Submit to God (4:7a)

    B. Resist the devil (4:7b)

    C. Draw near to God (4:8a)

    D. Confess and repent of your sins (4:8b-10)

Repentance must occur because Jesus will judge the world (4:11-12).

## THE ROOTS OF RELIGIOUS FANATICISM

### James 4:1-5

¹What causes quarrels and what causes fights among you? Is it not this, that your passions are at war among your members? ²You desire and do not have, so you murder. You are zealous and cannot obtain, so you fight and make war. You do not have, because you do not ask. ³You ask and do not receive, because you ask wrongly, to spend it on your passions. ⁴You adulterous people! Do you not know that friendship with the world is enmity with God? Therefore, whoever wishes to be a friend of the world makes himself an enemy of God. ⁵Or do you suppose it is to no purpose that the Scripture says, "He yearns jealously over the spirit that he has made to dwell in us"?

Here James narrows the focus of his arguments. He is addressing what he understands to be specific sins in the congregations to whom he writes. Indeed, in some ways, we can understand the whole of chapter 4 to be James's application of his argument in 3:13-18 that there are only two ways to live: according to the wisdom from above or according to the wisdom that is "earthly, unspiritual and demonic" (3:15). Now in chapter 4 James outlines some of the particular ways that his readers have begun to embrace earthly, demonic wisdom and guides them toward repentance and renewed trust in the wisdom that is from above, the way of Jesus, and the vindication of God.

James begins by asking a pointed question, "What causes wars and what causes fights among you?" In this question, he shifts the focus of his teaching from the more theoretical realm of 3:13-18 and turns it toward the current behavior of his readers. In 3:16 James noted that, "where jealousy and political ambition exist, there will be disorder and every vile practice." That prediction appears to be fulfilled in the quarrels and fighting of the congregation that he addresses. As James's readers have given themselves over to earthly wisdom that prizes zealotry and political ambition, their community has come to be more and more characterized by disorder and malice (1:21). This disorder and misdirected ambition is revealed in James's answer to his question: "Is it not this, that your passions are at war among your members?" (4:1b). As the community has given itself over to worldly wisdom, passions have inflamed within individual members as well as within their corporate body, leading to division and factions.

In verse 2, James shifts from questioning his readers to addressing them directly. To get a better feel for what he is saying, we can structure the passage like this:

> You desire and do not have,
>   so you murder.
> You are zealous and cannot obtain,
>   so you fight and make war."

Putting all vestiges of subtlety aside, James now confronts the sins of his readers directly. Desiring what they have not yet obtained, they have fought and even slaughtered in order to gain the object of their desire. Longing for what they had not yet possessed, their community is plagued by fights and wars, by all kinds of disorder and vile practices.

Since James does not name explicitly the unfulfilled desire of his community, it is left to us to fill in the blank as best we can. Nevertheless, because of the context of suffering, dispersion and persecution that forms the background for this letter, we can easily imagine what a community in this situation would have desired and coveted: an end to the threat posed against them, the return of their family members and friends who had been dragged off to prison, and peace and prosperity for their community. In other words, "the righteousness/justice of God" (1:20). There is nothing impious or necessarily worldly about these desires—indeed, protection from enemies and peace and prosperity are part of what God promises to his people throughout the Scriptures. Indeed, many centuries removed from the original context of James's epistle, we can resonate with the natural, human desires of his congregation—we also long for peace in our time, for protection for our families from death and sickness and for the blessing of God on our life's work.

James's complaint against his readers in these verses has little to do with the object of their desire (righteousness/justice), but rather with the *means* that they are employing to bring about the peace, prosperity, and protection for which they long. Instead of waiting patiently on the Lord to give them the blessings they yearn for, the readers of James's epistles have begun to adopt the tactics of their oppressors, and are using the worldly tools of violence, impassioned rhetoric, and political manipulation to bring about the peace they desire. Though living in this way seems wise to them, James intends to show his readers the destructive foolishness of this path, and its ultimate destination—rebellion against the one true judge of the world.

Throughout the Scriptures, it is undeniable that God plans good things for his children. But again and again we also see a pattern whereby God brings goodness and blessings to his people in his time, and in his way, rather than through their own effort or plans. Consider the story of Abraham, who was promised the blessing of descendants who would grow into a great nation, through whom all the nations of the world would be blessed. After years of waiting for God to make good on his promise to give him a descendant, Abraham listened to the counsel of his wife and followed earthly wisdom by sleeping with his wife's maidservant to gain for himself a son (Gen. 16). By grasping after the promise instead of waiting patiently for God to give it to him (an echo of the pattern of Adam's fall in Gen. 3), Abraham injected jealousy and division in his own family and set in motions events that would result in the creation of a nation that would plague the descendants of his covenant son Isaac for generations.

Though Abraham is of course an exemplar of faith in God (as demonstrated by James's references to him in chapter 2 of his epistle), he also stumbled in his dealings with Hagar in much the same way James's readers seem to be struggling at the time of this epistle. Like Abraham, they are reaching for the blessings promised to them in earthly wisdom, mimicking the tactics used by their Jewish tormentors to gain their own peace and power. In doing so, they rebel against the law of Jesus, but more fundamentally, they betray their lack of trust in the humble and meek life of Jesus as well as the sureness of the future vindication of God. At this point, James's repeated admonitions of patience and long-suffering throughout his epistle (James 1:2-4, 12, 19-20; 3:18) begin to make more sense—for at least some in the communities he is addressing, rejecting steadfastness and embracing violent action and rhetoric is not only a temptation, but apparently an ongoing struggle.

Indeed, according to verse 2, it is likely that at least some are engaged in violence to the point of homicide against their oppressors as a way of gaining for themselves the peace and protection they desired. Some may be tempted to read the Greek verb *phoneuw* (φονευω, "you murder") as simply *metaphorical* murder, perhaps by reading "murder" here through the lens of Jesus's words regarding anger in Matthew 5:21-22 and understanding that some in this church have grown so angry with their persecutors that they are metaphorically "murdering" them in their hearts. But this interpretation is unlikely for several different reasons:

**1.** *It does not do justice to the lexical use of* phoneuw.

This Greek word occurs ten times in the New Testament, and in every other case without exception means literal murder, including twice in James's own epistle (James 2:11, 5:6). James accuses the church's oppressors of "murdering the righteous one" (5:6). That's not something their persecutors are doing "in the hearts." They are physically torturing and killing disciples of Jesus. Is it really all that surprising that some would want to fight back by killing oppressors? It would be very unusual for James to use this word literally elsewhere in his epistle and here intend it to be understood metaphorically without giving some clue in the verse itself.

**2.** *It does not do justice to the exegetical context of the passage.*

In verses 1 and 2b, James accuses his readers of engaging in "fights" and "battles." Both of these words are used to indicate violent action throughout the New Testament.

**3.** *It fails to do justice to the historical context of James's epistle.*

Though we can hardly imagine engaging in murder in order to secure peace and protection for our families or communities in twenty-first-century America, our context is far removed from the one faced by the original readers of this epistle. At the time of his writing, James's audience found themselves in a situation that was truly desperate. According to Acts 8, after the death of Stephen, the Jewish authorities began to systematically and violently persecute those who had received baptism in the name of Jesus and believed that because of his resurrection from the dead, he had been vindicated as the long-promised Messiah.

The Jews moved in force against the followers of Jesus because they understood that the Gospel they proclaimed was a message that threatened the security and prosperity of Israel that they had worked so hard to create and maintain. Though the Jewish leaders did not believe that Jesus was truly risen from the dead, they still understood that his followers constituted a threat to their own power because of their insistent proclamation that Jesus was the rightful king of Israel, the replacement of the Temple system for the forgiveness of sins, and that he would certainly come again to judge his enemies. As Paul testified before the Jews at the temple, at one time he was at the head of this effort, and "persecuted this Way to the death, binding and delivering both men and women... and bring[ing] them in bonds to Jerusalem to be punished" (Acts 22:4-5).

In the desperate context of this intense persecution, it is not surprising that some in the community of new Christians were tempted to engage in murderous violence in defense of their families and to secure the justice they desired. Remember, these early Christians lived in a world far different from our own, not just in terms of the mortal danger they faced, but also how poor they were in biblical and theological terms. Consider that the church that James writes to does not possess the vast majority of the New Testament. It is possible that they had a copy of the gospel of Matthew, but unlikely that their Bible consisted of anything else other than the Hebrew Scriptures, and they also did not have the benefit of centuries of Church history and theology. Two thousand years later, it is easy for us to look back and wonder how any group of Christians could truly consider assassination as a viable alternative in the face of persecution. But the readers of James's epistle were truly the "firstfruits" of the Church (James 1:18)—and they faced violence and persecution worse than we as Western Christians can today imagine, with none of the benefits of Church history and a complete canon that we enjoy.

> We have no right to explain away or tone down the author's statements about these troubles, as though he exaggerated or did not mean to be taken seriously (as some expositors do out of respect for the early church, or for other reasons). Historical honesty demands that we acknowledge the situation as it was, rather than re-create it as we or others should like it to have been.... they strive to acquire what they claim as their due by violence and intrigue.[33]

But these early Jewish Christians were not tempted to fanatical violence simply because they faced intense violence or because they did not have the benefit of the complete canon or centuries of Christian history and theological development. They also faced the temptation to use violence to achieve their goals of peace and protection because they saw the peace and safety that the Jews who persecuted them enjoyed. It is no accident that James connects the violence (murder, fights, and quarrels) of his readers not only with their desire for peace, but also their covetousness (4:2b). At the time of the James's writing, the Jewish nation still seemed to be favored with the blessing of God. Though they were in subjugation to the Romans, Israel enjoyed enormous freedom to worship their God (and rebuild the Temple), while also benefiting greatly from the financial advantages of connection to the Roman empire. Add to this the protection of the Roman army, which kept order in their nation but also allowed them to carry out their own violent schemes against Jesus and his followers with impunity.

Confronted not only with the violence of the Jewish leaders against them, but also the peace, prosperity and protection that they seemed to enjoy, it is no surprise that these early Christians began to covet the power and prestige of the Jewish nation. And slowly, just as anyone who envies what his neighbor possesses, the followers of Jesus began to be tempted to imitate the behavior of the Jews in order to gain what they possessed. Believing that

---

33 Bo Reicke, *The Epistles of James, Peter, and Jude, The Anchor Bible*, Willam Albright and David Noel Freedman, eds., Volume 27 (New York: Double Day, 1964), 45.

peace could only be gained through violence and power, at least some of these early Christian brothers coveted after security and comfort so deeply that they took matters into their own hands and used the tools of violence and intrigue to gain for themselves what they desired. It is no accident that in the Ten Commandments given to Israel, "Do not covet" is included along with prohibitions against murder, adultery, stealing, and lying. All of these other sins flow out first from the sin of covetousness, and by allowing their hearts to covet the position and power of the Jews, the Christians to whom James writes have opened the door to a whole host of other sins, including murder (4:2), and spiritual adultery (4:4).

There is yet another reason for taking James's language of homicidal violence seriously. Related to what we have said already, there was the historical reality of zealotry among the Jews. The first-century Jews despised the Romans who ruled over them. But they also were strongly attracted to the power and authority Rome exercised over the Mediterranean world. This love-hate relationship led to a passion among many Jews to be like Rome, to achieve the authority that Rome had by means of similar tactics of military prowess. There were factions of Jews that resorted to insurgent violence in order to weaken Rome. They were called zealots.[34] There is strong evidence that this "mimetic rivalry" infected even the Jewish leaders as they surreptitiously supported the methods of the zealots.[35] Just four decades after James penned his epistle the rivalry of the Jews led to a full-scale insurrection that had to be quelled by Rome when they laid siege to Jerusalem and destroyed the temple. All of this means that when the Christians were expelled from Rome after the martyrdom of Stephen and then violently pursued by Saul

---

34 See Hengel, *The Zealots*.

35 Barabbas was one such rebel insurrectionist, which the Jewish leaders encouraged the crowds to ask Pilate to release rather than Jesus (Matt. 27:20). Moreover, the chief priests were easily swayed to adopt the tactics of the zealots to have the apostle Paul assassinated (Acts 23:12-15).

and other agents of the Jewish council, some of them seem to have readily adopted the tactics of the zealots to fight back against their oppressors. Such violent rhetoric and behavior on the part of these Christians was the motivation for James's anti-zealotic circular letter. Later on, Paul in his letter to the Roman Christians warns against similar tendencies to "zeal" (Rom. 12:18–13:14; 16:17-20). To sum up: the angry Christians in these exiled communities have become religious fanatics.

After identifying the sin of murder, fighting, and quarreling that at least some of the church is involved in, and then identifying the root of this sin in their zealous desire for peace that refuses to wait patiently for the good timing of their Father to be fulfilled, James turns his attention to the issue of prayer, writing, "You do not have because you do not ask. You ask and you do not receive, because you ask wrongly, to spend it on your passions" (James 4:2-3). In these verses, James echoes the words of Jesus, who taught his disciples,

> Ask, and it will be given to you; seek, and you will find; knock, and it will be opened to you. For everyone who asks receives, and the one who seeks finds, and to the one who knocks it will be opened. Or which one of you, if his son asks him for bread, will give him a stone? Or if he asks for a fish, will give him a serpent? If you then, who are evil, know how to give good gifts to your children, how much more will your Father who is in heaven give good things to those who ask him! (Matt. 7:7-11).

Given the promises of Jesus and the words of James, what is it that these Christians who murder, fight, and quarrel do not have because they do not ask their Father? They want deliverance from the enemies, rescue from the peril of their oppressors, and the vindication of their righteous God. But if they are petitioning God for the destruction of their enemies, they are definitely not relying on him for the promise of their security and for an end to their trials. Rather, they asked God for strength and opportunity forcefully to defeat their enemies. And for this reason—because their prayers are driven by zealotry and impatience for the righteousness of God to be established in their communities—their prayers were not answered. "Blessed are those who hunger and thirst for righteousness, for they shall be satisfied" (Matt. 5:6).

Let's be clear. It is not that asking God to judge their enemies is wrong. As we noted earlier in our exposition of James 3, there are good number of such petitions for judgment modeled for us in the Psalms (Pss. 5, 7, 58, 109, etc.). Rather than waiting patiently for God to deliver them in his time and walking in the way of Jesus, trusting that "a harvest of righteousness is sown in peace" (James 3:18), at least some brothers in these churches have given up on this seemingly impotent agenda and have turned their prayers and their actions to bringing about the promises of God in their own time, by their own aggressive methods. Imitating the way of apostate Israel and pagan Rome, their prayers to God have fallen on deaf ears. The language James uses here ("to spend it on your passions/desires") indicates that their motives are skewed. They want personal revenge and retribution rather than the "harvest of righteousness" promised for the Messianic kingdom of Jesus.

## A Prophetic Accusation: You Adulterous People!

Now having exposed the sin of violence and covetousness that plagues these Christian communities and exposing their unfaithfulness by pointing out the fact that their prayers to God remain unanswered, James now strongly rebukes his readers, writing, "You adulterous people! Do you not know that friendship with the world is enmity with God? Therefore, whoever wishes to be a friend of the world makes himself an enemy of God" (James 4:4).

Here James clearly echoes language used by God to describe his relationship with Israel in the book of Hosea when he instructs Hosea, "Go again, love a woman who is loved by another man and is an adulteress, even as Yahweh loves the children of Israel, though they turn to other gods and love cakes of raisins" (Hos. 3:1). Just as Israel was unfaithful to Yahweh by turning to worship other gods, so now these Christians, who have rejected the way of Christ and embraced insurrection and power struggles to gain their peace and security, have become adulterous in their relationship to the one true God.

Interestingly, Israel is called adulterous in the Old Testament specifically for the sin of idolatry—that is, for engaging in worship and sacrifice to the gods of other nations. Now, in the Messianic age, James levels the charge of adultery against these Christians not because they are worshipping actual idols of wood and stone but rather because their actions betray the reality that their hearts are given over to the "idols" that plague the Jewish nation— comfort, security and peace obtained at any cost, including violence and political scheming. Though these Christians would not dream of bending their knee to a statue of a Roman god, some at least in their midst have given in to the more subtle temptation of submitting their allegiance to the narrative of power gained through worldly strength that stands behind those idolatrous pagan statues.

Clearly, James is laying out two options for his readers to choose between: either they will befriend the world and breed enmity with God, or they will remain faithful to God and reject the world. Of course, by "befriending the world," James does not mean going buying or selling in the marketplace, wearing colorful clothes, or drinking wine with friends. Rather, what James means by "friendship with the world" is to adopt that world's values and patterns in regard to how to make things right in their communities, which is the immediate question these Christians are dealing with (cf. James 3:18). In other words, friendship with the world means to live according to wisdom that is "earthly, unspiritual and demonic" (James 3:15) and embrace zealotry, violence and misdirected political ambition as the manner of working to change things in society.

In demanding that his readers not befriend the world, James repeats a theme from earlier in the epistle when he defined pure religion as "to visit orphans and widows in their afflictions and to keep oneself unstained by the world" (James 1:27). James is not calling his readers out of the physical world. Worldliness here does not mean being overly involved in the material creation. Instead, he is encouraging them to work for real, physical change in the cities and communities in which they find themselves. He is solemnly instructing them to live in a way that is radically unworldly, in the sense that it is a complete rejection of worldly assumptions regarding power, authority, and the means of transforming society.

Instead of relying on the power of their tongues or the power of their politics or the power of their organized, aggressive violence, the Christians to whom James writes are called to rely solely on the power of God to vindicate them in his time and to trust in his Fatherly manner of bringing about their maturity through obedience, so that they might rule his world in the way of Jesus—through service and suffering. In this way, they participate in the blessing pronounced by Jesus for the pure in heart. For it is not in our sinlessness, but in our rejection of the ways of the world that we see God, who brings about his righteousness in the world in a manner that is a mystery to those whose hearts are stained by the world. But as the hearts of those who follow Jesus are made pure, our eyes are opened so that we might see the hand of God in every aspect of our lives, including our simple obedience and even our suffering.

The man who lives according to worldly values of violence and anger, as James puts it, "makes himself an enemy of God." He is God's enemy because his way of life is in opposition to the way of Jesus, even though his goals (bringing about the righteousness of God on earth) are nominally the same. There is not a hint of compromise in James's words—there is no room for synthesizing the teachings of Jesus with pagan cultural assumptions of power and prestige that the first-century Jews have adapted. Jesus brings a new kingdom not simply because he is a new king, but because his kingdom brings the ways of heaven to earth (Matt. 6:10).

But God is not content simply to allow those who have been baptized in his name to become his enemies. In the Old Testament, God assured Hosea that he loved Israel despite her adultery and would reclaim her as his own (Hos. 3:1-5). And though some in his church have begun to adopt the worldly, pagan values and tactics in bringing about the righteousness of God, James writes to them, "Or do you suppose it is to no purpose that the Scripture says, 'The Spirit he has caused to dwell in us is intensely jealous?'" (James 4:5). Because of their baptism and faith in Christ, the Holy Spirit has come to dwell in the followers of Jesus to whom James writes in this epistle. The recipients of this letter have been united to Christ, and because of that reality, God yearns jealously for his Spirit to work his full effect in their individual hearts and communities. In other words, God has joined himself to his people, like a husband to a wife, and the Spirit is the bond of that union. And the divine Husband is jealous for his wife's faithful love and submission. The very next imperative fits nicely with the marriage imagery: "Submit yourselves therefore to God" (4:7).

At least some of these Christians are on the brink of apostasy (indeed, James already calls them adulterers), rejecting their faith in Christ in order to return to the power and compromised history of faithless Judaism. But James does not merely chastise his readers for their faltering faith. He also reminds them that it is not to no purpose that God yearns jealously for them. In doing so, he causes them to remember their baptism, remember their status as the dwelling place of the Holy Spirit, and also to recall the whole of the story of Yahweh's jealous love for his bride Israel and his refusal to allow her to embrace other gods without his constant pursuit and relentless and effective effort to bring life out of the spiritual death of his people. James's words to these first-century Christians is also a promise to us today—though our temptations toward apostasy might not involve fights and murder, still we are sometimes drawn to forsake covenant with our God. To us, James also speaks these words, "Or do you suppose it is no purpose that the Scripture says, 'He yearns jealously over the spirit that he has made to dwell in us'" (James 4:5). There is indeed a purpose. Our divine Husband is faithful to us even when we are unfaithful to him.

## THE MEEK SHALL INHERIT THE EARTH

*James 4:6-10*

> ⁶But he gives more grace. Therefore it says, "God opposes the proud, but gives grace to the humble." ⁷Submit yourselves therefore to God. Resist the devil, and he will flee from you. ⁸Draw near to God, and he will draw near to you. Cleanse your hands, you sinners, and purify your hearts, you double-minded. ⁹Be wretched and mourn and weep. Let your laughter be turned to mourning and your joy to gloom. ¹⁰Humble yourselves before the Lord, and he will exalt you.

After reminding his readers that God has made his Spirit to dwell in them and therefore yearns jealously for them to return to the way of Jesus, James outlines for them the path which will bring them back into pure fellowship with God, writing, "But he gives more grace. Therefore, it says, 'God opposes the proud, but gives grace to the humble'" (James 4:6). First, assuring his readers of the grace of God that awaits their repentance, James then describes how this repentance is expressed: in *humility*. Though their sin against Christ their King runs as deep as murder, still the grace of God is extended to those that will reject the way of pride and earthly wisdom and humble themselves before their God. Of course, we know from Acts 9 that God's grace did extend to the fanatical murderer Saul. But this epistle is likely written during the time of Saul's solitary rehabilitation (Gal. 1:21-22), so they may even be aware of his conversion.

In verse 6, James loosely quotes the Greek translation of Proverbs 3:34, which reads, "Toward the scorners he [Yahweh] is scornful, but to the humble he gives favor." This reference back to Proverbs is significant, because Proverbs is the advice given by Solomon to his son in preparation for the day when he will rule over Israel. In the same way, James is rebuking these early Christians for the misguided way in which they are seeking to rule with Christ over his kingdom. The pursuit of humility is commended not only because it is the path of repentance and forgiveness of sin for these Christians, but also because it is a summation of the basic posture of the wisdom and maturity that will be required of them—not only in respect to this sin of worldliness and violence, but in every aspect of their individual and corporate lives. In humility, those who follow Jesus will rule over his kingdom by their suffering and service for the world. "Blessed are the meek, for they shall inherit the earth . . . . Blessed are the peacemakers, for they shall be called sons of God" (Matt. 5:5).

After calling his readers to humility, James then goes on to explain the details of the repentance that he demands from them, writing, "Submit yourselves therefore to God. Resist the devil and he will flee from you. Draw near to God, and he will draw near to you. Cleanse your hands you sinners, and purify your hearts, you double-minded. Be wretched and mourn and weep. Let your laughter be turned to mourning and your joy to gloom. Humble yourselves before the Lord and he will exalt you" (James 4:7-10). Taking each of these commands in turn will help give us a more fully textured understanding of the nature of the repentance God requires from his people, not only in respect to their particular situation and specific sins, but also even for our own calling to repentance for our contemporary sins, as individuals and as Christian communities.

**A.** *"Submit yourselves therefore to God" (verse 7a)*

In this command, James instructs his reader to embody their humility in submission to God. The submission that James requires means that these Christians must abandon immediately the violence and worldly power that they have so far pursued and return to the "wisdom from above" mentioned in 3:17 and begin again to sow peace by making peace and waiting patiently for the harvest of righteousness that God promises. But James is not simply giving a harsh order that he expects to be obeyed without question. Instead, he reasons with his readers, arguing that they must submit themselves therefore to God, referring back to the promise of grace that God offers to the humble as the motivation for their submission.

This is a significant point, for it shows us that despite the reality that Jesus is king, he is not a tyrant, and his kingship is fundamentally different from how it was misconceived by their Jewish contemporaries—the humility that he requires of those who would serve with him he models first himself. We might also note that the submission that God requires from those who would repent from their sins is itself an actual rejection of the sins associated with worldly fanaticism that they have committed. Submission to another without qualification is something that the world views as absurd and foolish. In submitting to God, these Christians reject the earthly wisdom they have become entranced by and begin to live according to the wisdom that comes from above.

**B.** *"Resist the devil and he will flee from you" (verse 7b).*

Submission to God necessarily entails resistance to the devil. Either we will live according to demonic wisdom or we will submit to heavenly wisdom (James 3:15). Remember, Jesus was tempted in the wilderness with submission to the devil in order to receive the fulness of his kingdom:

> Again, the devil took him to a very high mountain and showed him all the kingdoms of the world and their glory. And he said to him, "All these I will give you, if you will fall down and worship me."

Jesus responded with "Be gone, Satan," and "then the devil left him." There is no in-between path available either to the readers of James's epistle or to us today. This command also teaches us that the devil's power is largely overstated in popular Christianity today. James does not advise his readers to perform complicated rituals or prolonged psychological warfare in order to repel the devil. Rather, as with Jesus, all that is required is simple submission to God and resistance to Satan in order to drive him away. Those who follow Christ should be confident that this verse is not only a command to resist the devil, but also a promise by God that he will flee in response to our steadfast obedience and submission to the world's true king. This is a consistent theme in the New Testament:

> Be sober-minded; be watchful. Your adversary the devil prowls around like a roaring lion, seeking someone to devour. Resist him, firm in your faith, knowing that the same kinds of suffering are being experienced by your brotherhood throughout the world (1 Pet. 5:8).

**C.** *"Draw near to God and he will draw near to you" (verse 8a).*

This admonition serves as the opposing pair to the previous one. While those who would submit to God must resist the devil, they must also draw near to God. And just as our obedience to repel the devil will be rewarded by his departure, so also our coming close to God will result in his coming close to us. Interestingly, the Greek word for "draw near" is a translation of a fairly technical term in the Hebrew Scriptures that is often used to describe coming into Yahweh's presence. Over and over, this term is used to underscore the point that only duly ordained priests may "draw near" God's presence without risk of his wrath (Exod. 19:21-22; 24:2; Lev. 10:3; 21:21, 23).

James now commands all of his readers to "draw near" to God, promising not only that God will not destroy them in his anger, but that God will actually "draw near" as well to them. Considering that James's audience is made up primarily of Jews who have converted to faith in Jesus, neither the radically new significance of his command nor the connection between the instruction to "draw near" and the priestly actions of the Levites would have been missed by his readers. The implications of James's statements for Christians are startling: in our baptism in the Triune name and union with our priest, the Lord Jesus, we also have been made priests in God's household and given unfettered access to God's presence. As saints (holy ones) we have full sanctuary access. As we draw near to him, the Creator and Ruler of the universe draws near also to us. Once Jesus resisted the devil, not only did the devil flee from him, but his Father sent angels to come and minister to him in the wilderness (James 4:11). That promise of help and service stands for his disciples who are tempted in similar ways in their own wilderness.

**D.** *"Cleanse your hands, you sinners, and purify your hearts you double-minded" (verse 8b).*

James challenges his readers to cleanse their hands in light of their sin. In the Hebrew Scriptures, having "clean hands" is a frequent picture of righteousness (2 Sam 22:21; Job 9:30; 17:9; Pss. 18:20, 24; 24:4; 73:13). By commanding these Christians to cleanse their hands, James is pointing out that because of their worldliness, they have broken covenant with God, thus they are "sinners," not in the generic sense that all humans are, but in the sense that their rebellion has made them unrighteous covenant breakers. He is calling them to repentance—to confess the wrongness of their affections and consequent actions and return to obedience to Jesus. In addition to cleansing their hands, James's readers need to purify their hearts. Again, to be "pure in heart" is an image drawn from the Old Testament to describe a righteous, covenant-keeping person—that is, not a sinless man or woman, but someone who is faithful in covenant with Yahweh (Pss. 24:4; 73:1).

In Psalm 24:3-4, David writes, "Who shall ascend the hill of Yahweh? And who shall stand in his holy place? He who has clean hands and a pure heart, who does not lift up his soul to what is false and does not swear deceitfully." Clearly, this stands behind James's commands in verse 8, given the numerous verbal links. What is particularly fascinating regarding the connection between these verses is that Psalm 24:3-4 helps explain the logic of James 4:8. In Psalm 24:3-4, we see that in order to "ascend the hill of Yahweh" and enter his presence, one must have "clean hands and a pure heart." In James 4:8, James commands his readers to "Draw near to God." But what should these Christians who have become sinners against the Lord do before they come into his presence? As Psalm 24 teaches, they must cleanse their hands and purify their hearts. That is to say, the commands in James 4:8b serve as the necessary condition for fulfillment of the command (and promise) of James 4:8a. Ascending to the mount of Yahweh implies ruling with him as his vice regents. Jesus has ascended to the mount of Yahweh, and sits at his right hand, ruling the world. This promise is also for those united to Christ, as is repeatedly promised by Jesus in the Gospels and in the New Testament epistles (e.g., Matt. 19:28; Eph. 1:20; Col. 3:1; 2 Tim. 2:1; Rev. 20:4, 6).

There is no doubt that Jesus's beatitudes once again stand behind the words of James in this verse. The command to "purify your hearts" echoes Jesus's declaration that "Blessed are the pure in heart, for they shall see God" (Matt. 5:8). Noting this connection, we see that James is calling his readers to embody the beatitudes and teaching of Jesus in their community by embracing his conditions of blessedness. In this way, they again reject worldly wisdom and standards of blessedness (power, prestige, security) and follow the heavenly wisdom of Jesus by living according to the confession that the pure in heart are truly blessed—because they will surely ascend the hill of the Lord, draw near to his presence and finally see God.

James not only addresses his readers as "sinners," but also as "double-minded." This is a reference back to James 1:7-8, where James argues that the man who asks for wisdom but doubts is a "double-minded man." Just as the man who desires wisdom but is unwilling to go through the process of steadfast and joyful obedience in the midst of suffering in order to gain the wisdom he desires is also "double-minded." These Christians, who desire the righteousness of God to be made manifest in the world, are double-minded because they have rejected the way Jesus has promised all things will be restored (obedience, suffering, the power of God). Rather, they have pursued the world's assumptions regarding change and renewal (manipulation, violence, political power moves, etc.). As James says in 1:7, "That [double-minded] person must not suppose he will receive anything from the Lord."

**E.** *"Be wretched and mourn and weep. Let your laughter be turned to mourning and your joy to gloom" (verse 9).*

Having reminded his readers that they must have clean hands and pure hearts in order that they might draw near to God, James now instructs them in the ritual nature of the repentance through which they might actually be cleansed and purified. The path of repentance for these early Christians who have rebelled against Christ by embracing worldliness in their desire to bring about the promises of God in their communities and cities is simple: they must mourn their sin. Instead of self-confident laughter and triumphal joy in the seeming success of their misguided wisdom, the community to which James writes must be conformed to the teaching of Jesus and express their repentance in mourning and weeping over their foolish ways. Rejecting gladness for mourning is the typical pattern of repentance in the Hebrew Scriptures. For example, in Lamentations 5:15, Jeremiah writes after the destruction of Jerusalem, "the joy of our hearts has ceased, our dancing has been turned to mourning" as Judah realizes the extent of her rebellion against God.

But James does not command his readers to "mourn and weep" to simply prove that they are truly sorry for their sin. Their mourning is also a demonstration of their rejection of earthly wisdom (is there any posture less valued by the world than that of humiliation, mourning, and repentance?) and their allegiance to heavenly wisdom. Indeed, these Christians are called to mourn because to mourn is to live by faith according to the promises of Jesus, to live as though it really is true that "blessed are those who mourn, for they shall be comforted" (Matt. 5:4). It is a ritual enactment that Jesus in fact came to the world, "to comfort all who mourn; to grant to those who mourn in Zion—to give them a beautiful headdress instead of ashes, the oil of gladness instead of mourning, the garment of praise instead of a faint spirit; that they might be called oaks of righteousness, the planting of Yahweh, that he be glorified" (Isa. 61:2b-3).

When we mourn our sins, we are defenseless and cast ourselves wholly on the mercy and power of God. Therefore, when James commands these Christians to repent of their sins he is not only asking them to humble themselves so that God will forgive them—he also asks them to proclaim with their lives the reality that Jesus is Lord and King, able not only to forgive sins, but also to put all things to right and usher the righteousness of God into the world.

**F.** *"Humble yourselves before the Lord, and he will exalt you" (v. 10).*

James now explains the nature of the grace that God will give to the humble (cf. verse 6)—his grace is displayed in their exaltation. Significantly, James here echoes Mary's triumphant song of praise in Luke 1:52 ("He [God] has brought down the mighty from their thrones and exalted those of humble estate") as well as the words of Jesus himself, who instructed his disciples, "Whoever exalts himself will be humbled, and whoever humbles himself will be exalted" (Matt. 23:12).

Seeing this connection between humility and exaltation elsewhere in the New Testament is helpful because it shows us that this sequence (humility before exaltation) is a consistent theme throughout the Bible. Everywhere in the biblical narrative, faithful men and women who have endured suffering and lived in humility have been subsequently exalted by God.

Consider the story of Joseph, who was sold into slavery, then thrown into prison before he was raised up to a position of power and influence in Egypt and exalted over his brothers. Or consider Moses, who ran for his life from Egypt and wandered in the wilderness forty years before Yahweh appeared to him in the burning bush and established him as the leader of Israel. Or David, who fled from Saul for many years before being made king of God's people. Or especially, Jesus himself, who endured the threats and accusations of his enemies and finally suffered death at their hands before being exalted in his resurrection and ascension to his throne in heaven at the right hand of God.

By commending humility to his readers, James is not only showing them the path of repentance and restoration to God's presence. He also is inviting them to follow the pattern of biblical maturity and righteousness by living humbly and trusting that God will exalt them. In the context of the exiled Christians to whom James writes, this means that they must confess and repent of their sins, but it also means that they must reject the way of violence they have previously embraced and sow peace after the pattern of Jesus by blessing their enemies instead of cursing them and enduring suffering with steadfast joy rather than angry violence. It is remarkable how consistent this message is both in the Old and the New Testaments. If they truly desire to see the enemies of God humbled they will follow the instruction that will later be described by the apostle Paul:

> Bless those who persecute you; bless and do not curse them. Rejoice with those who rejoice, weep with those who weep. Live in harmony with one another. Do not be haughty, but associate with the lowly Never be wise in your own sight. Repay no one evil for evil, but give thought to do what is honorable in the sight of all. If possible, so far as it depends on you, live peaceably with all. Beloved, never avenge yourselves, but leave it to the wrath of God, for it is written, "Vengeance is mine, I will repay, says the Lord." To the contrary, "if your enemy is hungry, feed him; if he is thirsty, give him something to drink; for by so doing you will heap burning coals on his head." Do not be overcome by evil, but overcome evil with good (Rom. 12:14-21).

## THE PERILS OF HASTY JUDGMENTS

*James 4:11-12*

[11]Do not speak evil against one another, brothers. The one who speaks against a brother or judges his brother, speaks evil against the law and judges the law. But if you judge the law,

you are not a doer of the law but a judge. ¹²There is only one lawgiver and judge, he who is able to save and to destroy. But who are you to judge your neighbor?

Having rebuked his readers for their adulterous affinity for earthly wisdom and worldliness in 4:1-5 and shown them the way of repentance in 4:6-10, James now instructs them in how they must now live in light of that repentance. Instead of relying on angry rhetoric and zealotry to accomplish their desires, James's readers should bite their tongues and put their trust in Jesus to bring about the justice and peace for which they long. Instead of grasping after security and comfort and an end to the persecution that has come against them, they must be content to wait for God's timing in bringing about his righteousness in their world.

In verse 11a, James instructs his readers, "Do not speak evil against one another, brothers." James prohibits evil speech in this community of Christians because they have lately been dominated by "quarrels" and "fights" (4:1). Though we do not know the exact nature of these quarrels, we may surmise that it is likely that they have to do with whether to follow earthly or heavenly wisdom in response to the persecution against them (3:15). In other words, the community was apparently so divided over whether to use subversive measures against their oppressors that even their congregation has become disorderly and troubled within itself. In response to this conflict, James forbids them to speak evil against one another, gently reminding them of his admonitions regarding the tongue in 3:1-12. Because the whole community is guided by the words that are exchanged within it, James rightly understands that lasting repentance will come for these churches only when their speech is reformed. This reading, of course, fits nicely with the overall message of James about the power of the tongue.

After his command ("Do not speak evil against one another…") James goes on to explain further the reason for his exhortation, writing, "The one who speaks against a brother or judges his brother, speaks evil against the law and judges the law. But if you judge the law, you are not a doer of the law but a judge" (11b). To speak evil against another member of the covenant community is to set oneself up as a judge—one who has the authority to determine and administer good and evil. James's logic moves in this way: 1) if you speak evil about or judge your brother you are also speaking evil against and judging the law; 2) if you judge the law, then you are no longer subject to it (that is, "a doer of the law," 1:25; 2:12) because you have set yourself over it as a judge (that is, one who applies the law by calling others good and evil). With this in mind, we should examine what James means by the terms "speak evil," "judge," since these words play such a prominent role in this verse, which in turn will help us understand verse 12.

What James means by "speak evil" is easy enough to understand in the larger context of his epistle. It means angry, intemperate speech (1:19) spoken by an unbridled tongue (1:26). To "speak evil" means to allow the fire of our tongues to burn freely against one another so that the whole community is stained and enflamed (3:6). It means to poison those we do not agree with by spewing curses at them instead of blessing and praying for them, despite the reality that they are created in the image of God (3:8-9). Perhaps one way to summarize what it is to "speak evil" in James is to say that it means to freely speak angry curses against others.

In verses 11-12, James uses the word "judge" three times as a verb and once as a noun. What does he mean by this? This is not the first time in his epistle that James has named his readers as "judges." In chapter 2, James asserts that if his readers honor and pander to the rich oppressors in their communities while ignoring the poor, then they have "become judges with evil thoughts" (James 2:4b). James also refers to judgment in 2:12-13, where he exhorts his readers to truly love their neighbors without partiality because they (who have set themselves up as judges) will be judged on the basis of the mercy they show to others.

The issue James has with his readers acting as judges in chapter 2 is that they act as though they have the authority to distinguish between men based on their own wisdom and knowledge (i.e., judging the rich to have the power to help them, they serve and pander to the rich, and judging the poor to be useless in ending their persecution, they ignore the poor). In doing this, they have assumed the role of God—a point that James brings home when he reminds his readers that they themselves will be judged one day. We may summarize that what James means by "judge" is proudly to set oneself up as an authority and execute power that one does not posses.

After admonishing his readers to cease speaking evil (that is, freely using their tongue to speak angry curses against one another), James goes to explain the reason for this command, writing, "The one who speaks evil against a brother or judges his brother speaks evil against the law and judges the law." Clearly, James considers speaking evil against a brother and judging a brother as comparable actions—which fits with his earlier usage of these terms, for to freely and angrily speak against another brother is to falsely set oneself up as an authority over him.

In doing so, James argues, such a person has actually spoken evil against and judged the law. The reason for this is at least two-fold. First, because the law has said that men and women are made in the image and likeness of God (James 3:9). To speak evil against a man or woman is to speak evil against the law, which has declared men and women as bearers of God's image and thus worthy of respect and honor. Second, because the law demands love of neighbor as self (3:8). Speaking evil against or judging (as James is using this term) other men or women in our communities is a breach of the law of love. Therefore, to speak evil against or judge a brother is to speak evil against or judge the very law of God.

James proceeds in his argument, writing, "But if you judge the law you are not a doer of the law, but a judge" (verse 11b). To judge the law in the way described by James in this passage means that you are unable also to be a doer of the law—because speaking evil against or judging a brother is a violation of the law that we are commanded to keep. If this kind of harsh and hurtful speech characterizes our lives, it is a sign that we have ceased to be a doer of the law and instead have become simply a hearer of the law that forgets what it says and does not persevere in obedience to its demands (1:25). This is a hard-hitting rebuke to these first-century Jewish Christians who have convinced themselves that their speech and actions are the epitome of faithfulness to the law of God.

In verse 12 James concludes this section of his argument, writing, "There is only one lawgiver and judge, he who is able to save and to destroy." Clearly, the one that James refers to in this verse is Jesus Christ, the Lord of Glory (2:1). He is the one who is able to save and to destroy, the one that will one day judge without mercy those who refuse to be doers of the law and withhold mercy from others by showing partiality in their dealings with the rich and poor (2:1-7), ignoring those who are in need (2:15-16), failing to bridle their tongues and cursing other men who are made in God's image (3:1-12), and use disorder and evil practice to protect themselves against their oppressors (3:16). Just as in 2:12-13 and 3:1, James locates the grounds for his readers' obedience to his exhortations squarely in the promise of the future judgment of Jesus. It is because Jesus is Lord and King that we listen to and obey his words. As the apostle Paul says elsewhere, "we must all appear before the judgment seat of Christ, so that each one may receive what is due for what he has done in the body, whether good or evil" (2 Cor. 5:10).

Without the promise of a future judgment, it is possible to imagine ourselves as rightful judges of others, to see it as our responsibility to differentiate between rich and poor, to speak harsh curses against those who offend us. But because Jesus is the only judge with the power to both save and destroy, we rightly understand ourselves as the objects of judgment, not those with the power or authority to judge others. As James puts it in verse 12b, "But who are you to judge your neighbor?" contrasting the behavior of his readers with the royal law's command to "love your neighbor" (James 2:8).

Of course, there is a proper way to make judgments about other people. After all, James himself is critiquing these folks pretty severely. We should not lift strong statements like "who are you to judge your neighbor" (4:12) out of context and make them into absolute moral dictates. The context of James 3 and 4 inform us that some leaders in these communities are cursing others (3:10-12) and *irresponsibly* speaking "evil" (4:11) of others. Probably the most famously misused passage in the Gospels is our Lord's warning, "Judge not, that you be not judged" (Matt. 7:1). It is often used to squelch all criticism as somehow unchristian. But the very next verse contextualizes the maxim: "For with the judgment you pronounce you will be judged, and with the measure you use it will be measured to you." Jesus says something similar in John 7:24, "Do not judge by appearances, but judge with right judgment." James is condemning unrighteous judgments arising from our misdirected passions and desires.

## Summary & Reflections

As we reflect on the message of James's words in his letter's fourth chapter, consider how this passage fits into the overall flow of the epistle as a whole. In the first chapter of his letter, James explains the theme of his book, summarizing his thesis with these words: "Count it all joy my brothers, when you meet trials of various kinds, for you know that the testing of your faith produces steadfastness. And let steadfastness have its full effect, that you may be perfect and complete, lacking in nothing" (James 1:2-4). In the first chapter, James reiterates this main thesis (1:12), while also beginning to introduce some key themes that will reappear throughout his epistle: godly wisdom (1:5-8), the future exaltation of the humble (1:9-12), the necessity of bridling the tongue for maturity (1:19, 26), the futility of anger to achieve the righteousness of God (1:20), the necessity of faith expressing itself in works (1:22-25), and the dangers of worldliness (1:27).

In the second and third chapters, James addresses each of these themes in more detail. He first shows how the exiled Christian communities have slipped into worldliness by currying the favor of their rich inquisitors at the expense of the poor among them (2:1-7), and then explaining the necessity of true faith to be matured by obedience to the commands of Jesus (2:14-26), thereby underscoring the stark choice that stands before his readers in the midst of their persecution: worldliness or submission to Jesus. In the first part of chapter three, James considers the destructive power of the tongue and rebukes the leadership of the "brothers" for the harm it has caused in their communities (3:1-12) before returning again to the theme of the different lifestyles earthly and heavenly wisdom demand (3:13-18), again showing his readers the contrast between the way of the world and the way of Jesus.

Turning to his letter's fourth chapter, James continues to develop themes that he has introduced throughout his epistle. He rebukes his readers for how they have allowed their passions to rule them and how they have given into the worldly lie that violence and anger will bring about the peace and righteousness that they long for (1:1-4). James then shows them the way of repentance (1:5-10), and instructs them in how to live in submission to Jesus: by refusing to misjudge and speak evil against one another.

What does James's teaching in this chapter have to do with us today? At least in the Western world, there are no communities of Christians who are tempted to demonstrate their affection for worldly values by conspiring to murder their enemies. Indeed, today we face nothing like the persecution suffered by the original readers of James's epistle. Even so, that time may come, and perhaps sooner than we think. In the West, however, where Christian influence has been so beneficial for political and cultural prosperity and stability, Christians and basic Christian moral standards are increasingly marginalized. Traditional believers are being exiled from positions of leadership in government, business, and entertainment. That being the case, we should expect some believers to be tempted to "fight back" in ways that violate James's warnings.

Besides addressing the problem of worldliness, James also gives contemporary communities of Christians an outline for repentance. In this he shows us to live in a way that is consistent with the kingdom of Jesus—through confession and submission to the true king. As we purify our hearts, cleanse our hands and mourn, we will be exalted and raised to true conflict with worldly power, but now are able to rule with Christ, entering into the service and mission of Jesus. As Lesslie Newbigin writes,

> [We cannot] accept the view that the only task of the church is to provide for individuals a place in the private sector where they can enjoy an inward religious security but are not required to challenge the ideology that rules the public life of nations. The privilege of the Christian life cannot be sought apart from its responsibilities. The Christ who said, "Come unto me and I will give you rest," also said to those same disciples, "As the father sent me so I send you," and showed them the scars of his battle with the rulers of the world[36]

Given the accelerated marginalization of Christians in the modern world, some church leaders have outlined various options available to beleaguered believers who desire to see the "righteousness of God" (re)established in their communities. Though we are not currently tempted to use murder and outright violence to achieve our goals, we are still confronted with the possibility of giving ourselves over to worldly tactics in order to bring about the renewal of our society and the changes for which we long. The question of how in particular we are tempted to imitate the world changes with every generation. But from the letter of James, we can understand that we are always to resist partiality towards the rich and strong for the sake of gaining favor

---

36 Lesslie Newbigin, *Foolishness to the Greeks: The Gospel and Western Culture* (Grand Rapids: Eerdmans, 1988), 124.

with those who are powerful, reject overheated rhetoric designed to tear down our enemies (both in and outside the church) and inflame other Christians to unwise, aggressive action to achieve our ends.

These problems have plagued the church from its inception, and if our worldliness is not as obvious as that of the early church, then it is at least as insidious. The letter of Clement to the church in Corinth in the first century reminds us of the danger of escalating worldliness in Christian communities. Clement writes to the Corinthians, who have been experiencing conflict and division with these words,

> All glory and enlargement was given to you, and that which was written was fulfilled: "My loved one ate and drank and became large and fat and kicked out his heels." From this came jealousy and envy, strife and faction, persecution and disorderliness, war and captivity. And so the dishonorable rose up against the honorable, the disreputable against the reputable, the senseless against the sensible, the young against the old. For this reason, righteousness and peace are far removed, since each had abandoned the reverential awe of God and become dim-sighted in faith, failing to proceed in the ordinances of his commandments and not living according to what is appropriate in Christ. Instead, each one walks according to the desires of his evil heart, which have aroused unrighteous and impious jealousy—through which also death entered the world (The Epistle of Clement to the Corinthians, 3:1-4).

Despite the good gifts that were given the Corinthian church—the preaching of the gospel, the Scriptures themselves, the waters of baptism, and the bread and wine of the Eucharist—still they began to imitate the world around them, striving for power and giving themselves over to jealousy and envy.

Though much has changed in the centuries since these ancient letters were written, our temptations today are not that different from the ones that faced the audience of James and Clement. We are still tempted to mimic those in power, even though we ought to know better than imitate the tactics used by the ungodly to secure and maintain power. We remain attracted to the potential these seemingly effective methods offer to reform our culture according to the commands of Christ. We still wonder if the reason the wicked prosper and the righteous suffers is because it is the wisdom of the world that truly offers good things, and we slowly begin to imitate the very people we criticize.

But the kingdom of Christ is not a shadow of the kingdom of the world. Jesus did not imitate the first-century scribes, Pharisees, and chief priests. He supplanted him. The new world brought into existence by the death and resurrection of Jesus is a whole new order. His kingdom is God's new way of ordering humanity under the Lordship of Christ. Jesus exposed the mimetic rivalry and the escalation of violence in first-century Judaism by humbly submitting to death at the hands of his persecutors. And by gloriously rising from the dead his righteousness was vindicated and the pagan violence of the Jews and the Romans exposed for what it was.

> The Resurrection is not only a miracle, a prodigious transgression of natural laws. It is the spectacular sign of the entrance into the world of a power superior to violent contagion. By contrast to the latter it is a power not at all hallucinatory or deceptive. For from deceiving the disciples, it enables them to recognize what they had not recognized before and to reproach themselves for their pathetic flight in the preceding days. They acknowledge the guilt of their participation in the violent contagion that murdered their master.[37]

The epistle of James is proof that the disciples did recognize the pagan, worldly roots of the mimetic violence that had led to Jesus's death. James unmasks it. His letter is copied and distributed to the churches. They heed his wisdom. That violent system has been exposed and defeated. Early Christians embraced

---

37 Girard, *I See Satan Fall Like Lightning*, 189.

the new life in Jesus's righteous kingdom. This is our challenge today. It is not the strong and powerful who are blessed, but the meek and merciful. The old systems have been definitively torn down, and new ones thrown up in their place. Indeed, the allure of worldliness is not in its progressiveness, for it is stuck irretrievably in the past. We must come, with Jesus, into the new world he has created.

## 10

# THE PROPHET JAMES

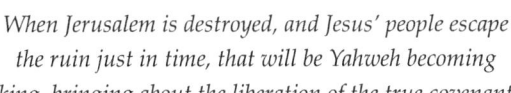

> *When Jerusalem is destroyed, and Jesus' people escape the ruin just in time, that will be Yahweh becoming king, bringing about the liberation of the true covenant people...the beginning of the new world order.*
>
> – N.T. Wright[38]

### James 4:13–5:6

<sup>4:13</sup>Come now, you who say, "Today or tomorrow we will go into such and such a town and spend a year there and trade and make a profit" — <sup>14</sup>yet you do not know what tomorrow will bring. What is your life? For you are a vapor that appears for a little time and then vanishes. <sup>15</sup>Instead you ought to say, "If the Lord wills, we will live and do this or that." <sup>16</sup>As it is, you boast in your arrogance. All such boasting is evil. <sup>17</sup>So whoever knows the right thing to do and fails to do it, for him it is sin.

<sup>5:1</sup>Come now, you rich, weep and howl for the miseries that are coming upon you. <sup>2</sup>Your riches have rotted, and your garments are moth-eaten. <sup>3</sup>Your gold and silver have corroded, and their corrosion will be evidence against you and will eat your flesh like fire. You have laid up treasure in the last days. <sup>4</sup>Behold, the wages of the laborers who mowed your fields, which you kept back by fraud, are crying out against you, and the cries

---

38 N.T. Wright, *Jesus and the Victory of God* (Minneapolis: Fortress Press, 1996), 364.

of the harvesters have reached the ears of the Lord of hosts. ⁵You have lived gloriously on the land and in self-indulgence. You have fattened your hearts in a day of slaughter. ⁶You have condemned; you have murdered the righteous person. He does not resist you.

In his letter's fourth chapter, James called the exiled Christian communities to repentance from their sin of worldliness—that is, submitting to the world's authority by living according to its maxims as they work to achieve the peace and prosperity they seek. Instead, they should follow the way of Jesus and trust in God's timing and vindication. After this strong rebuke, James described the form their repentance should take: submission to God and humility before him, patiently allowing him to exalt them. Finally, James instructed his readers again in how they must live as repentant sinners—by reforming their tongue, resisting the temptation to speak evil against one another, and refusing to boast in their own strength and wisdom (thus submitting to the authority of Jesus in their speech and rejecting the authority of the world).

Now, beginning in 4:13, James concludes his epistle with a pointed prophetic parable (4:13-17) and an announcement of severe judgment against the wicked oppressors of the church (5:1-6). Then he encourages his readers to remain patient and steadfast because of the sure promise of the coming judgment of Jesus against their enemies (5:7-12). In conclusion he gives some final practical instruction on how to live in patient trust while they wait for their vindication (5:13-20).

Remember that James is addressing Jewish Christians presently in the midst of violent and intense persecution that has driven them from Jerusalem and has put even their lives at risk. But instead of advising these young Christians to form allegiances with the rich and powerful or form communities oriented toward aggressive retribution, James has commanded them to follow in the difficult and vulnerable path of Jesus. In the midst of their persecution, James has commanded his readers to joyfully remain steadfast (1:2-4), be "slow to speak, slow to anger" (1:19), bridle their tongues (1:26), show no partiality toward those that seem to have the power to help them (2:1-7), refuse to curse their enemies (3:9), work for peace in the face of violence (3:18), and reject the worldly wisdom of attaining power as a way of preventing persecution (4:1-4).

It is not an exegetical leap to imagine that for a believer in the community that James addresses, submission to these commands would have seemed burdensome and nearly impossible in the context in which they lived. How would they possibly find the capacity and strength to walk as Jesus walked, to stop their tongues and love their enemies instead of using rhetorical and even physical violence against them? James answers this question in part by promising that they will grow in wisdom and maturity as they patiently submit to the wisdom of God (1:4-5), that the "implanted word" they received in their baptism and in the reading of God's Word in their assemblies will work its fruit in them, that as they meditate and act on the word of God, they will be blessed and strengthened (1:25), and that the presence of the Spirit within them means that God will continue his work in their lives (4:5).

But the dominant answer that James gives again and again to the question of how and why his readers should submit to the authority of Jesus and reject violence against their enemies is because Jesus himself is Messianic Lord, and he will judge and destroy those who oppose him. Throughout his epistle, James has often used this theme of Jesus's judgment to compel obedience in his readers to his commands because they themselves will be judged (2:12-13; 3:1; 4:12), but now at the end of chapter four and the beginning of chapter five, James draws out the ethical consequences of Jesus's judgment—warning their oppressors of their arrogance and calling them to repentance (4:13-17) and reassuring his readers that they are able to patiently remain steadfast in their suffering because Jesus has promised to destroy their enemies (5:1-7).

## The Parable of the Traveling Merchants

*James 4:13-17*

<sup>13</sup>Come now, you who say, "Today or tomorrow we will go into such and such a town and spend a year there and trade and make a profit" — <sup>14</sup>yet you do not know what tomorrow will bring. What is your life? For you are a mist that appears for a little time and then vanishes. <sup>15</sup>Instead you ought to say, "If the Lord wills, we will live and do this or that." <sup>16</sup>As it is, you boast in your arrogance. All such boasting is evil. <sup>17</sup>So whoever knows the right thing to do and fails to do it, for him it is sin.

There are two options available to us when we seek to understand the meaning of this passage. The first is to see it connected in some way with what James has written in 4:1-12. The "come now" exhortation would then be understood as applying to traveling Christian merchants among the exiled Christian communities. This reading has James instructing his hearers on how they must live out their repentance in ordinary business endeavors. Just as some in the community James addresses were tempted to grasp power and security for themselves through political machinations and even violence, so also some were tempted to create stability for themselves by shrewd business planning and trading. Some form of this interpretation has been adopted by most commentators. In addition, most have also understood the prophetic warning against "the rich" in 5:1-7 to be directed at Christian land- or plantation-owners who were mistreating their laborers.

I believe there is another, better interpretation of these two connected paragraphs (4:13-17; 5:1-6), one that I think fits more closely with the overall theme of the epistle as whole. And since this epistle is "wisdom literature" it is fitting that James closes his incisive rebukes in chapter four with a "dark saying," that is, a parable. The wisdom literature of the Hebrew Scriptures is full of parabolic "riddles" that require some careful deciphering in order to understand the thrust of the intended message. And the prophets often propound parables (*mashalim*) as the rhetoric of judgment. Job's final speech (Job 26-31) is cast in the form of a parable to minister judgment against his three accusers. Jotam, the youngest of Gideon's sons, and the only survivor of Abimelech's murderous coup, declaims a parable from Mt. Gerizim, against his bastard brother—the parable of the trees (Judg. 9). Jotham does not speak plainly, but craftily as a judgment against Abimelech. Nathan the prophet is sent by the Lord to rebuke David after his adulterous affair with Bathsheba. The first words out of his mouth are the parable of the ewe lamb (2 Sam. 12:1ff.). Without any explanation David understands it to refer to someone else. The parable has masked the truth. Nathan must speak plainly: you are the man! The prophet Isaiah sings a parable to the people of Israel, one his most famous, the parable of the Vineyard (Isa. 5). It is spoken in righteous indignation as a judgment against Israel. These are just a few examples of how parables (*mashalim*) are used as the rhetoric of judgment in the Hebrew Scriptures (cf. Ezek. 17:1-24; Mic. 2:3-4).

Jesus also uses parables as dark sayings designed to confound the foolish. Quoting Isaiah 6:9-10, Jesus explains to his disciples:

> To you has been given the secret of the kingdom of God, but for those outside everything is in parables, so that they may indeed see but not perceive, and may indeed hear but not understand, lest they should turn and be forgiven (Mark 4:11-12).

Stop and remember that even the disciples were baffled by the parables. Jesus's use of parables is much more complex than what is commonly taught today—that he was artfully adopting his teaching by using quaint and recognizable imagery so that people would understand him better. No. The parable was a literary medium of judgment, the grammar of God's wrath against his obstinate people. Parables are propounded to people that deserve his judicial blinding. Parables hide as much as they illustrate.

And unless one is predisposed to search out and understand the meaning and unless you are graciously enlightened by God, as the disciples eventually were, the parables will serve as a judgment against you.

This particular parable in James 4:13-17 should be interpreted as an incisive warning directed against the arrogant, rich Jewish oppressors headquartered in Jerusalem. If that is the case, then James is warning against the hubris involved in their traveling "business ventures"—that is, their pursuit of Christian converts, their "travel across sea and land to make a single proselyte" (Matt. 23:15). Unfortunately, the connection between the "traveling merchants" at the end of chapter four and the "rich" at the beginning of chapter five is obscured in our English Bibles because of an infelicitous chapter break at the end of this parable. But this paragraph at the end of James 4 commences the "prophetic denunciations" James continues in his letter's fifth chapter. Both 4:13 and 5:1 begin with "come now" and are best understood as pointed squarely at apostate Jewish oppressors, which would be comforting to these beleaguered Christian exiles. Comforting to be sure, but also a warning to the Christian zealots that mimicking their tormentors will result in judgment for them as well.

Doing "business"—buying and selling, trading and commerce—is often used in Scripture as a metaphor for "spiritual commerce," if you will. Quite a few of Jesus's parables make use of economic transactions to deliver penetrating messages about the coming kingdom.

> "The kingdom of heaven may be compared to a king who wished to settle accounts with his servants" (Matt. 18:23).

> "The kingdom of heaven is like a master of a house who went out early in the morning to hire laborers in his vineyard. After agreeing with the laborers for a denarius a day, he sent them into his vineyard" (Matt. 20:1-2).

"Hear another parable. There was a master of a house who planted a vineyard and put a fence around it and dug a winepress in it and built a tower and leased it to tenants and went into another country" (Matt. 21:33).

"Woe to you, scribes and Pharisees, hypocrites! For you travel across sea and land to make a single proselyte, and when he becomes a proselyte, you make him twice as much a child of hell as yourselves" (Matt. 23:15).

"So it will be like a man going on a journey, who called his servants and entrusted them with his property" (Matt. 25:14).

"There was a rich man who had a steward and charges were brought to him that this man was wasting his possessions" (Luke 16:1).

These examples are just a sample of Jesus's parables using economic relations to communicate his displeasure with the way the Jewish leaders had mishandled the "wealth" given to them. Parabolic rhetoric like this is also used freely by Jesus and John in Revelation.

To the church in Laodicea: "For you say, I am rich, I have prospered, and I need nothing, not realizing that you are wretched, pitiable, poor, blind, and naked. I counsel you to buy from me gold refined by fire, so that you may be rich . . ." (Rev. 3:15).

The sea beast requires a mark "so that no one can buy or sell unless he has the mark. . . . This calls for wisdom" (Rev. 13:16-18).

The condemnation of "Bablyon the great" (which is apostate Israel) includes this indictment: ". . . the kings of the earth have committed immorality with her, and the merchants of the land have grown rich from the power of her luxurious living" (Rev. 18:1-3).

> One of the lamentations for fallen Jerusalem is that "the merchants of the earth weep and mourn for her, since no one buys their cargo of gold, silver, jewels, pearls . . . . that is, human souls" (Rev. 18:11-13).

That interpretive comment at the end of Revelation 18:13 tells us that these merchants are not being condemned for unjust business practices (although that was surely involved), but rather, their condemnation has to do with squandering the theocratic wealth the Lord had given them for service among the nations. It's not about monetary transactions per se, but about "human souls."

These passages ought to be enough to alert us to the parable-like nature of James's warning to the "traveling merchants" in James 4:13-17. He is addressing the faithless Jewish authorities that are pursuing exiled Christians from city to city, doing what they thought was their spiritual business—to eradicate what they considered a new departure from Judaism. The Pharisee Saul was not the only deputized inquisitor that was sent out from the Sanhedrin "ravaging the church, and entering house after house, dragging off men and women and committing them to prison" (Acts 8:3). His travels are highlighted because of his later conversion. But he was surely one of many who were being authorized by "the high priest" with letters to the various synagogues in city after city to bring "any belonging to the Way, men and women, bound to Jerusalem" (Acts 9:1-2). After Saul's conversion, interrogators were being sent from Jerusalem, traveling from city to city, seeking to undermine Saul's ministry (Acts 9:23). This program of interrogation and even extermination began with the banishment of the Jewish converts from Jerusalem after the martyrdom of Stephen (Acts 8:1; 11:19) and only increased in severity as the Christian church expanded and grew. These "apostles" from Jerusalem are what we now call "Judaizers," because their mission, their business, was to re-incorporate these new disciples of Jesus back into the community of apostate Judaism (1 Thess. 2:14-16; 2 Cor. 11:5).

Again, this narrative of the traveling Jewish persecutors of the church situates James's parable such that we can discern its deeper meaning. The arrogance of the early church's oppressors is highlighted. They fail to understand that they are "vapor" and will shortly disappear (4:14), blown away by the judgment of the Lord (James 5:1-6). He cautions them to reflect on whether their business has the Lord's approval or not. They appear to be oblivious to the arrogance of their endeavors so that they "boast [glory] in their hubris" (4:16). Such haughtiness is evil. Having heard the Gospel of Jesus's Lordship, they know what is right, but they refuse to heed the Lord's call and so are guilty of heinous sin (4:17).

Why is this parable placed here in James's epistle? There are at least two reasons. The first is to give these oppressed Christian exiles some hope. They need to have some confidence that James understands, that the Lord understands, the kinds of people that are harassing them. This is especially necessary in the light of their own frustration and failed attempts to bring justice to bear on the haughty, powerful enemies of the church. James has told them to cease and desist meeting the violence of their persecutors with violent action of their own. But they need to have some assurance that James understands how arrogant their persecutors are and that God will hold them accountable for their sin.

Verse 17 is a segue into the first paragraph of James 5 and the promise of the coming judgment. "Whoever knows the right thing to do and fails to do it is sin." We might ask if these Jewish zealots really know what they are doing? On the cross Jesus prayed to his Father, "forgive them for they know not what they do" (Luke 23:34). At that time the Jewish leaders only had the testimony of Jesus. That should have been enough to establish their culpability. But the Lord determined to be gracious and give them a second witness, the coming of the Holy Spirit speaking through the apostolic proclamation of Jesus's Messianic vindication in his resurrection and ascension. According to the early chapters of Acts, we know that many thousands of Jews repented and believed the Gospel, even many among the priests in Jerusalem

(Acts 2:41, 47; 4:4; 6:7). This testimony of two witnesses (Deut. 17:6)—Jesus's three-year ministry and the Spirit's testimony through the apostles—left those that refused to repent without excuse. Peter and John (Acts 4) and later Peter and all the apostles stood before the Jerusalem elders and proclaimed to them the truth of Jesus's Messianic identity (Acts 5). In his first appearance before the Jewish leaders Peter even said to them, "I know that you acted in ignorance" (Acts 3:17). But he was speaking of a time before the resurrection, before the coming of the Spirit. This fits with what Jesus says about the blasphemy against the Holy Spirit:

> For everyone who speaks a word against the Son of Man will be forgiven, but the one who blasphemes against the Holy Spirit will not be forgiven. And when they bring you before the synagogues and the rulers and the authorities, do not be anxious about how you should defend yourself or what you should say, for the Holy Spirit will teach you in that very hour what you ought to say" (Luke 12:10-12).
>
> Then Peter, filled with the Holy Spirit, said to them, "Rulers of the people and elders. . ." (Acts 4:8).

Therefore, after the apostolic testimony to the Jewish authorities they could no longer claim ignorance or a lack of sufficient evidence. They were now guilty of "blasphemy against the Holy Spirit," according to Jesus, an unforgivable sin.

But there is another, a second reason why this parable is here. By exposing the evil traveling merchants from Jerusalem, James also warns the Christian zealots against mimicking the same sort of behavior that their pursuers are engaged in against them. As we have seen throughout this epistle, angry Christian leaders were attempting to right things by aggressive, violent action against their enemies. This kind of mimetic rivalry is endemic to social conflicts in a fallen world. It is precisely what Jesus warned his disciples against when he said, "Beware the leaven of the Scribes and the Pharisees" (Matt. 16:6, 11, 12). He was training a new kind of leadership so that no one in his new kingdom would say something like, "Meet the new boss, same as the old boss." The righteousness of Christian leaders had "to exceed the righteousness of the scribes and Pharisees" (Matt. 5:20). For the leadership of Jesus's kingdom here was no place for pride and arrogance, for ruling as the Gentiles (Matt. 20:20-28; Mark 10:35-44): "Whoever would be great among you must be your servant."

In other words, Jesus's followers had to adopt a different form of leadership than both Rome and Judaism. First-century Jewish leaders were mimetic rivals with Rome. They hated Rome, but they loved and coveted Rome's power. They wanted the power that Rome possessed, and they thought that acting like Rome was the way to achieve it. This is one of the chief reasons the Jewish authorities would not recognize Jesus as the promised Messiah. They thought their Messiah would rule "as those who are considered rulers of the Gentiles" but Jesus solemnly informed his disciples, "It shall not be so among you" (Matt. 20:26). Throughout this epistle James has been imploring them to follow a better way, to pick up their cross and follow Jesus.

## The Coming Judgment

*James 5:1-6*

¹Come now, you rich, weep and howl for the miseries that are coming upon you. ²Your riches have rotted and your garments are moth-eaten. ³Your gold and silver have corroded and their corrosion will be evidence against you and will eat your flesh like fire. You have laid up treasure in the last days. ⁴Behold, the wages of the laborers who mowed your fields, which you kept back by fraud, are crying out against you, and the cries of the harvesters have reached the ears of the Lord of hosts. ⁵You have lived on the earth in luxury and in self-indulgence. You have fattened your hearts in a day of slaughter. ⁶You have condemned; you have murdered the righteous person. He does not resist you.

The initial exegetical question we need to answer as we consider this passage is the identity of the "rich" that James addresses in 5:1-6. James has already referred to the "rich" in two other places in his epistle and considering the identity of those references will enable us to understand to whom he refers in chapter five.

The first time James refers to the rich in his letter is in 1:9-11, where he writes that the rich, "like a flower of the grass…will pass away…so also will the rich man fade away in the midst of his pursuits." In his epistle's second chapter, James refers again to the rich, chastising his readers for deferring to the rich at the expense of the poor. The rich man who walks into their assembly has the ring and robe of authority (2:2). James leaves little doubt that these are their powerful enemies. "Are not the rich the ones who oppress you, and the ones who drag you into court? Are they not the ones who blaspheme the honorable name which was invoked over you?" (2:6-7). Currying favor with them with the hope of moderating their opposition is foolish. God has not chosen these rich apostate Jewish rulers. Rather, he has "chosen those who are poor in the world to be rich in faith and heirs of the kingdom" (2:5).

From these two references earlier in James's epistle, we see James's depiction of the "rich" as those who are engaged in persecuting and oppressing his readers. His polemic is not against all of the wealthy and powerful, but only to those that are using their wealth and power to do violence against the followers of Jesus. In his letter's fifth chapter, James gives no indication that he refers to a different kind of rich person than he has already spoken of earlier in his letter. Therefore, it is best to assume that the rich addressed in 5:1-6 are the same rich referred to in 1:9-11 and 2:6-7. Indeed, we might understand 5:1-6 as describing the manner in which the rich man will "pass away" as described in 1:9, thus bookending the prophecy of James 1. Recall the chiastic structure of the letter and how C and C' are related:

A. 1:2-8 - Trials, Faith, Steadfastness
 B. 1:9-27 - Suffering, Patience, Piety
  **C. 2:1-7 – The Rich and "the Poor Man"**
   D. 2:8-13 - Love, Liberty, & Mercy
    E. 2:14-26 - Justification & Works
     F. 3:1-12 - The Teacher's Tongue
    E' 3:13-18 - Wisdom & Works
   D' 4:1-12 – Enmity, Adultery, & Pride
  **C' 4:13-5:6 – The Rich & "the Righteous One"**
 B' 5:7-18 - Suffering, Patience, & Fruit
A' 5:19-21 - Wandering, Sin, Death

Given the overall context of James's epistle, and the description of the persecution of the early church after the death of Stephen in Acts 8, we may also assume that the rich oppressors James cries out against in James 5:1-6 are the Jewish authorities in Jerusalem who have set themselves against his readers because of their allegiance to Jesus (the "honorable name" that the rich blaspheme; 2:7). These are the rich rulers who have "condemned and murdered the righteous one" (5:6). The identity of the "righteous one" may be ambiguous. Is it Jesus or his followers? But in either case, that statement can hardly refer to simply rich landowners in Judea or to wealthy Christian plantation owners. James is prophesying judgment against their Jewish oppressors headquartered in Jerusalem.

Having established the most likely identity of the "rich" in James 5:1-6 as wealthy Jewish oppressors of the Christian readers of James's epistle, what does James say to them? James writes, "Come now, you rich, weep and howl for the miseries that are coming upon you" (5:1). Consider the sheer audacity of these words in their original context. At the time that he penned this letter, James was hiding in Jerusalem with the rest of the apostles, attempting somehow to shepherd the new and growing group of baptized followers of Jesus over whom they had been given care.

The vast majority (perhaps all) of these followers of Jesus were Jewish converts who had left behind Judaism and were proclaiming that the resurrection of Jesus meant that he was indeed Messiah and Lord. After the murder of Stephen, however, these Christians were exiled from Jerusalem and were now suffering through violent persecution at the hands of the wealthy and powerful Jews. Though it may be hard to believe in today's world where the Christian church is strong and powerful, at that time the Jews had all the power, and they were exercising every ounce of it against this new heresy that they understood as a threat to their own religion. These Christians' only hope was that Rome would step in to protect them, and Rome seemed to show no interest in doing so.

And yet, during this terrible situation where the future existence of the Christian church appeared to be in doubt because it faced the very real possibility of being exterminated and intimidated into apostasy and non-existence, James shamelessly prophesies not only that the church will indeed survive, but also that their oppressors will be destroyed. Only one thing could compel James to make such an unlikely prophetic declaration—the conviction that Jesus was indeed raised from the dead and that his prediction of the destruction of Jerusalem would come about as he promised.

James calls on the Jewish oppressors to "weep and howl" for the misery and hardship that is about to fall upon them. This manner of commanding a people to wail and mourn for the judgment of God that they are about to experience is typical Old Testament prophetic language. For example, in Isaiah's oracles against the nations that will soon feel the brunt of God's judgment, he tells Babylon, "Wail, for the day of the Yahweh is near; as destruction from the Almighty it will come!" (Isa. 13:6), and to Philistia, he says, "Wail, O gate; cry out, O city; melt in fear, O Philistia, all of you!" (Isa. 14:31). He employs similar language in addressing Moab (Isa. 15:2-3; 16:7) and Tyre (Isa. 23:1,6).

What is significant about James's use of Isaiah is that when Isaiah used this kind of language, he directed it against gentile nations who had set themselves against Yahweh. James uses the same kind of language, but now it is directed against Israel herself—because Israel has now become the one that is set against Yahweh revealed in the incarnate Son.

James's words in James 5:1-6 have a double purpose. On the one hand, he is calling upon the Jewish oppressors of the church to repent of their persecution of God's new people and to turn to trust in Jesus, just as Saul later would do (cf. Acts 9). James is setting before the Jews a choice between two alternatives: repentance or destruction. Just as the Christians James addresses must repent of their worldliness, so also the Jewish oppressors must "be wretched and mourn and weep" (James 4:9) and thus repent and leave behind their wickedness.

But James is undeniably addressing his Christian readers here as well. In his prophecy against their Jewish oppressors, James gives his church a concrete hope of the vindication they will soon experience. Their suffering is not in vain, and it is not pointless. Rather, like Jesus who was vindicated before his enemies in his resurrection from the dead, these early Christians who now experience persecution and suffering because of Christ will receive protection and deliverance from Jesus himself when he judges the Jewish nation for their apostasy and rebellion against him and his people. Ultimately, because of this hope, those who now suffer should find the strength to endure.

James continues to call the rich oppressors of his church to repentance in verses 2-3: "Your riches have rotted and your garments are moth-eaten. Your gold and silver have corroded, and their corrosion will be evidence against you and will eat your flesh like fire. You have laid up your treasure in the last days." In these phrases James again echoes the words of the prophet Isaiah, who, speaking in the voice of the suffering servant, compared the fate of his enemies with that of a moth-eaten garment: "Behold, Master Yahweh helps me; who will declare me guilty? Behold all of them will wear out like a garment, the moth will eat them up" (Isa.

50:9). Thus James shows his readers (as well as their oppressors) that they are following in the path of Jesus, the suffering servant prophesied by Isaiah, for like Jesus, their enemies will also fade away like a garment eaten up by moths.

Likewise James's words also point back to Isaiah 51:7-8, where Yahweh exhorts Israel to faithfully pursue righteousness by assuring them of the destruction of their oppressors, and speaking through the prophet Isaiah, says, "Listen to me, you who know righteousness, the people in whose heart is my law; fear not the reproach of man, nor be dismayed at their revilings. For the moth will eat them up like a garment, and the worm will eat them like wool; but my righteousness will be forever, and my salvation to all generations." By prophesying that the oppressors of the followers of Jesus are clothed in moth-eaten garments, James reveals that these exiled believers have become the new and true Israel. The promises of the Hebrew prophets apply to them, not to the Jews who have rejected Jesus. This is a striking rebuke to the persecutors of the church, who now share the same fate as those who troubled the righteous remnant in Israel in times past. James's words reiterate Jesus's own prophetic denunciation of the Jewish authorities:

> Woe to you, scribes and Pharisees, hypocrites! For you build the tombs of the prophets and decorate the monuments of the righteous, saying, "If we had lived in the days of our fathers, we would not have taken part with them in shedding the blood of the prophets." Thus you witness against yourselves that you are sons of those who murdered the prophets. Fill up, then, the measure of your fathers. You serpents, you brood of vipers, how are you to escape being sentenced to hell? Therefore I send you prophets and wise men and scribes, some of whom you will kill and crucify, and some you will flog in your synagogues and persecute from town to town, so that on you may come all the righteous blood shed on earth, from the blood of innocent Abel to the blood of Zechariah the son of Barachiah, whom you murdered between the sanctuary and the altar. Truly, I say to you, all these things will come upon this generation (Matt. 23:29-36).

## The Prophet James

Why is it that these miseries are coming down upon apostate Israel? Against the command of Jesus (Matt. 6:19-21) they have hoarded, for their own use and benefit, the physical and spiritual treasure they have been given. Instead of sharing the riches that God has given them and acting in obedience to the Father of lights by themselves being lights to the world, Israel opposed God's Son throughout his ministry, and now opposes his followers, even as they give themselves for life of the world.

Israel was called as a nation so that through them, "all the families of the earth shall be blessed" (Gen. 12:3). But in these last days, Israel has loved power and prominence over service and suffering. As Jesus taught the crowds and his disciples regarding the leaders of Israel, "They tie up heavy burdens, hard to bear, and lay them on people's shoulder, but they themselves are not willing to move them with their finger. They do all their deeds to be seen by others. For they make their phylacteries broad and their fringes long, and they love the places of honor at feasts and the best seats in the synagogues…[but] the greatest among you shall be your servant" (Matt. 23:4-6, 11). Because Israel has forgotten that she exists for the sake of the world, rather than the world for the sake of her, misery is coming upon her. The rust and corrosion of her stored-up riches testify against her, and as Jesus prophesied, the location of Israel's treasure has revealed the location of her heart—it is on earth rather than in heaven.

Jesus's prophetic critique of the lust of Israel's leaders for wealth and power is expanded when he warns the crowds against the scribes: "Beware of the scribes, who like to walk around in long robes and like greetings in the marketplaces and have the best seats in the synagogues and the places of honor at feasts, who devour widows' houses and for a pretense make long prayers. They will receive the greater condemnation" (Mark 12:38-40). As Jesus points out, Israel has come to love her great garments and her gold above all things (cf. Matt. 23:16-22), and even thinks that her increasing power and wealth is evidence of God's favor upon her, begetting even more lust for these things. These "garments" or "robes" are those that are worn by the high priests and the priests in the Temple. They are also the robes that the scribes, Pharisees, and other Jewish authorities love to wear as they strut around Jerusalem. The reference to "gold and silver" cannot but bring to mind the location of huge amounts of gold and silver—the Temple. Although some plantation owners and merchants surely possess some gold and silver, such holdings are nothing compared to the way the Temple is adorned with these precious metals. All the language here—robes, gold, silver, treasure, living gloriously on the land—confirms that James is speaking of the wealth given to the Jews. They are the theocratically, covenantally rich that are being addressed in this passage.

James turns the tables on Israel, arguing that in fact these signs of wealth and power, rather than functioning as public displays of God's blessing on their nation, are actually evidence against Israel's covetousness and wickedness and the corruption of their material riches will spread into their own bodies, eating their flesh like fire—an image that recalls Jesus's description of hell as the place where the "worm does not die and the fire is not quenched" (Mark 9:48).

But Israel will be judged by God not only because of the way she has lusted after power and hoarded wealth and riches for her own benefit. James continues to prophesy against Israel, writing, "Behold, the wages of the laborers who mowed your fields, which you kept back by fraud, are crying out against you, and the cries of the harvesters have reached the ears of the Lord of hosts. You have lived on the earth in luxury and in self-indulgence. You have fattened your hearts in a day of slaughter. You have condemned; you have murdered the righteous person. He does not resist you" (James 5:4-6).

The obvious question that comes to mind when reading this is the identity of the laborers and the harvesters who cry out against the rich oppressors. Though of course there is a sense in which these warnings may refer simply to economic injustice in Israel and the laborers and harvesters might be physical workers who are denied fair wages (and these warnings certainly apply to the plight of oppressed workers in our contemporary context), it is much more likely that the laborers James describes are those who work for a spiritual harvest (a connection made by Paul in 1 Cor. 3:6-9).

Jesus himself used this kind of language to describe those who would minister in his name to Israel. As Matthew tells us, "When [Jesus] saw the crowds, he had compassion for them, because they were harassed and helpless, like sheep without a shepherd. Then he said to his disciples, 'The harvest is plentiful, but the laborers are few; therefore pray earnestly to the Lord of the harvest to send out laborers into his harvest'" (Matt. 9:36-38, cf. Luke 10:2). Jesus makes this connection between the work of the disciples and harvesting fields even more explicit when he teaches them in the gospel of John, "Do you not say, 'There are yet four months, then comes the harvest'? Look, I tell you, lift up your eyes, and see that the fields are white for harvest. Already the one who reaps is receiving wages and gathering fruit for eternal life, so that sower and reaper may rejoice together" (John 4:35-36). It is the cries of *these* laborers, *these* harvesters, the apostles and prophets of the book of Acts, that reaches the ears of the Lord of Armies. John Peter Lange's comment on James 5:4 is worth reading:

> This denotes that Israel at this time has become ripe unto harvest; on the one hand unto the harvest of judgment; on the other, unto the harvest of salvation. The latter idea predominates here. The harvest of Israel was the ripened spirit-produce of the Old Testament, as manifested in the work of Christ; in the reapers we may aptly see the Apostles (according to Jn 4:35) and the first Christians in general. From them the rich in Israel kept back their wages in that they rejected their testimony in unbelief. And thus the voices of those reapers cried into the ears of the Lord of hosts, in other words, their sin against them cried out to God, even to God, the Lord of those hosts which were already on the point of approaching in order to execute the judgment of God on Israel.[39]

---

39 John Peter Lange, *A Commentary on the Holy Scriptures: James*, trans. Philip Schaff (New York: Scribner, 1884), 120.

Given the way Jesus uses the language of harvest and laborers to describe the work of his followers, it is abundantly clear that the laborers and harvesters James refers to in verse 4 are the apostles as well as the readers of his epistle. Because the church preached the gospel of Jesus in Jerusalem after the day of Pentecost, the Jews killed Stephen and began to persecute those who believed in Jesus, driving them out of the city and into exile. But they did not cease from preaching the gospel even in their exile from Jerusalem. As Luke records in Acts 11:19-21, "those who were scattered because of the persecution that arose over Stephen traveled as far as Phoenicia and Cyprus and Antioch, speaking the word to no one except Jews. But there were some of them, men of Cyprus and Cyrene, who on coming to Antioch, spoke to the Hellenists also, preaching the Lord Jesus. And the hand of the Lord was with them, and a great number who believed turned to the Lord." The Christians to whom James writes are the laborers and harvesters whose wages have been held back by the rich, they have been defrauded and oppressed, and are now crying out to the Lord of Hosts.

In writing that the voices of the persecuted Church are joining together to cry out to the Lord, James affirms the reality of the suffering of his readers and recognizes their need for deliverance. His epistle is not simply an exhortation for these Christians to suffer endlessly without purpose, but rather to show his readers that their suffering is meaningful and seen by their Father in heaven. Throughout the Old Testament, God's people would cry out to the Lord in the midst of their oppression and again and again God heard their cries and delivered them (cf. Gen. 4:10, Exod. 2:23, Judg. 3:9, etc.). For James to prophesy that the cries of the oppressed Christians "have reached the ears of the Lord of hosts" is to put the Christians in the place of God's people and Jews, in the place of God's enemies. In an ironic twist, the historically oppressed have now become the oppressors, and those who follow Jesus are, in James's prophecy, the new and true Israel.

## The Prophet James

Understanding the radical nature of James's prophecy helps us to see the great comfort his readers would have gained from his words—for they now are given the freedom to understand their current oppression as following in a coherent narrative of the historic suffering of the people of God, and a renewed trust to believe that Jesus, whom they serve, is the same God who delivered Israel from the oppression of Egypt, Midian, Philistia and Babylon, and that they also will experience the salvation of God's judgment. In the same manner, understanding the meaning of James's words here also helps us to see exactly why the followers of Jesus threatened the power and status of the rulers of Israel—because the totality of the claims of the Church was that they in fact were the remnant of faithful Israel, and those that rejected Jesus had rejected their own history and their own right to be called the people of God.

The primary reason that the wrath of God has now turned against the rich Jewish oppressors of the Christians is because they have killed Jesus. As attested by Stephen (Acts 7:52), Jesus is the "righteous person" whom the Jews condemned and murdered, even though he offered no resistance against them (5:6). Now the Jews persecute in the same way the followers of Jesus, condemning and murdering them as well, even as they walk in the way of Jesus in patience and longsuffering. And thus this Israelite generation fulfills the prophecy of Jesus, who said to the Jewish leaders shortly before his own death, "I send you prophets and wise men and scribes, some of whom you will kill and crucify, and some you will flog in your synagogues and persecute from town to town, so that on you may come all the righteous blood shed on earth, from the blood of innocent Abel to the blood of Zechariah the son of Barachiah, whom you murdered between the sanctuary and the altar" (Matt. 23:34-35).

Because the Jews have set themselves against Jesus, and now against his followers, because they have remained steadfast in their rebellion and their wickedness, they have "lived on the land in luxury and in self-indulgence," and they have "fattened [their] hearts in a day of slaughter." In less than forty years, the slaughter prophesied by James here will come upon the Jews, when Roman soldiers will march into Jerusalem and burn the city, destroying the temple and effectively destroying the Jewish nation. In the events of A.D. 70, not only was Jesus's prophetic ministry validated (Matt. 24), but the followers of Jesus were also vindicated, because in that event God acted in strength to destroy their oppressors and save his people from their suffering.

## Summary & Reflections

The two "come now" invitations give the oppressors an opportunity to repent and seek forgiveness before it is too late. The parable of the traveling merchants exposes their hubris and invites them to reflect on whether their "business" has approval of the Lord. They may boast about their righteous zeal, but James challenges them to do the right thing. They cannot plead ignorance.

The message of James 5:1-6 is that judgment and destruction are coming against the powerful and rich Jewish oppressors of the church, because they have violently killed and persecuted both Jesus and his followers, and so James's readers, who are now experiencing this persecution should take heart and look forward to the vindication of Jesus's prophecies in the destruction of their enemies. The glorious, enriched Temple will be torn down and those who have lived "gloriously on the land" will be destroyed.

Although Christians reject the idea that there can be any "poetic justice"—that all wrongs will be righted in this life—we nevertheless don't jettison all hope for some measure of justice in history. Of course, we confess that at the Last Day there will be a final judgment when the Lord adjudicates every historical event and every person who has ever lived (Matt. 25:31-46; John 5:27-29; Acts 25:24; Rom. 2:5-11; Heb. 9:27; 10:27; Rev. 20:11-15). That should provide us with a great deal of comfort, especially when we think of how many evil people seem to skate through life without experiencing any negative consequences for their immoral acts (Ps. 73). But can we expect God also to judge tyrannical nations and malevolent movements in history?

Shouldn't the answer to that question be obvious when we examine biblical history? Repeatedly we find God not just meting out justice to individuals, but also to "nations," "cities," and "peoples." He *acts* in history to bring down despotic, immoral governments—Egypt, the Canaanites, Moab, Edom, Philistia, Tyre, Sidon, Ammon, Syria, Assyria, Babylon, Persia, Rome, and Jerusalem, to name a few. The Lord is involved in the affairs of nations. He is not the detached Being of the philosophers or just a Big Idea that serves to comfort religiously inclined people. Yahweh is the "Lord of Hosts/Armies" (Isa. 1:24) and the incarnate Yahweh is now the "Lord of Lords and King of Kings" (Rev. 17:14; 19:16).

The recipients of the epistle of James should be encouraged and comforted that their oppressors will be judged. The "coming of the Lord" and therefore the destruction of Jerusalem "is near" (5:8). Not everyone who hears this letter read in the assembly will live to see the historical judgment enacted. Some will die before that great event. But the certainty that it will happen is important for them to hear. James believes that the assurance of the Lord's judgment will help them abandon their schemes for retaliation. The righteousness of God will be manifest when Jesus's prophecy is fulfilled, and his church is vindicated.

This message ought to encourage Christian dissidents today. The Lord Jesus will act to defend his oppressed people. Historical judgments are not comprehensive. We must wait until the Last Day for perfect justice. Historical judgments are, however, genuinely helpful for God's people—not just to see God's enemies dealt with; but they also bring to beleaguered Christians some measure of peace and security.

## 11

# PATIENCE, PRAYER, & RESTORATION

*Religion must be defended not by killing but by
dying, not by violence but by patience.*
– Alan Kreider[40]

### James 5:7-20

[7]Be patient, therefore, brothers, until the coming of the Lord. See how the farmer waits for the precious fruit of the earth, being patient about it, until it receives the early and the late rains. [8]You also, be patient. Establish your hearts, for the coming of the Lord is at hand. [9]Do not grumble against one another, brothers, so that you may not be judged; behold, the Judge is standing at the door. [10]As an example of suffering and patience, brothers, take the prophets who spoke in the name of the Lord. [11]Behold, we consider those blessed who remained steadfast. You have heard of the steadfastness of Job, and you have seen the purpose of the Lord, how the Lord is compassionate and merciful. [12]But above all, my brothers, do not swear, either by heaven or by earth, or by any other oath, but let your "yes" be yes and your "no" be no, so that you may not fall under condemnation.

[13]Is anyone among you suffering? Let him pray. Is anyone cheerful? Let him sing praise. [14]Is anyone among you sick? Let him call for the elders of the church, and let them pray over

---

[40] Alan Kreider, *The Patient Ferment of the Early Church: The Improbable Rise of Christianity in the Roman Empire* (Grand Rapids: Baker Academic, 2016).

him, anointing him with oil in the name of the Lord. [15]And the prayer of faith will save the one who is sick, and the Lord will raise him up. And if he has committed sins, he will be forgiven. [16]Therefore, confess your sins to one another and pray for one another, that you may be healed. The prayer of a righteous person has great power as it is working. [17]Elijah was a man with a nature like ours, and he prayed fervently that it might not rain, and for three years and six months it did not rain on the earth. [18]Then he prayed again, and heaven gave rain, and the earth bore its fruit.

[19]My brothers, if anyone among you wanders from the truth and someone brings him back, [20]let him know that whoever brings back a sinner from his wandering will save his soul from death and will cover a multitude of sins.

Patience is a virtue. How many times in our lives have we been asked, "Please, be patient" or "Please, wait." Think of how often we have said to our children, "Wait" or "Just wait your turn. Be patient." If someone is going to comply with the request to "be patient," three conditions must exist:

    **1.** You must believe that the one asking you to wait is trustworthy.

    **2.** You must also believe that the wait won't be too long or so long as to make the wait not worth your time.

    **3.** You must be willing to behave yourself while you are waiting or you might forfeit your right to whatever it is you are waiting for.

These three conditions came to me one day while I was watching old videos of our children when they were young. There were more than a few times when either my wife or I asked the children to wait or be patient. So I watched for these three conditions:

    **1.** If mom tells a child, "You need to wait your turn," the child must believe that mom would in fact give them a turn in due time. They had to *trust* her. You can often see it in their eyes when they look at mom. They know she's told them to wait before and she has kept her word. If she had not kept her word in the past, well, then that could be a problem.

**2.** If they were waiting to play with a toy because some other sibling was playing with it at the time, they not only had to trust mom would eventually give them a crack at it. They also had to believe that their chance to play would be soon and not four days from now or next week.

**3.** If they were going to get their turn, they had to behave themselves during the wait. If they started to throw a temper tantrum or began to take swings at the sibling who was currently enjoying their time with the toy, then the child would forfeit their right to use it.

Now these three conditions (trust, wait time, and behavior) hold true whether we are waiting a few minutes for a toy or some years for something more substantial—like waiting for our driver's license, or waiting for the right woman or man to marry, or waiting for justice to be done when we have been wronged. In the case of these early disciples, James commands them to "be patient" (5:7) and to "wait" (5:8). They are to be patient and wait for their oppressors to be brought to justice. They are to wait patiently for the Lord to act in their behalf and begin to make things right and liberate them from their suffering. And so in order to comply with this imperative they . . .

**1.** had to believe that what James is prophesying is trustworthy—that the Lord's promise is trustworthy. . .

**2.** had to believe that the promise of the Lord's coming in judgment was actually near and not somewhere far off in the distant future. . .

**3.** and they had to behave appropriately, that is stop the aggressive, violent rhetoric and behavior toward their persecutors, stop fighting with one another, stop taking rash oaths, and so on.

James has covered all these conditions throughout his epistle. This entire concluding section (5:7-20) should be understood as a summary of the main themes of James's epistle: the blessedness of remaining patient in the midst of trials (5:11), along with an explanation that part of the motivation for this patient waiting is the promised future vindication of the righteousness of these suffering Christians, demonstrated by the destruction of their enemies (5:1-6), along with more practical instruction in what it will mean for James's readers to remain steadfast in their sufferings (5:13-20).

## Jesus in a Pickle Jar

James shifts back to speaking to his Christian readers directly, addressing them as "brothers" (v. 7). Having assured these brothers of the destruction of their enemies, James now exhorts them to be patient until the coming of the Lord in judgment against their enemies. Indeed, as James says, his readers must "therefore" be patient—their patience is directly related to the promise of God's judgment on their enemies. It is the trustworthy promises of God to judge our enemy that enables us to turn the other cheek, to resist violence and political manipulation and await the vindication of our father. Though the patience of the church appears to be weakness, in reality it is strength, because our longsuffering is borne out of the vengeance of God.

In Douglas Bell's zany novel *Mojo and the Pickle Jar,* some people get their hands on a pickle jar that they later find out contains the heart of the Virgin Mary. And her heart is mystically connected to the entire cosmos. Holding in their hands this pickle jar means they hold in their hands the fate of the world. The "brothers" James addresses are acting like they've got Jesus in a pickle jar. They think they can open the lid now and then and use him to control their situation. They will bring an end to their suffering and trials in their own way with the help of Jesus.

Though his readers desire an end to their suffering and persecution and have even begun to grasp after power and violence as a means for bringing about the end of their long tribulation (cf. James 4), it is not given for them to be their own agents of deliverance. They do not have Jesus at their beck and call in a pickle jar. They must be *patient* and wait for the moment when their Father in heaven, who cares for them, deems the length of their suffering is sufficient and saves them from it. The peace that James's readers long for so desperately will indeed be given to them, but not nearly as quickly as they would like. And certainly not in the way they have sought it.

To illustrate this reality, James gives as an example a parable of the farmer, who "waits for the precious fruit of the earth, being patient about it, until it receives the early and late rains" (5:7b). The farmer cannot bring about the harvest that he desires purely through his efforts. All he can do is plant the seed in the ground, tend to the sprouts and pray for the rain and sun that God sends to do its work. No matter how hard he might try, he cannot speed the day of the flowering of his crop. In the same way, the Christians to whom James writes desire a "harvest of righteousness" (3:18), but they must be content to wait for God to grow to fruition the peace they desire. And so James says to his readers: "You also, be patient. Establish your hearts, for the coming of the Lord is at hand."

Indeed, the suffering of these early Christians is very much like a farmer who plants a seed in the ground. Like the farmer, their work of patience and suffering at first seems to have no impact at all. There is no fruit that is evident as they are afflicted by their enemies and experience distress of all kinds. Time goes by and their suffering continues, and still, there is no fruit to be seen. Day after day, week after week, year after year, still there is nothing.

Luke's account in Acts tells us that the persecution of the Christians at the hands of the Jews began soon after Pentecost, and we know from historical documents that it continued for nearly forty years before the destruction of the Jewish nation in 70 AD.

The suffering experienced by these early Christians was neither easy nor glorious—it was slow and difficult and painstakingly long. James's readers still had many years to wait before their vindication, and so his exhortation for them to be patient must be read not simply as pious advice for a moment, but rather a description of the normative behavior that must characterize their whole lives as well as the lives of their children.

There are many Christians in the world today who also experience the kind of suffering felt by these earliest Christians. There are very few press conferences for the thousands of Christian martyrs who are killed every year in Islamic and Communist nations. In those countries, many Christians suffer anonymously, and their pain is known only to those in their immediate communities and to God himself. Though James's epistle is centuries old, the application of his message for those Christians who today suffer persecution and even death remains the same. Walking in the way of Jesus, Christians all over the world today await the destruction of their enemies and the judgment of Jesus to deliver them.

But James's exhortation to remain patient during suffering has application even for those of us who do not currently experience the same kind of violent persecution as James's first readers. For even now, in our everyday experience, we are constantly tempted to grasp after victory over those people and things that trouble us. Our lives are plagued by plans that are frustrated, desires that are thwarted, attempts to guarantee security and comfort for ourselves and our families that crumble even as we struggle after them. Though our culture would tell us the opposite is true, there is still so much in modern life that is outside of our control.

When someone we love is diagnosed with a terminal illness, or our community experiences a natural disaster, we realize anew how little power we have to craft our own future and protect our own interests. But this inability to manipulate the realities of our lives is not limited to these kinds of cataclysmic events. Rather, it is the normative way of our lives in this world. All around us, written in the front page of the newspapers and heard in the drone of talk radio is the message that wisdom and power is expressed in exerting the greatest amount of control over the unknown and unmanageable. Whether it's protection from our national enemies, greater economic prosperity, or simply a better marriage, gurus and talking heads prove their wisdom by analyzing and predicting the unpredictable.

But though we might find ourselves longing for this kind of infallible wisdom, when we allow our hearts a moment of honesty, we know that this quest for control and security is tenuous. Consistently, the message of the Scriptures is that true wisdom is learning to live in light of our frailty and inability to sequester mastery over our lives. In other words, wisdom is not found in increasing our manipulative abilities, but rather by learning humility and trust in the One who is Lord of all things—by holding loosely to our dreams and joyfully delighting in what has been given to us today.

The difficulty inherent in James's instruction in these verses must not be underestimated. The natural response for these early Christians who were so badly abused by their powerful and rich oppressors would be to strike back against their persecutors, burning their storehouses or ambushing them to intimidate their oppressors and force them to stop their violence. Indeed, this kind of violent, guerrilla action has shown again and again to be an effective means for an oppressed minority to gain the peace and freedom they desire. This kind of violent reaction to violence is natural human behavior. Consider the way children retaliate and hit back at their siblings or friends—an eye for an eye, a tooth for a tooth is the way of the schoolyard and the playground. From their earliest days this kind of vindictive attitude is drilled into children by their communities.

But James tells these Christians abused by rich unbelieving Jewish religious leaders to put aside concern for their rights. Their need for protection and sustenance and housing is right and good, and the men who are attempting to deny them these things are truly wicked. And yet James exhorts his readers to be patient, to submit humbly to God, and not to resist their tormenters by using worldly power in the name of Jesus. James's words are stunning in terms of the response they call forth from his readers—a total submission to God and a refusal to be intimidated into returning violence for violence against their persecutors.

Of course, this admonition to embrace patience does not only apply to putting aside physical violence. When we feel the brunt of someone's unjust anger, or we experience the pain of slander spread against us by others, or even when we hear a sharp word spoken to us by our friend or spouse, there is a natural and human temptation to respond to the destruction and humiliation we feel by destroying and humiliating in kind. James's words should sting in our ears today just as sharply as they did in the ears of his readers in the first century whenever we are tempted to return anger for anger, slander for slander, humiliation for humiliation: "Be patient."

What does James mean by his admonition to "be patient"? In the first chapter, James explains that in the midst of trials, his readers are blessed when they remain "steadfast," so it seems that this sense of enduring in an unmovable manner is part of what he means by "be patient." In 5:8, he again instructs his readers to "be patient" and then goes on to instruct them to "Establish your hearts, for the coming of the Lord is at hand." Whatever James means by "be patient," it seems that it is linked to the command to "establish your hearts."

The phrase "establish your hearts" occurs twice in the writings of Paul, in 1 Corinthians 7:37 (where the original Greek phrase is very similar) and 1 Thessalonians 3:13 (where the Greek is the same). Both of these passages are helpful for us in understanding what James means in his exhortation to his readers in James 5:8. In 1 Corinthians 7:36-37, Paul instructs his unmarried readers with these words: "But whoever is firmly established in his heart, being under no necessity but having his desire under control, and has determined this in his heart, to keep her as his betrothed, he will do well." In this passage, for one's heart to be established means that one's desire are "under control" and what has been determined in the heart will be carried out in the body.

In 1 Thessalonians 3:12-13, Paul instructs the Thessalonians, writing, "May the Lord make you increase and abound in love for one another and for all, as we do for you, so that he may establish your hearts blameless in holiness before God and Father, at the coming of our Lord Jesus with all his saints." In this passage, to "establish your hearts" seems to mean to prepare oneself for the return of Jesus, so that you will be ready to face his judgment.

So what does James mean when he instructs his readers to, "Establish your hearts, for the coming of the Lord is at hand"? Given the context of this passage in James (following after sharp rebuke of those Christians who have angrily struck out against their oppressors and a prophetic announcement of the judgment of God on the wicked) as well as the way in which Paul uses this phrase elsewhere in the New Testament, we may confidently conclude that what James intends by this metaphoric exhortation is that his readers would: 1) Stand steadfast in the midst of their trials; 2) control their fleshly desire to return violence for violence; and 3) prepare themselves for the return of Jesus, so that they will be vindicated in his judgment.

Again in James 5:8, we see that James continues to ground the motivation for his readers' obedience to his exhortations squarely in Jesus's pledge to return to earth and exercise his authority to judge all men (cf. 2:13-14, 3:1, 4:12). Even though James has just promised in 5:1-6 that his readers' enemies will surely be judged and destroyed, he is careful to remind his audience that they are not exempt from Jesus's judgment. When the Lord comes to judge, he is impartial in his judgments; he deals not only with the wicked oppressors, but he also will judge his people. And the same standard will be used for both.

Given the stress that the New Testament places (both in the words of Jesus himself as well as the teaching of his apostles) on the judgment of Jesus and the motivating force this should be in the life of the believer to lives righteously, it is interesting that in modern Western Christianity, when we hear exposition of the final judgment (which itself is rare) it is almost always explained in terms of what that judgment will mean for the wicked. In other words, in Western Christianity the promise of the final judgment is often used as a stick to "beat" the wicked, and sometimes used as a carrot to encourage the righteous, but rarely is it used as a stick to warn the righteous to remain steadfast in their belief and obedient to Jesus's law—even though this use is often found in the New Testament. One of the great challenges of the church is to consistently emphasize those things Jesus, through Scripture, emphasizes, and not emphasize those things he does not stress. In this area, it seems that our typical way of discussing and teaching on the final judgment fails to match the emphasis of Jesus.

In verse 9, James explains some practical implications of what it means for his readers to be patient and establish their hearts as they wait for their Lord, writing, "Do not grumble against one another, so that you may not be judged; behold, the Judge is standing at the door." In the midst of the suffering that James's readers are experiencing, the temptation for division and arguing against one another in order to advance divergent agendas in response to the Jewish persecution must have been tremendous. But James directly addresses this problem in words that are reminiscent of Jesus's instruction to his disciples, "Judge not, that you be not judged. For with the judgment you pronounce you will be judged, and with the measure you use it will be measured to you" (Matt. 7:1-2). Again, James instructs his readers to live righteously so that they will stand in the judgment of Jesus.

## EXEMPLARY FOREFATHERS

James goes on to encourage his readers with an illustration, writing, "As an example of suffering and patience, brothers, take the prophets who spoke in the name of the Lord. Behold, we consider those blessed who remained steadfast." (James 5:10-11b). Amid the fear and confusion experienced by the community to whom he writes, James points his readers back to the stories of God's people in the Old Testament, showing how the pattern of their lives forms a pattern for his readers to walk in. Just as the prophets in the past suffered persecution and violence against them and persevered so that they are now called blessed in their steadfastness, so also the followers of Jesus must be patient to walk in the same path, knowing that future generations will also call them blessed.

But James does not point back to the stories of the prophets simply to inspire his readers to obedience in their present situation. Connecting the experience of the these followers of Jesus with the stories of Israel's exemplary forefathers also has the dramatic effect of advancing the claim that they are actually the true Israel, and the Jews who oppress them are no longer the rightful inheritors of those stories. By putting his readers in the place of the Old Testament prophets, James has identified those who follow Jesus as the faithful remnant of Israel, and their oppressors as apostate and wicked Israel. What James does in these verses is to subvert the propaganda of the Jewish leaders who had set themselves against the church, claiming that they are "purifying" Israel by driving the apostate from their midst and protecting the religion of their forefathers. At the time this letter was written, it seemed that the Jewish leaders have God on their side in the argument, since he was allowing (and implicitly, it seemed, blessing) their persecution of these renegade Jews who claim to follow the resurrected Son of God. James's readers need assurance, and he gives it to them by linking their story with the story of their righteous forefathers, and by promising that God will decisively act in judgment against their apostate enemies (5:1-6).

After generically referring to the Hebrew prophets, James narrows in on one figure in particular. "You have heard of the steadfastness of Job, and you have seen the purpose of the Lord, how the Lord is compassionate and merciful" (5:11b). Some commentators argue that James cannot be referring here to the biblical story of Job, but rather to the apocryphal "Testament of Job" because of the way the biblical Job responds to his suffering. During his misery, Job was not afraid to cry out to God in wonderment and complaint, cursing even the day of his own birth (3:3-16), and mourning the absence of God in his suffering (23:2-9). And yet, surprisingly to many modern Christians, James uses Job as an example of "suffering and patience."

Perhaps the reason we are surprised that Job is upheld as an example of righteous suffering and patience is because our conception of righteous suffering is a stoic acceptance of whatever hardship comes into our lives. Indeed, read through a certain kind of lens, the epistle of James can be interpreted as commending this kind of detached and deterministic acceptance of evil as righteousness. When James says to his readers to count their suffering as joy and to "remain steadfast" and "be patient" even as they experience incredible pain and violence done against themselves and their families, we might be tempted to imagine that he is instructing them to shut up, be quiet and take the harsh medicine of suffering in their lives.

But the fact that James cites Job as his Old Testament example of suffering is a powerful corrective to this temptation. Job was not content to simply sit back and take the misery and grief that came into his life. Rather, Job cried out in his tribulation, honestly declaring,

> God gives me up to the ungodly and casts me into the hands of the wicked. I was at ease, and he broke me apart; he seized me by the neck and dashed me to pieces; he set me up as his target; his archers surround me. He slashes open my kidneys and does not spare; he pours out my gall on the ground. He breaks me with breach upon breach; he runs upon me like a warrior. I have sewed sackcloth upon my skin and have laid my strength in the dust. My face is red with weeping, and on my eyelids is deep darkness, although there is no violence in my hands, and my prayer is pure (Job 16:11-17).

The vicious honesty of Job's outbursts throughout his misery is almost frightening. He cries out to God, wondering why he suffers while the wicked prosper. He questions whether God is even present with him and loudly mourns the deaths of his children, the destruction of his livelihood, and the physical pain he himself experiences. And Scripture tells us that, "in all this Job did not sin with his lips" (Job 2:10b), and God blessed him because of his perseverance (Job 42:10-17).

James cites Job as a model of patience and suffering because God does not desire his children to face pain and evil with a stoic acceptance or detachment. Rather, God expects that when suffering comes into our lives, it causes us to wrestle with the hard questions suffering brings, and to wrestle even with God himself. Remember that the Psalms are given to Israel and the Church as a prayer and song book. They contain fully authorized models of prayer for God's people. Then consider how often the Psalmist cries out with passion to God, asking questions, making petitions, and expressing his frustration with their situation (e.g., Pss. 3, 4, 6, 7, etc.). Moreover, in our wrestling with the Lord and refusal to shrink back into stoicism and detachment, God uses our suffering to make us mature. Indeed, as James says, in the story of Job we not only see an example of righteous suffering, but also the purpose of God when he brings pain into our lives: to display for us in a new and deeper way his compassion and mercy.

The promise of these verses, and the promise of the story of Job in our lives is that our suffering is not the end of the story. It is the promise that in the end, God will transform and use our suffering not for evil, but for his gracious and merciful purposes. It is the same promise that upheld Joseph as he stared into the cold dark of his Egyptian prison cell, the same promise that David clung to as he ran for his life and hid in the wilderness from Saul, and it is ultimately the same promise Jesus held to as he faced his own innocent death and looked forward to the resurrection.

In the end, the faithfulness of God in the resurrection of Jesus that is a pledge not only that we ourselves will rise from the dead, bodily and in glory, but also that every death, large and small, in our lives, be it sickness or poverty, depression or disappointment, or even the untimely suffering and death of a child or father or husband or wife is not without meaning or purpose and indeed, will be transformed and renewed and made beautiful in the hands of God our father—that every death is a good and perfect gift from above, "coming down from the Father of lights with whom there is no variation or shadow due to change" (James 2:17).

## Oaths & Zealotry

James concludes this section by writing, "But above all, my brothers, do not swear, either by heaven or by earth or by any other oath, but let your 'yes' be yes, and your 'no' be no, so that you may not fall under condemnation" (5:12). At first glance, the placement of this verse during an exhortation to patience is confusing. But we must consider the reality that in the ancient world, when men banded together to form a violent or political conspiracy against an oppressive government, they came together and swore oaths to one another in private, thus forming an underground resistance party. This was quite common in first-century Judaism. This is precisely what a Jewish zealot was—someone who had sworn to act to cripple Rome's power over the Jews. Simon, one of Jesus's twelve disciples was called a "zealot," probably because he was recruited from the ranks of zealotry (Luke 6:15; Acts 1:13).

By prohibiting his readers from swearing oaths, James is ensuring that they do not establish or join resistance movements against the Jewish oppressors. We have an example of this kind of oath-taking in the book of Acts. After the apostle Paul had been arrested and appeared before the Jewish ruling council to defend himself, a band of zealous Jews (approved by the council) swore an oath to kill Paul:

> When it was day, the Jews made a plot and bound themselves by an oath neither to eat nor drink till they had killed Paul. There were more than forty who made this conspiracy. They went to the chief priests and elders and said, "We have strictly bound ourselves by an oath to taste no food till we have killed Paul. Now therefore you, along with the council, give notice to the tribune to bring him down to you,

as though you were going to determine his case more exactly. And we are ready to kill him before he comes near" (Acts 23:12-15).

From all accounts, this kind of oath-taking by bands of zealous men was common among resistance fighters against Rome. It is therefore not surprising that such a tactic would be repurposed to eliminate the threat of the apostle Paul. And if this was common among the Jews in their struggle against Rome, it stands to reason that newly converted disciples of Jesus would be tempted to use similar tactics in their struggle with the Jewish leaders in Jerusalem who have turned out to be oppressors. If this is not the case, then accounting for James's inclusion of this warning against swearing oaths at this point in his letter makes little sense. But if we remember the overall context and purpose of this letter, then this admonition fits nicely James's desire to address the violent and fanatical words and actions employed by some of the brothers in these exiled Christian communities.

It is not by violence that the oppression of the church will be transformed into victory and come to an end, but James knows that the temptation to live by the sword in these times of persecution is immense, and so he protects his readers against the seduction and condemnation of ill-gained political power by preventing them from swearing oaths.

## CARING FOR THE SUFFERING & INJURED

*James 5:13-16*

<sup>13</sup>Is anyone among you suffering? Let him pray. Is anyone cheerful? Let him sing praise. <sup>14</sup>Is anyone among you sick? Let him call for the elders of the church, and let them pray over him, anointing him with oil in the name of the Lord. <sup>15</sup>And the prayer of faith will save the one who is sick, and the Lord will raise him up. And if he has committed sins, he will be forgiven. <sup>16</sup>Therefore, confess your sins to one another and pray for one another, that you may be healed.

In the concluding verses of his epistle James ends with some general exhortations to his readers, including instruction for the sick or injured in the congregation. First, notice that James does not act as though there ought not to be sickness in the people of God, as though the new life found in Jesus promises an end to the struggles and sicknesses of our earthly lives. James also does not criticize the sick person in the congregation as though their illness is related to a deficiency in faith or piety. James honestly admits the reality that his readers live in a damaged and sin-sick world, and he instructs them in how to respond, as a community, to the physical suffering members of their congregation will surely experience.

What is the nature of the sickness that James sets out in these verses? The Greek word that James uses for "sick" in verse 14 is *asthenew* (ασθενεω), an expansive word that can describe a physical illness or weakness. Given that James implies that the elders of the church must come and visit the "sick" person, it is likely that the sickness or condition that James discusses in these verses is one that is serious and/or chronic, such that the sick person is unable to travel.

Remembering the context of James's epistle, it seems likely than many of the "sick" that he describes owe their physical affliction to the Jewish persecution his readers are experiencing. We might translate verse 13 as "Is anyone injured?" or even "Is anyone wounded?" The apostle Paul includes *asthenew* in his list of what he has suffered from his persecutors (2 Cor. 12:10). Even so, the language James uses in James 5:14 to talk about the "sick" person is intentionally broad so as to provide the church with a pattern of ministering to all of those in its community who are weak and sick and troubled by darkness and depression, and even intense spiritual doubt.

The first instruction James gives to the injured or sick person in the congregation is to "call for the elders of the church" (verse 14). James does not say that they should "call the faith healer in the church" or "wait until the itinerant faith healer visits your town and then bring the sick person to him." Of course, at times the apostles were given the power to heal the sick instantly, after the pattern of Jesus (e.g., Acts 3:1-10). But this kind of apostolic healing was usually done in public contexts to stand as a miraculous sign of Christ's power over the devil, and as a token of his resurrection from the dead. But this passage in James's epistle is striking evidence that ministry to the sick in the church, apart from the special gift of healing given at times to some of the apostles, has properly been given to the elders of the church, not to some self-appointed "healers."

James also does not say, "If anyone is sick, let him cry out alone in prayer for healing." Even though all believers are filled with the Holy Spirit, this does not mean that we have the wherewithal to suffer through our illnesses by ourselves. Often, in American evangelicalism, the doctrine of the "priesthood of all believers" is taken to mean that we all can be our own priests. This is a reversal of Martin Luther's original teaching on this subject. In the words of Timothy George, what Luther meant by the doctrine of the priesthood of all believers is that "Every Christian is someone else's priest, and we are all priests to one another."[41] During times of persecution and oppression the experience of the priesthood of believers becomes crucial for the health of a community. Individuals cannot by themselves bear the unjust burdens tyrannical powers inflict upon them. We cannot hear Hannah Arendt's warning and not fear for our future:

> What prepares men for totalitarian domination in the nontotalitarian world, is the fact that loneliness, once a borderline experience usually suffered in certain marginal social conditions like old age, has become an everyday experience of the ever-growing masses of our century.[42]

---

41 Timothy George, *Theology of the Reformers* (Nashville: Broadman, 1988), 96.

42 Hannah Arendt, *Origins of Totalitarianism* (New York: Harcourt, 1973), 339.

Rather than a conformation of the importance of our individuality in the Christian life, the doctrine of the priesthood of all believers is an affirmation that we need one another, that our communal and shared life with one another is significant and essential to our spiritual health. James's instruction for the sick to call for the elders to pray for him is not simply a statement about the office and responsibilities of elders in the church, rather it is more centrally a statement about the import of the church itself in the life of the believer. For the prayers of the elders, as the authorized representatives of the body, are simply the prayers of the church and embody the petitions of the entire congregation.

After explaining that the sick person ought to call for the elders of the church, James then goes on to describe what it is the elders should do in this situation, "let them [the elders] pray over him, anointing him with oil in the name of the Lord" (verse 14). We are not surprised that the elders are commanded to pray over the sick person. But why ought they also to anoint him with oil? First, it is very unlikely that the elders are instructed to anoint the sick with oil because of any perceived medicinal power in the oil itself. After all, if the oil is supposed to restore the sick person to health, why must it be the elders who anoint him? Why not the family or friends of the one who is sick? Indeed, verse 15 makes it explicit that it is the Lord who will raise up the sick man, not the medicinal power of oil.

If the oil does not act as a primitive medicine for the sick person, why are they to be anointed? Anointing the sick with oil is a symbolic ritual. In the Hebrew Scriptures, priests and kings are anointed with oil in order to set them apart for their new vocation, and the dead are also anointed in order to prepare them for their new resurrection life (Mark 16:1; Matt. 26:6-13). In Mark 6:13, we see that the apostles, acting on the command of Jesus, "anointed with oil many who were sick and healed them." Given the pattern of how anointing oil is used throughout the Bible, the primary reason James commands the sick to be anointed by the elders is as ritual sign that the sick person needs the ministry of the Holy Spirit for healing and comfort. Olive oil being poured on the head symbolizes the descent of the Spirit (e.g., 1 Sam. 16:13). The olive oil ritual anoints the sick person and sets him apart for the prayers of the church.

We also see that in the Bible, people are anointed with oil as a sign of cheerfulness and joy—as a visible sign of the abundance of God's blessing (Pss. 23:5; 45:7; 133:2). And so, the anointing of the sick in James 5 is, in a broad sense, sacramental. When the elders gather around the bed of a sick person and anoint him or her with oil in the "name of the Lord" the oil is used by the Holy Spirit, through the prayers of the elders and the church, to bring relief to the sick. The invisible work of the Spirit is made manifest for our eyes to see and our skin to feel.

The one who is injured or sick is usually isolated from others. He or she is not able to gather with other believers for worship. Often those who are ill are confined to their rooms and beds. This separation from others leads to dark thoughts in many people. "I am alone. Nobody cares about me. Maybe God has abandoned me. I have been cut off from the life of the church." When the elders gather at the bedside of someone like this, they bring the community, as it were, to the sick believer. Their simple presence ministers peace to the one isolated from the community. But the oil also serves to remind them that they have not been cut off from "the olive tree" of God's people. The Glory Spirit, represented by the oil, has not departed from them. As they are "anointed in the name of the Lord" they should be assured of the Lord's care for them as part of his body, the Church.

James goes on to explain the effect of the prayer of the elders, "And the prayer of faith will save the one who is sick, and the Lord will raise him up. And if he has committed sins, he will be forgiven" (verse 15). Embedded in James's instruction to pray for the sick is the promise that that prayer will save him, and he will be raised up. Though we no longer live in the apostolic age, when miraculous healing was a sign of God's favor on the followers of Jesus, we should be careful not to limit the power of God to heal his people miraculously and mysteriously in response to the prayers of the church. Of course, we must also resist the opposite temptation of assuming that God will always miraculously heal believers, and the absence of a miracle is proof of God's displeasure or of some deficiency of faith or piety in the one offering or receiving prayer. Sometimes, healing will come through the "natural" means of a doctor's skill or the human body's restorative functions—but this is no less God's work than an instantaneous miracle.

And, sometimes, healing will not come at all, and the sick person will weaken and even die. In all the pain and sorrow of death, where is James's promise that "the prayer of faith will save the one who is sick"? The promise James offers is located and fulfilled in the ultimate promise of the resurrection of the dead, in the promise that salvation of the sick is found in day when the "Lord will raise him up" (v. 15).

It may be tempting to see the argument that the resurrection of the dead is the ultimate fulfillment of the promise of verse 14 as a case of special pleading—as a way of minimizing the power of God in the present age. Nevertheless, even if a sick person calls for the elders of the church who pray for and anoint him with oil, resulting in his immediate healing, his ultimate hope and fulfillment of God's promise to deliver him is still found in the resurrection. Even the man who is healed will one day die, and God never promises complete restoration or healing in this life, but only in the age to come. Even though we experience glimpses of resurrection life in this age through physical healing, our true and full hope looks forward to the day when all things will be made new.[43]

The healing promised by James is not only physical but also includes the forgiveness of sins. Are the sins here connected with the sickness? That's hard to say definitively. But given the context of the letter and the possibility that someone has been

---

43 Some have argued that the anointing commended here by James is akin to last rights for the dying. The person calls for the elders because he is near death. The forgiveness of sins is held out to him along with the resurrection of his body at the Last Day. See C. John Collins, "James 5:14-16a: What is the Anointing For?" *Presbyterion* 23/2 (1997): 79-91.

"wounded" (and not simply contracted a generic illness), it is not out of the question to think that this person's engagement in sinful, aggressive behavior caused his injuries. A few sentences after James says, "confess your sins to one another. . ." (v. 16) he concludes the letter with a promise to those who restore "a sinner from his erring path." This work of recovery will "deliver his life from death and cover a multitude of sins" (v. 19). Perhaps we should not press the connection between the infirmity suffered by this person and his sins, but there is enough in the context to suggest that some have wandered from the narrow path, engaged in violent retribution against their enemies, and then suffered injuries because of their behavior.

Even so, to suggest that there is always a connection between anyone's illness and particular sins is manifestly unbiblical. The Scriptures are clear that God does not punish us tit for tat when we sin, as if every illness we suffer is a result of some particular sin or sins we have committed. There are many examples in Scripture of people suffering without it being a punishment for sin. Job is a great example. He suffers because he is righteous (Job 1:6-12). And there is the man born blind in John 9. The disciples asked Jesus, "Teacher, who sinned, this man or his parents, that he was born blind." Jesus answered, "It was not that this man sinned, or his parents, but that the works of God might be displayed in him" (John 9:2-3).

Why then does James promise healing from sickness as well as forgiveness of sin? Because sickness, especially life-threatening sickness, almost always tempts a Christian, especially those with tender consciences, to fabricate a connection in their own minds between their physical suffering and their own sin. Forgiveness of sin is offered to the sick as an assurance that their suffering is part of God's providence and good will in their life, not as penalty for something they have done.

Forgiveness of sin is also promised because the person who is sick in the manner described by James is likely to have been cut off from the larger body of which they are a part. Because of their physical condition, it is likely that the sick person has been secluded and alone. If someone is isolated from the Christian community, they don't have access to the assurances of God's love that come from worship and fellowship with the body of Christ. Through worship, the sick and lonely person is assured their sins are indeed forgiven so that their joy and comfort in their identity as part of the bride of Jesus will be restored. Indeed, as the sick person is anointed with oil, they receive a powerful physical reminder that they are being regrafted—in heart and mind—into the olive tree of the Church, the community of Jesus. Someone in this weakened state needs the elders to proclaim God's love for them, his forgiveness, and care. Through the care of the elders and the church itself, doubt, and darkness, as well as sickness, is driven away.

Though it may be unusual today for the elders of the church to gather at the house of a sick person in the church, or to bring a sick member to the church building itself so that the elders can pray over him or her, this is an historic and biblical practice of the church that we would do well to restore to our regular life together as the body of Christ. When the leaders of the church submit to the practice of praying personally (with physical contact and anointing) and regularly for the sick and needy, it is a dramatic affirmation of the reality of our need for one another, and of the unity of the body, as well as our reliance on God as the source or our life and hope.

In verse 16a, James writes, "Therefore, confess your sins to one another, and pray for one another, that you may be healed." Even in our modern world, we all feel the need for a deeper community life together. We feel the isolation and loneliness that is apparently inherent in the human experience. Indeed, Christians everywhere are rediscovering that our own peculiar modern malaise is the absence of genuine community. Though the Church will never be the perfect community that will meet all of our needs, it is intended to be a foretaste of the renewal and healing promised in the new earth.

In these verses, James describes the way in which the Church is meant to function as the new humanity in Jesus—by mutual dependence on one another, through regular confession of sin and forgiveness and constant prayer. It may seem odd or awkward for us to commit to this practice of confessing our sins to one another, or confessing privately to our pastors, but it is in confession that we are able to come to grips with our brokenness and articulate our needs to one another. Indeed, this kind of mutual dependence is the heart of true community, for as we learn to depend on one another we learn to trust and then to love.

## Petitioning for the Harvest

*James 5:16b-20*

> [16b]The prayer of a righteous person has great power as it is working. [17]Elijah was a man with a nature like ours, and he prayed fervently that it might not rain, and for three years and six months it did not rain on the earth. [18]Then he prayed again, and heaven gave rain, and the earth bore its fruit. [19]My brothers, if anyone among you wanders from the truth and someone brings him back, [20]let him know that whoever brings back a sinner from his wandering will save his soul from death and will cover a multitude of sins.

The reason that the church must be a community that is characterized by prayer for one another is that the "the prayer of a righteous person has great power." It is tempting to read this verse and assume that by calling the person in question "righteous," James is referring to a man or woman of extreme moral purity, someone who is sinless and not prone to struggle or failure. The problem that many of us have in correctly interpreting what James means here by "righteous" is that righteousness has become something one builds up or accumulates. For example, someone might be "more righteous" than another person and thus will resist some sin in which another "less righteous" person would be prone to indulge.

But in the Scriptures, to be "righteous" is to be a certain kind of person—not a moral quality to accumulate. To be righteous, according to the Bible, is simply to be a faithful covenant keeper with God. Luke, for example, tell us that John the Baptizer's parents Zechariah and Elizabeth "were both righteous before God, walking blamelessly in all the commandments and statues of the Lord" (Luke 1:6). That's quite a statement. Does this mean they were sinless or perfectly obedient? No. But they were true to their covenantal obligations. When they sinned they were obedient to the law and offered a sacrifice and confessed their sin. To be a faithful covenant keeper is like being a faithful husband—it does not mean that you never sin against your wife (of course!) but that you repent of your sin, and you refuse to abandon her, or to violate your marriage covenant. In other words, the physical and earthly church that you are a part of is made up of "righteous persons," and when this church community begins to live a life of prayer and confession with one another, their prayers for healing and wholeness will be answered.

It is power that James's readers are grasping after throughout his epistle by way of violence and plotting and earthly wisdom. They long for peace, and they long for protection. James now points out to them that true and lasting power is not found in those things—rather it exists in the simple and loving prayers of the church, and it is through this life of confession and prayer that powerful change is brought about in our own hearts and lives, and indeed, in the culture around us.

After referring his readers back to the example of the prophet Job's obedience and suffering earlier in chapter 5, James now points to Elijah as an exemplar for their prayer and action. Elijah is an example for these early Christian leaders not only because his prayers to God were answered, but because his situation was remarkably similar to their own. Like the readers whom James addresses, Elijah suffered under the rule of the apostate rulers of Israel, Ahab and Jezebel. Like the early Christians, Elijah was forced to go into hiding because of the persecution of these leaders and run for his life. But instead of beginning an insurrectionist movement designed to bring down the ungodly leadership of Israel, Elijah patiently ministered to the widow in Zarapheth, providing food for her and healing her son. Instead of making angry speeches to his fellow countrymen, Elijah pleaded with God for the healing of his nation, and because of his prayers, the rain stopped, and then returned, and brought with it the fruit of the earth (like the "harvest of righteousness" promised in James 3:18). Indeed, Elijah is referenced here by James because his life is paradigmatic for the new Israel that James addresses—they are to suffer as Elijah suffered, to embrace his patience and care for the poor in the face of persecution, to pray as he prayed, and ultimately, to trust that God will answer their prayers just as he answered those of Elijah.

James concludes his epistle simply, without the typical benedictions or greetings that are characteristic of Paul's letters. Rather, James reminds his readers of the purpose for which he writes with these words, "My brothers, if anyone among you wanders from the truth and someone brings him back, let him know that whoever brings back a sinner from his wandering will save his soul from death and will cover a multitude of sins" (5:19-20). James caps off his epistle by admonishing the brothers to join with him in doing what he has tried to do in his letter—bring back those who are wandering from the truth. If you join with me in doing this, you will deliver the sinner from his wandering, rescue his life from death, and cover a multitude of sins. Sins which the wayward disciple will encourage in others by his angry, inflated rhetoric and corrosive example.

The purpose of James's epistle, as revealed in his closing words to his readers, is that those to whom he writes will form a community that suffers, obeys, waits, and prays together, and thus protects its members from apostasy. In the face of persecution and evil faced by this early church, the temptation to leave the Christian faith, to forsake one's baptism and return to one's old beliefs was immense. The joy and patience, and ultimately, the maturity, that James longs for in his readers (as described in 1:2-4) is possible only in the context of community. Indeed, what the apostle James desires is not simply mature and patient and obedient followers of Jesus, but rather a community of those who follow Jesus that is mature and patient and obedient.

## 12

# FINAL REFLECTIONS & SUMMARY

*As for that in the good soil, they are those who, hearing the word,
hold it fast in an honest and good heart, and bear fruit with patience*
– Luke 8:15

In 1980 a friend approached me after church and handed me a manila file folder. "Read these and let me know what you think," he said. I did. It turned out the folder was filled with samples of 3 or 4 Christian newsletters. These were newsletters giving Christian commentary on contemporary cultural issues—abortion, economics, art, and politics. After reading them, I mailed in a donation and a request for subscriptions to all of them.

I had just come out of a severely dispensational Christian community where everyone was convinced that the end of the world was upon us. Hal Lindsey's *The Late Great Planet Earth* was a Christian best seller. Because the world was ending you don't polish brass on a sinking ship. You wait for the ship to begin to sink and then Jesus will swoop down *deus ex machina* to snatch up Christians off the tilting deck and rapture us into heaven. This meant that careful thinking about what might be happening in American society and how Christians might make a difference was new to me. But I was 23 years old with a wife and newborn daughter which meant I was motivated to think about the future.

Well, we thought things were bad back then. Christians in the early 1980s were worried about the increasing secularization of American culture. A few months ago, we renovated our basement and I had to box up three walls of books. I had an entire bookshelf of books from the 1980s that analyzed the anti-Christian drift that was occurring in American society.

Today, however, the marginalization of Christians in education, culture, and politics has accelerated faster than anyone could have imagined even ten years ago, let alone in 1980.

And this has led to some interesting proposals from Christian leaders on how Christians ought to respond. Everything from the call to "faithful presence" by James Davidson Hunter, to the "Benedict Option" by Rod Dreher.[44] And then there's the Trump-inspired populism of the last few years. Now Dreher is prepping us to suffer as martyrs in his recent book, *Live Not By Lies*.[45]

As I said in my introductory remarks, for Christians who want to change the world the apostle James puts up some guardrails — how we should *not* respond to our increasing marginalization and cultural exile in America. I believe that the misbehavior exposed in James's letter will become a serious temptation to Christians as the cultural malaise continues to accelerate.

But when I preached and taught on this book in the past it sometimes felt like what we do when we are surfing through YouTube videos and come across a very interesting "how-to video" about changing the headlights in your car, or maybe someone showing us how to install a new kitchen faucet. You watch it for a while, but since your car's headlamp doesn't need changing and your kitchen sink is working just fine, you make a mental note to come back to those instructional videos when you need them.

---

44 James Davidson Hunter, *To Change the World: The Irony, Tragedy, and Possibility of Christianity in the Late Modern World* (Oxford: Oxford University Press, 2010). See also the helpful critiques of Hunter's thesis in *Revisiting 'Faithful Presence': 'To Change the World,' Five Years Later*, ed. Collin Hansen (Deerfield, IL; The Gospel Coalition, 2015). Rod Dreher, *The Benedict Option: A Strategy for Christians in a Post-Christian Nation* (New York: Penguin, 2017).

45 Rod Dreher, *Live Not by Lies: A Manual for Christian Dissidents* (New York, Penguin, 2020).

## Final Reflections & Summary

But today it seems to me that the first-century situation which called forth this letter is remarkably like what we are now experiencing in this country in at least two ways: 1) the marginalization, the exile, if you will, of Christians from mainstream culture, and 2) the call for justice.

When we see that things appear to be going from bad to worse in American culture, indeed, as there appears to be an escalation of moral, legal, and political degeneration that often breaks out into violence, and when increasingly Christian believers are targeted as the enemy, what action should Christians take? What should we do?

The best way to answer questions like these is to pay attention to the teaching of James in his letter. James has answered the question: what we need to be careful to avoid in our zeal to turn things around. Much of his letter is about how *not* to change the world.

There are certain temptations that readily present themselves to Christian leaders with a passion to change the world (doctors, teachers, pastors, elders, deacons, school teachers, cultural leaders, movement leaders, etc.), who hunger and thirst for righteousness, who long for God to rescue their lives and others' lives from their oppressors.

These temptations are not from God. And to give into them does not bring about divine justice. They arise when we are lured and enticed by our own angry desire, which when conceived gives birth to sin, and when it is fully grown brings not peace and justice, but breeds zealotry, political ambition, disorder, anarchy, violence, and ultimately death. This is exactly what James warns against in chapter 3:14-16.

In closing this commentary, let me give a quick summary of the temptations James warns against in his epistle.

The first temptation is to fail to listen carefully to the words of Jesus concerning the character of his kingdom and justice and the way it will be established in human communities. This is the "implanted word" (1:21) these disciples have heard and hopefully hid in their hearts so that they might not sin against the Lord.

What they have of the Word of God is what they remember hearing. Because they have been dispersed from Jerusalem and the apostolic ministry, they have been cut off from the normal hearing of the Gospel and the life and teachings of Jesus. This letter is also chock full of references to the Gospel of Matthew, particularly Jesus's Sermon on the Mount—the first Gospel written very early on and likely the one they have all heard read in their assemblies. They don't have copies of it. No one does yet. But they have heard it read aloud and James hopes it has been implanted like a seed in their minds and hearts.

Of course, we have so much more. We have multiple copies of the Bible. We hear the Word of God read every week in church and hear sermons explaining the meaning and application. Even so, we don't always carry Bibles around with us when we are living normal lives in the world. We also must remember what we heard and read. The Word has been implanted as a seed and we have to allow it to grow without hinderance, as Jesus tells us in the parable of the sower. "As for what was sown on good soil, this is the one who hears the word and understands it. He indeed bears fruit and yields, in one case a hundredfold, in another sixty, and in another thirty" (Matt. 13:18).

James's readers were listening to the wrong sorts of words—angry words spewed out by immature "brothers" and instigating aggressive, violent action against their enemies. He admonishes them to listen to "the mature instruction" that "brings liberty" (2:8-13). Put away "filthiness" and rampant malice. The word "filth" in Greek is related to a medical term describing earwax. Our ears need to be opened. Ears to hear. Priests had to have their ears opened. Bondservants volunteered to have their ears circumcised, opened so that they would hear the voice of their master.

There is a direct relationship between the openness of people to God's instruction and the state of the world. I remember coming back into the church community when I was in college in the 1970s. Everyone brought their Bibles to church. Everyone was in some Bible study. Christians were eager to hear the Word read and expounded. We came to church and Sunday school with wide-margin Bibles and notebooks to record what we were hearing. I still have my old New American Standard Bible filled with highlights, underlining, and copious notes in the margin.

Something changed over the years. I suspect it has to do with the glut of information available now online. But today most Christians don't even carry Bibles to church. They mostly don't take notes either. I don't want to be overly nostalgic about those "good old days" and think that the answer is a return to a note-taking congregation on the Lord's Day. Some of it is the fault of the church's leadership. Most churches don't have long Scripture readings on Sunday anymore. Why don't we have an Old Testament, a Gospel, and an Epistle reading every Lord's Day? Why don't we recite and sing the Psalms every week? Why are people content with a single Bible verse or two projected in a PowerPoint presentation? The pastor then gives a Christian TED talk that is somehow related to the verse but usually contains more emotional stories than it does biblical exposition. Is that all we need every week?

So are we faithfully responding to the first temptation? The first temptation is to fail to listen carefully to the words of Jesus concerning the character of his kingdom and justice and the way it will be established in human communities. As long as Christian people do not hear regularly the "royal instruction" from all of Scripture, we will continue to be misled about the nature of Jesus's kingdom and the methods of advancing it.

The second temptation typically dogs opinion leaders in the church, those called to speak and guide other Christians with their tongues. What is that? It is to fail to attend to our personal growth in grace and maturity while we are engaged in public teaching and leadership. James's letter is written to the leaders of these exiled Christian communities. Twelve times at key junctures in the letter James addresses "the brothers." They are "the teachers" (3:1) whose tongues are guiding the entire body of believers for whom they are responsible (3:1-12). But their behavior betrays their lack of maturity. They are "double-minded" and therefore "unstable" (1:7). They speak without thinking and are quick to react in anger and malice against their enemies (1:19-21). They have not grown in their obedience because they are "deceiving themselves" (1:22). They hear the Word, but do not respond in obedience (1:23-25). They think that the authenticity of their "religion" will be evident in what they say, rather that by what they do (1:26-27). These brothers are misbehaving on every level, but their unbridled tongues proclaim their faith nonetheless (2:1-26). By the time we reach the end of chapter 3 and the first half of chapter 4, the magnitude of misbehavior among these brothers is shocking—zealotry, selfish ambition, anarchy, vile practices, covetousness, murder, violence, pride, and idolatrous spiritual adultery.

It is striking to compare the disgraceful duplicity among these early-church Christian brothers to the hypocrisy of the Jewish leaders in the Gospel accounts. The nascent church was in danger of ignoring everything Jesus taught about leadership in his kingdom. Would it come to this—meet the new boss, same as the old boss? This challenge is addressed all through the New Testament epistles. Paul warns Timothy, "Watch your life and teaching closely. Persist in this, for by doing so you will save both yourself and your hearers" (1 Tim. 4:16).

There are certain predictable traps that pastors who want to be "movement leaders" fall into. We think we are on a higher plane because we have this altruistic social vision for peace and justice. We are above the law, above common morality. Since our cause is righteous, and in our minds will eventually benefit the masses, some liberties could be taken in the pursuit of these righteous ends.

The challenge for Christian movement leaders is that we want to spin out grand theories about why things are going wrong and what needs to be changed, and we want to inspire others to action for the sake of the kingdom. . . but then we ourselves will ignore the more common, ordinary acts of charity and obedience. This is a huge concern of James all through his letter. Christian leaders and pastors that style themselves instructors and visionaries will exult in rhetoric designed to move others to act but we ourselves ignore obedience in common life, if you will, because we are called to greater deeds (James 2:26-27, 14-17).

What is worse, leaders too often will secretly look down their noses at these ordinary activities as not powerful enough, and come to despise anything that does not directly engage the larger theater of political and governmental affairs. James, however, challenges us to remember that the way of the cross is the way of transformation, the way that God has ordained to change the world. And the way of the cross necessarily involves self-denial, sacrifice, treating others better than ourselves, loving those that God has put in our path, in our lives— not loving some *ideal* husband or wife or child or parent or neighbor or friend or fellow workmate. Rather it is being kind and longsuffering and patient toward that flesh-and-blood person right there before us in our home or in our office. We are tempted to think that these ordinary activities are not effective, not powerful, that they won't get the job done.[46] But we forget that our primary calling in *this* world is in fact to create a social reality, a civilization, and kingdom that is precisely characterized by this kind of loving, charitable, peaceful behavior (3:13-18).

The third temptation is to cozy up to our enemies thinking that we can win their favor. If we can get them to like us, maybe they will leave us alone. This is the "partiality" problem James criticizes in 2:1-13. It is not simply that they are favoring the rich over the poor. That would be bad enough. But the man who is being catered to in their assembly is the one who wears the right of authority and the robe of office (2:20). He is explicitly identified as an oppressor, someone who drags them into court, and a blasphemer against the name of Jesus (2:6-7). To "judge" the rich oppressor as someone more deserving of special care than the poor believer is "to become judges engaging in an evil conspiracy" (2:4). That evaluation from James is not just about individual "evil thoughts" but about the way the brothers have conspired together

---

[46] See Epilogue, "Fire From Heaven," for a sermonic illustration of this.

to appease their rich enemies. They have thereby dishonored those poorer disciples whom "God has chosen . . . to be rich in faith and heirs of the kingdom" (2:5).

The appeasement option ought not to be on the table for conscientious Christian leaders. To turn a blind eye to immorality and abuse with the hope of getting a hearing from some powerful government or academic figure would be to betray our allegiance to the Lord. Not only is such schmoozing mostly ineffective—the more we give, the more they will take—but such behavior runs counter to the examples of the prophets and of Jesus himself. The prophets denounced the rich and powerful, even, maybe especially, when they were in positions of authority in Israel. Elijah, Isaiah, Jeremiah, and others did not cozy up to corrupt, immoral leaders. Neither did Jesus.

Fourth, the most insidious temptation, according to James, is to use the power of our words to guide the church toward aggressive and violent action thinking we are acting thereby as agents of God's justice. As we have argued, James 3:1-12 is at the heart of the letter. And the key passage that unlocks the entire letter is James 1:19-20, "Know this, my beloved brothers: let every man be quick to hear, slow to speak, slow to anger; for the anger of man does not produce the righteousness of God." Anger against their oppressors has fueled impetuous speeches with the intent to rally the disciples to make things right by means of aggressive, retributive action (3:13-16; 4:1-12). This kind of Christian "zealotry" will not make things right. Rather, such speech and behavior is not of the Spirit but demonic (3:15). These angry and violent responses have been fueled by the immature rhetoric of their teachers, the brothers responsible for leading their communities. They want freedom, but they are going about achieving liberty in the wrong ways.

In contemporary, twenty-first century America things have not degenerated to the point where Christians are tempted with the lure of violent zealotry. Or have they? In some circles the desire for "social justice" has become more than simply prophetic speech. We seem to be moving from political theatre (marches, protests, etc.), which is appropriate when moderate, to unrestrained, violent action (riots, destruction of property, etc.). In the modern world where everything seems to be immediately available (or at the most two-days away when delivered by Amazon Prime), Christians are tempted to want justice now. James warns against that kind of intemperate impatience.

Fifth, it is critical that Christians who have a passion for changing the world not lose heart and grow impatient when God does not act according to our timetable. Although James has warned them against the intemperate use of their tongues in their struggle for justice and freedom (3:1-12), he does not hold back words of prophetic condemnation against their oppressors (5:1-6). He is not inciting violence, but prophesying God's just retribution. These harried and mistreated Christians needed to hear this prophetic judgment against Jerusalem just as much as they needed to hear James's rebuke of their unwise words and zealous behavior. They needed to hear James's own justifiably angry denunciation of the leaders in Jerusalem and hear his assurance that the days of their oppressors are numbered, and the Lord is coming in judgment soon (5:8).

Christians today also need to be reminded of God's righteous judgment, not just at the Last Day, but also in history. James comforted his flock with the promise that "the coming of the Lord was near" (5:8). He was not talking about the end of history and the final judgment. His words in the first part of James 5 are designed to remind them of Jesus's prophetic promise that the Temple would be destroyed, and Jerusalem judged (Matt. 24). This promised destruction was on the horizon and they needed to be reminded so they would wait for their coming vindication patiently. Although we don't have such definitive prophesies regarding our nation as these early Christians did, we should expect the Lord to act in history against the enemies of the church. The Scriptures are clear: the Lord has repeatedly judged haughty, unjust nations and rulers—Pharaoh, the Canaanites, Nineveh, Egypt, Samaria, Moab, Babylon, Persia, Greece, Rome, and even Jerusalem. Why would we think that corrupt, immoral modern nations are exempt from God's just recompense? We don't have the assurance of a quick timetable, as the early church did ("this generation will not pass away until all these things take place," Matt. 24:34). Nevertheless, we do have the timeless promises from the prophets that the Lord will act:

> If at any time I declare concerning a nation or a kingdom, that I will pluck up and break down and destroy it, and if that nation, concerning which I have spoken, turns from its evil, I will relent of the disaster that I intended to do to it. And if at any time I declare concerning a nation or a kingdom that I will build and plant it, and if it does evil in my sight, not listening to my voice, then I will relent of the good that I had intended to do to it (Jer. 18:7-10).

Sixth, not only does James warn us against inflammatory rhetoric that leads to violent action, but because of the Lord's coming judgment against his enemies, he also commends patience under trial, prayer for wisdom, mercy toward our persecutors, and special care for those in the community adversely affected by the tribulations. Attending to these challenges is how the kingdom of Jesus is advanced during times of opposition and persecution. This is how mature "brothers" lead their congregations. Maturity comes from faithfulness under trial (James 1:2-4). Growth in obedience to the "royal law" brings true "liberty" (2:22-25). Muzzling one's tongue and then taking care of orphans and widows is evidence of true religious observance (2:26-27). As we have already noted, paying closer attention to the impoverished in our own Christian communities is much more productive than attempting to influence powerful enemies by obsequious favors (2:1-9).

Even when talking about "justification" James zeros in on their behavior not so much what they say. For all the public talk about their "faith" they have neglected the simple obedience implied in the posture of "trust" Christians profess. There are brothers and sisters in dire need because of their banishment. They need to be cared for, not just talked to (2:15-17). When parents are called to put their faith in God even though their children are being "sacrificed" in the turmoil of the on-going persecution, that kind of loyal resignation to God's will is evidence of living, genuine, justifying faith (2:20-24). And just as Rahab was vindicated as a true believer when she deceived Jericho's secret police about the whereabouts of the Israelite spies, so also believers who risk their lives to help others escape from their Jewish inquisitors manifest a living, active trust in the Lord (2:25-26).

James's final words are all about patience when suffering and the assurance that God will act to deliver and vindicate them (5:7-11). They should meditate on the prophets and on the story of Job and stop grumbling and contemplate the Lord's goal in the trouble they are experiencing (5:10-11). Cultivating genuine Christian community is crucial—join with one another to sing, praise, and weep together (5:13). Take special care to minister to those who are injured in the on-going suffering meted out by the enemies of the Gospel. Give your wounded and sick the assurance that they are full members of the body of Christ by anointing them with oil, providing them with an opportunity to confess their sins, and reminding them of the promise of the resurrection of the body (5:16). But don't stop praying for the Lord to act. Remember Elijah and pray for the Lord's judgment and blessing (5:17-18). And the last admonition from James to these brothers in leadership is to work hard to restore those that have wandered from the way of the cross to mimic the ways of their oppressors. That kind of wandering on the part of Christian leaders can lead to a multitude of sins. Work to deliver such people from behavior that will end in their death (5:19-20).

If we consider everything that James has commended to his readers, we will have enough to do in our Christian communities and families, even during times of severe persecution. What James has given us is a fleshed-out version of Jesus's Sermon on the Mount. There are so many allusions to Jesus's sermon in James that the two might be formatted in side-by-side columns to see all the correspondences.⁴⁷ In fact, I encourage you to read the whole sermon for yourself and see how closely James follows our Lord's "royal instruction" regarding his coming kingdom. But in closing ponder the beatitudes:

> And Jesus went throughout all Galilee, teaching in their synagogues and proclaiming the gospel of the kingdom.... Seeing the crowds, he went up on the mountain, and when he sat down, his disciples came to him. And he opened his mouth and taught them, saying:
>
> "Blessed are the poor in spirit, for theirs is the kingdom of heaven.
>
> "Blessed are those who mourn, for they shall be comforted.
>
> "Blessed are the meek, for they shall inherit the earth.
>
> "Blessed are those who hunger and thirst for righteousness, for they shall be satisfied.
>
> "Blessed are the merciful, for they shall receive mercy.
>
> "Blessed are the pure in heart, for they shall see God.
>
> "Blessed are the peacemakers, for they shall be called sons of God.
>
> "Blessed are those who are persecuted for righteousness' sake, for theirs is the kingdom of heaven. Blessed are you when others revile you and persecute you and utter all kinds of evil against you falsely on my account. Rejoice and be glad, for your reward is great in heaven, for so they persecuted the prophets who were before you" (Matt. 4:23, 5:1-12).

The verdict of history commends the apostolic and post-apostolic church for their conformity to James's instructions and warnings. They were patient, steadfast during four centuries of severe trials. Kreider argues persuasively that the virtue of patience was the key that led to the cultural dominance of the

---

47 For a detailed account of all the allusions to Jesus's sermon in James see Virgil V. Porter, Jr., "The Sermon on the Mount in the Book of James, Part 1," *Bibliotheca Sacra* (2005): 344-60. And "The Sermon on the Mount in the Book of James, Part 2," *Bibliotheca Sacra* 162 (2005): 470-82.

## Final Reflections & Summary

Christian church over the Roman empire.[48] The church resisted the temptation to respond with violence against their persecutors, patiently waiting for vindication from the Lord, and all the while maintaining a clear prophetic criticism of both the apostate Jews and the pagan Roman authorities. That mature balance is precisely what Jesus and James his apostle calls us to today. The epistle of James contains just the sort of ancient wisdom that today's Christian dissidents need to hear and heed.

---

48 Alan Kreider, *The Patient Ferment of the Early Church*.(Grand Rapids, MI: Baker 2016).

# Epilogue

# Fire From Heaven

*If I speak in the tongues of men and of angels, but have not love, I am a noisy gong or a clanging cymbal. And if I have prophetic powers, and understand all mysteries and all knowledge, and if I have all faith, so as to remove mountains, but have not love, I am nothing. If I give away all I have, and if I deliver up my body to be burned, but have not love, I gain nothing.*
– 1 Corinthians 13:1-3

*The following is a wedding homily I delivered on January 9, 2021, at the marriage ceremony for Jacob & Sarah Skogen.*

In his novel *That Hideous Strength*, C.S. Lewis is able to masterfully illustrate in narrative form so many of his insights about the subversive dangers of Leftist political dogma to Christian civilization. Perceptive essays from Lewis like "The Abolition of Man" and "The Inner Ring" are fleshed out in the story of Mark and Jane Studdock. The elitist social engineers of Belbury, intent on remaking and controlling England and all of humanity, hide behind what appears to be a harmless bureaucratic, administrative organization called N.I.C.E (National Institute for Co-ordinated Experiments). But over against demonic Belbury stands the domestic estate of St. Anne's-on-the-Hill, with wise Ransom as the Director.

The battle lines are drawn. On one side—the good, the true, and the beautiful. And on the other—the evil, the powerful, and the hideous. St. Anne's household vs. the Belbury hive. Christian domesticity vs. Satanic domination. And as I said, it is a war to preserve Christendom.

So how will the battle be fought and won? What strategy will Ransom and his household at St. Anne's employ? Well, not what you might expect. In the penultimate scene we have a divine intervention that confuses Belbury's attempt at a new tower of Babel. But how does that come about? What triggers that event? What brings the heavenly judgment down on Belbury? As it turns out, some very ordinary, very common-place triggers.

When the beastly conspirators of Belbury are finally defanged and sent packing, there's a celebration at St. Anne's estate. One of the members of the St. Anne household, Andrew MacPhee, a Scot, something of a Scottish common-sense realist, is dumbfounded at just how this victory was accomplished and exactly what part any of the household of St. Anne might have had in it. The others are all wondering how the history of this great triumph will be recorded.

"Aye," said MacPhee, "and it could be a right good history without ever mentioning you and me or most of those here present. I'd be greatly obliged if anyone would tell me what we have done—apart from feeding the pigs and raising some very decent vegetables."

"You have done what was required of you," said the Director [Ransom]. "You have obeyed and waited. As one of the modern authors has told us, the altar must often be built in one place in order that the fire from heaven may descend somewhere else."

And right there is a profound lesson for all of us crusaders for Christendom. The most powerful weapon we wield against the forces of evil is ordinary Christian faithfulness. And I want to stress the adjective ordinary. Like the Scot MacPhee we often miss the centrality of simple godly living in order to pursue heroic, grandiose means to victory.

And if we had more time, I would point out that Lewis's story begins with two central characters—Jane and Mark. The opening scene is Jane contemplating the words of the Book of Common Prayer on marriage. The first sentences in the book are these words:

"Matrimony was ordained, thirdly," said Jane Studdock to herself, "for the mutual society, help and comfort that the one ought to have for the other." She had not been to church since her schooldays until she went there six months ago to be married, and the words of the service had stuck in her mind.

Sadly, Jane is contemplating these words because neither she nor her husband are experiencing any of this. As it turns out, they are each of them pursuing a fool's errand. They have been enticed to seek after the modernist promise of happiness through self-fulfillment. They must learn the hard way, not only how self-destructive this is, but also how the pursuit will further the campaign of the enemies of all that is good, true, and beautiful.

At end of the book both Jane and Mark abandon their self-centered quests and are united in an ordinary life of charity, love, and joy that brings true freedom.

What does all of this have to do with you two today? Well, you have probably already figured that out, as much as you are able to with so many things swirling around in your heads on the day of your marriage. I don't remember a single word of the homily given at my own wedding. But these days everything is recorded on video, so you can always return to this little homily when you have opportunity.

You are both warriors in the cosmic battle for Christian civilization. That's commendable. But don't think the battle is won primarily in high places of governmental power, with acts of gallantry in the public arena—whether in the university or conservative political organizations. There's certainly some help there, some advances to be fought for. Some selective victories to be won, for sure.

But remember Ransom's very wise, very biblical advice to MacPhee, " . . . the altar must often be built in one place in order that the fire from heaven may descend somewhere else." And the altar you must both erect is the altar of an ordinary Christian marriage and family. Perhaps everyone should know that this table behind me has been newly constructed and will be the table that this new family will gather around for meals when they return home. This is the altar that will be more powerful for the advancement of the kingdom of our risen Lord than any direct political, social, or educational activism. And it is fitting that this will be today the altar from which you all will receive the body and blood of our Lord for the first time together as husband and wife, father and mother, brothers and sisters.

I read from St. Paul's epistle to the Corinthian church earlier, especially his argument against the Corinthian Christians' pursuit of spiritual greatness. Chasing after the showiest gifts, even gifts of the Spirit, is not the most excellent way. You might be able to deliver a speech or podcast in angelic tongues, you might attain great intellectual powers of discernment so as to prophetically ascertain global trends, you could muster up enough faith to move political and educational mountains, or even offer yourselves as individuals to be martyred for the cause. But if you have not love, ordinary love for one another and for your children, you will accomplish nothing and you are nothing.

Psalm 131 gives us God the Son's posture in his incarnation.

> "O Yahweh, my heart is not lifted up;
> > my eyes are not raised too high;
> I do not occupy myself with things
> > too great and too marvelous for me.
> But I have calmed and quieted my soul,
> > like a weaned child with its mother;
> > like a weaned child is my soul within me.
> O Israel, hope in Yahweh
> > From this time forth and forevermore."

Our hope in Yahweh's promise to act on our behalf is grounded in our humility before him. After all, he loved us so much that he humbled himself. We are, therefore, called to be conformed to the image of our Savior. But we too often resist. As St. Augustine put it so well, "God has humbled himself, and still man is proud"

My prayer for you both is that you will humbly submit yourselves to the gracious discipline of the Lord in your marriage, so that you both can participate in the quality of love described in 1 Corinthians 13. This is a worthy expectation, a truly magnificent goal—to be remade in the image of God, to experience a mature love, a love that never fails, never disappoints, just as the love of our Lord for us. When we Christians learn to focus on building that kind of domestic altar, we can expect the Lord to call down his fiery judgment on the Belburys of our time.

Amen.

# Appendix

# Dating the Epistle of James

*Joshua Anderson & Jeffrey Meyers*

Evangelical scholars like Moo,[49] Johnson,[50] and Davids,[51] and McCartney[52] have given ample arguments in support of authentic authorship of the epistle of James by James the half-brother of Jesus.[53] But in expending so much energy in defending against a pseudonymous author and a late first-century date for the epistle, little real attention has been given to the possibility of an earlier date and consequently an earlier author for the epistle. But the apostle James, the brother of John, the son of Zebedee may be a more reasonable candidate for authorship of the epistle than has thus far been admitted. There doesn't seem to be any real basis to dismiss out of hand an earlier date for the epistle. When the name of James the apostle is mentioned in most commentaries he is usually dismissed with a simple "that would be too early"

---

49 Douglas Moo, *The Letter of James* (Grand Rapids, MI: Eerdmans, 2000).

50 L. T. Johnson, *The Letter of James* (Garden City: Double Day, 1995).

51 Peter H. Davids, *The Epistle of James*, in The New International Greek Testament Commentary (Grand Rapids, MI: Eerdmans, 1982).

52 Dan G. McCartney, *James* (Grand Rapids, MI: Baker, 2009).

53 Davids, *James*, 21-22. Davids holds a modified position on this point, arguing for a later redactor.

comment. Then no real reasons are given for rejecting the authorship of James and an earlier date. But as we shall see, there are some good reasons for believing that the epistle of James was written by the apostle sometime before his death in AD 42 (Acts 12:1-2).

Why study this issue at all? On the face of it, another discussion of another possible authorship and date for a brief New Testament letter (about four pages in my ESV Bible) may seem an odd topic for further academic effort. But far from being an esoteric question of academic specialty, deciding upon the most likely author, date and setting of the epistle of James (and indeed any work of literature) has important implications for its interpretation.[54] In this case the payoff can be quite clarifying. The entire character of the book takes on a different meaning once it is treated less as a loose connection of wise sayings and more like a circular letter written to deal with a specific crisis and "trials" faced by the letter's audience. Dating the letter early will also clarify the relationship between James and the apostle Paul, especially when we consider James's treatment of faith and works in chapter two. An early date answers so many questions raised by the text itself. It makes one wonder why the authorship of James the apostle has received only scant attention from the academic world.

*The writer of the letter identifies himself simply in the opening sentence as "James, a servant of God and of the Lord Jesus Christ" (James 1:1).*[55] But can this identification be trusted? Two alternative possibilities must be considered. The first is that the writer of the letter is only a *follower* of James—that is, that the letter is pseudonymous. On this point, however, we may confidently conclude that there is little or no evidence that pseudonymous

---

54 Moo, *James*, 12. On this point, Moo comments, "Identifying the James who wrote the letter may enable us to set the letter more accurately into its historical and canonical context...but the matter of authorship is important for another reason. Precisely because the letter makes a claim about the author, the truthfulness of the letter as a whole is at stake."

55 All scripture quotations are from the ESV, unless otherwise noted.

letters carried the authority the letter of James has been given in Church history, and so this option must be rejected.[56] The other possibility is that the introduction in 1:1 is a later addition and not original to the letter. However, on this point, we can take confidence in a strong textual tradition that attests to the integrity of 1:1 and the fact that 1:2 seems to require the identifications given in 1:1.[57]

*If the identification of "James" as the writer of the letter may be trusted, the next question that must be answered is to which James the letter refers.* Though there are multiple men called James in the New Testament,[58] only two by that name in early Church history held the authority necessary for such a letter: James son of Zebedee and James of Jerusalem (the brother of Jesus). Recent evangelical and moderate scholarship, while admitting the possibility of the first James as the author of the epistle, has deemed it improbable because of his early death.[59] On this point, Douglas Moo is representative of the scholarly consensus, commenting, "James the son of Zebedee is one of the most prominent apostles in the gospel narratives…but this James was put to death by Herod Agrippa I (Acts 12:2), perhaps in about A.D. 44. And we probably should not date the letter of James quite this early."[60] Peter Davids also dismisses this James with a similar argument, writing, "James the son of Zebedee probably died too early to leave any literary

---

56 On this point, see Moo, *James*, 20-21.

57 On these points, see J. A. T. Robinson, *Redating the New Testament* (Philadelphia: Westminster, 1976), 128-29.

58 Moo, *James*, 9. Moo lists James the father of Judas, James son of Alpaeus, James son of Zebedee, and James of Jerusalem.

59 Johnson, *James*, 93. Notably, Johnson adds to the problem of James's early death the fact that "this James' authority is not singled out by any source," underscoring the lack of patristic support for James the son of Zebedee's authorship of the epistle. This is an objection we shall have to consider later in the essay, as it has far more merit than the problem of James's early death..

60 Moo, *James*, 9.

remains," and adding, "Acts 12 indicates that he died before AD 44, ruling out the probability, although not the possibility, of his writing the epistle."[61]

Curiously, though Moo dismisses the authorship of James son of Zebedee because of the "improbability" of an early date for the epistle, he then promotes James of Jerusalem as a more likely candidate for authorship and finally dates the book according to a historical reconstruction of that James's life.[62] In other words, Moo seems to decide against one James because of the date of his death, but then bases the date of the letter on when it would likely have been written by the later James. If good reasons exist to firmly date the letter after James son of Zebedee's death, Moo has assumed the proof instead of showing it.[63] Indeed, there seems to be little reason to assume an absolute *terminus a quo* for the letter other than the birth of the Church at Pentecost.[64] J. A. Motyer seems to admit this lack of evidence when he comments,

> It is usually thought that James son of Zebedee was martyred at too early a date (AD 44) for him to have been the author of the letter [of James]. Even this, however, cannot be

---

61 Davids, *James*, 6, fn 26.

62 For Moo's rationale for the dating of the epistle, see Moo, *James*, 25-26. Strangely, Moo finally ends up with an early date for James, placing it in the "middle 40s." Even if we accept this date, given that James the son of Zebedee was killed in 44, it seems odd to dismiss him as improbable simply because he died at a too early date. Could not the "middle 40s," imprecise as such a statement is, easily be 42 or 43, when James the son of Zebedee would still have been alive?

63 It is difficult not to wonder if it is merely a pre-supposition of the impossibility of a very early date (i.e., late 30s) that keeps Moo and others from seriously considering the possibility of James the son of Zebedee's authorship.

64 Some have argued that James could be a pre-Christian Jewish work that was modified by adding 1:1 and 2:1 (see Davids, *James*, 3). Though there are good reasons to reject this theory—namely, the improbability of the Christian church accepting such a document under false premises—the fact that such a theory is given credibility is indicative of the lack of firm external evidence for the impossibility of very early date for James.

maintained for certain. Nothing in the letter absolutely forbids a date as early as James the son of Zebedee, and certainly the arguments proposed for later dates lack impressiveness.[65]

But if the date of James son of Zebedee's death ought not to prohibit serious consideration for his authorship, other important objections do exist. We must now consider their merits, moving from the least to the most persuasive.[66]

**1.** *Because of high level of Greek in the letter it is doubtful that a non-native speaker (such as a Galilean) could have written it.* The epistle indeed contains some of the most complex and developed Greek in the New Testament, and initially this might give us pause at accepting James son of Zebedee (or James of Jerusalem) as its author. But there are several weaknesses in this argument. First, while the nature of the Greek in the letter is indeed developed, it is still below the level found in Hebrews, and nothing like classical (literary) Greek.[67] Second, there is good and well-documented reason to think that Galilean Jews would have far better command of the Greek language than has often been assumed,[68] and indeed, there is no reason to conclude a first century Palestinian could not have written this letter.[69] The oft-heard canard that Jesus chose uneducated fisherman and workers to be his apostles just won't stand up to scrutiny. It makes for good sermon fodder, but the very fact that these literary productions—the four Gospels and the

---

65 J. A. Motyer, *The Message of James* (Downers Grove: InterVarsity Press Academic, 1985), 18.

66 It should be noted that, to my knowledge, no recent commentator has assembled a systematic argument against the authorship of James son of Zebedee, relying instead on an assumed late date to eliminate him from consideration. Therefore, these are my own imagined objections—other and better ones may exist.

67 See Moo, *James*, 14.

68 See J. N. Sevenster, *Do You Know Greek? How Much Greek Could the First Jewish Christians Have Known?* (London: Brill, 1968), 3-21.

69 On this point, see the defenses marshaled by Johnson, *James*, 116-18 and Moo, *James*, 14-15.

New Testament epistles—have been the subject of intense literary, historical, philosophical, and theological analysis in the West for two millennia testifies to the intellectual brilliance of these men. They were literate, smart men. They may not have been formally educated in the schools of the rabbis, but they nevertheless were brilliant authors and thinkers. The Holy Spirit did not zap them with literary prowess. He guided and directed each of the apostles so as to bring out their native and acquired acumen. There is no reason to think that James the son of Zebedee would be any less capable of writing sophisticated Greek than the later pastor of Jerusalem, James the Just.

**2.** *Because of the letter's discussion of faith and works in James 2, it is clear that the author is responding to Paul's teaching and therefore the letter must be dated after a time when his writings had circulated (at least the mid-40s).* On the surface, this might seem a valid argument. However, as Luke Johnson argues, "it is certainly as plausible to have Paul reading James as James (or pseudo-James) reading Paul."[70] There is no reason to assume a particular chronological relationship to Paul based solely on the content of James 2, and this objection to James the son of Zebedee's possible authorship must also be rejected. The truth is that reading James's arguments in chapter two for the necessity of good works makes so much more sense if it is not taken to be a polemic response to the apostle Paul. If the letter was written before the outbreak of the Jew-Gentile controversy, James's argument does not have to contradict Paul's polemic against "the works of the law/Torah" as necessary for a Gentile's justification. James is addressing an entirely different concern.

---

70 Johnson, *James*, 110. See also Robinson, who notes, "As a reply to Paul's position James' argument totally misses the point; for Paul never contended for faith *without* works. But as a reply, not indeed to James, but to the use made of him by the Judaizers in a subtly different context (that of the basis of salvation for *Gentiles*), the argument of Rom. 4 [i.e., by Paul] is very effective" (Robinson, *Redating*, 127-28).

**3.** *If James son of Zebedee had written the letter, he would have identified himself as an apostle in James 1:1.* The trouble with this objection is that is essentially an argument from silence, and a weak one at that. If we accept traditional theories of Pauline, Matthean and Johannine authorship, there is clear precedent for apostolic authorship without explicit identification of the apostolic title.[71] In any case, as Moo points out (regarding a similar objection to the case for James of Jerusalem's authorship), "the occasional nature of our NT letters renders any argument from what is included or not included in the letter quite tenuous."[72] If James the son of Zebedee was indeed the first "pastor" in Jerusalem and this circular letter is written to his flock that has been exiled from the city after the execution of Stephen (Acts 8:1-2; 11:29), then there would have been no need for long introduction. They all knew who he was.

**4.** *Patristic witnesses point almost exclusively to the authorship of James of Jerusalem.*[73] This is certainly the most troubling objection to the possibility of the authorship of James son of Zebedee. It must be pointed out, however, that the patristic evidence on this point is very late. As James Brooks shows in his excellent survey of patristic witness to James, the earliest explicit tie between James of Jerusalem and the letter is made by Eusebius, (c. 325 AD) in his *Church History* (2.23).[74] That's 250 years after the apostolic age!

---

71 In Matthew, John, and 1 John, the apostles write without even giving their name, much less the title of "apostle." In 2 and 3 John, John identifies himself as "elder," not "apostle," and in Philemon and Galatians Paul does not give his apostolic title.

72 Moo, *James*, 14.

73 There are exceptions to this rule. As Brooks notes, "the tenth century Latin Codex Corbeiensis (*ff*/66) and several Spanish writers including Isidore of Seville (d. 636) [attribute the letter to James son of Zebedee]" (James A. Brooks, "Introduction to James," *Southwestern Journal of Theology* 43.11 (Fall 2000): 11, fn 2. This evidence, however, cannot be given too much weight, because it is late, and, as many commentators have pointed out, James son of Zebedee became a favorite saint of Spain and this may have influenced their estimation of his authorship.

74 See Brooks, "Introduction," 12-16. Other commentators, including Davids

Though patristic witness after this date is nearly unanimous in attributing the letter to James of Jerusalem, the fact that Eusebius's claim is an original (at least to our knowledge) assertion made about something that happened two hundred fifty years in the past means that it must be approached with healthy suspicion. Indeed, it is not difficult to construe a scenario where Eusebius's opinion simply became the popular assumption of the church without any basis in historical fact. Although, in general, patristic witness ought to be given strong weight in considering questions of date and authorship of the New Testament, in this case the evidence is too meager to be conclusive or even very helpful in settling the matter in question.[75]

Having surveyed the major objections to James son of Zebedee's possible authorship,[76] there does not appear to be any conclusive evidence that he could not have written this letter. Now we must turn out attention toward internal evidence that may support his authorship.

---

1982, 7, have claimed that "Origen made the first clear reference to James as... being written by James the Just." However, as Brooks points out, Origen usually refers to the author as only "James" or "the apostle James," designations which could easily apply to either James (Brooks, "Introduction," 13, fn 9). The only time he explicitly ties the epistle to James the brother of Jesus is found in a Latin translation of his work performed by a later translator (Rufinus) who was known to "doctor" Origen's work and thus is less than trustworthy. Eusebius mentions the link almost in passing, summing up the James of Jerusalem's biography by noting, "Such is the story of James, to whom is ascribed the first of the so-called General Epistles." Eusebius, 2.23. Though Eusebius at least claims to be relying on earlier tradition and not simply his own speculation when he asserts the link between James of Jerusalem and the epistle, it is impossible to verify his claim. It would be helpful to know in this case who exactly ascribes the epistle to James, but Eusebius does not tell us.

75 As Brooks admits, "Certainly [the patristic evidence] does not support authenticity to the extent it does most other books in the New Testament" (Brooks, "Introduction," 16).

76 One positive argument for James of Jerusalem's authorship that must be dealt with is the supposed linguistic parallels between the epistle of James and James of Jerusalem's speech in Acts 15. But the supposed evidence is very meager and does not necessarily indicate anything about authorship. As Johnson

**1.** *The potential link between diaspora in James 1:1 and Acts 8 and 11.* According to James 1:1, the letter is written "to the twelve tribes in the dispersion" (ταις δωδεκα φυλαις ταις εν τη διασπορα). What is meant by this reference to the *diaspora*? Though the word is rare in the NT, its verbal form is found in Acts 8:1, 4 and 11:19, referring there to the dispersion of Jewish Christians from Jerusalem due to Jewish persecution after the stoning of Stephen.[77] Allowing Scripture to interpret Scripture, it is almost certain that James had in mind the same dispersed Jewish Christians that Luke describes in Acts.[78] The death of Stephen took place during the first year of the church's birth (AD 30-31), and the persecution of the church by the Jews began soon after that date. If James 1:1 and Acts 8:1 refer to the same general dispersion of the Church, it is far more

---

comments, "No support for authenticity [of James of Jerusalem's authorship] is offered, however, by the convergence of language between this letter and the statements attributed to James in Acts 15:13-21 or the letter attributed to the Jerusalem leadership in Acts 15:23-29." Johnson 1995, 118.

77 The word *diaspora* is used three times in its nominal form in the NT (John 7:35; James 1:1; 1 Pet. 1:1) and three times in its verbal form (Acts 8:1,4; 11:19). In John 7:35, it clearly refers to the historic dispersion of the Jews among the nations after the Babylonian exile. In the Acts references, it clearly refers to the dispersion of Jewish Christians from Jerusalem because of the Jewish persecution. The use in 1 Peter 1:1 seems to be to refer to a more "spiritual" dispersion of Christians, that is, not in response to a specific persecution, but referring to the spiritual status of Christians. In James, the sense is debated, and some have argued that it is impossible to tell for sure if it refers to a physical dispersion or a spiritual one. Significantly, however, when *diaspora* is used in the LXX, it always refers to a physical dispersion (see Schmidt 1964, 99), and given James's strong reliance on the LXX, (see Johnson 1995, 7) this seems to tilt the evidence in favor of *diaspora* describing a physical dispersion in James 1:1 (the "twelve tribes" would then refer to the new Israel). Interestingly, Moo agrees, describing the *diaspora* in James 1:1 as a literal dispersion (2000, 23), but does not make any consequent connection to the use of the word in Acts.

78 This is exactly the argument made by the Church father Bede (d. 735), who writes, "We read that when Stephen was martyred a great persecution of the church broke out at Jerusalem...James then wrote this letter to those who had been scattered because they had suffered persecution for the sake of righteousness." Quoted in Bray, 2000, 2.

likely that the letter would have been written during the 30s or early 40s and thus the likely author would have been James son of Zebedee.[79]

**2.** *The many connections between James and the sayings of Jesus.* Ralph Martin has well documented the numerous connections between the content of James and the sayings and teachings of Jesus in Matthew.[80] While it is possible, as Martin suggests, that these parallels point to literary dependence for the letter on Matthew's gospel (though the order could be reversed, of course), these parallels may also point in another direction. If we take the early church position on the relative composition and dating of the synoptics Gospels—that Matthew was written and disseminated first, then Mark, and finally Luke—then James's use of Matthew's material makes a lot of sense.[81] Matthew's gospel was either already composed and beginning to circulate or was in the process of being written. That means James, as a member of the apostolic brotherhood, had some access to Matthew's material. McCartney comes to a similar conclusion:

> It is as though James is imbued with the wisdom teaching of Jesus, but not in the written form in which we now find it. All this points to a time quite early in the life of the church, prior to the theological reflections of Paul, prior to the circulation of the Gospels, and prior to the authors of Hebrews, 1 Peter, and the Johannine materials, or at least prior to the time when these

---

[79] Indeed, before the death of James son of Zebedee in c. 42-44 AD, it seems more likely that any letter written with only the name "James" would have been first attributed to him, as James of Jerusalem did not rise in prominence until around 42 AD.

[80] Martin 1988, lxxiv-lxxvi. For example, see connections between James 1:2 and Matthew 5:12; James 1:5 and Matthew 7:7; James 1:4 and Matthew 5:48; James 3:17-18 and Matthew 5:5,9; James 1:12 and Matthew 24:13. See also Davids 1984, 66-67 for a detailed list of parallels.

[81] For arguments that the canonical order of the Gospels is the order in which they were written, see John Wehham, *Redating Matthew, Mark, and Luke* (Downers Grove: IVP, 1992), and also Peter Leithart, *The Four: A Survey of the Gospels* (Moscow, ID: Canon Press, 2010), pp. 105-115.

other writings began to have widespread and determinative influence... James represents a state of Christian thinking that has not yet been determined by them, and hence is logically prior.[82]

We would add that James is not merely grounding his admonitions on the "wisdom teaching" of Jesus, but he is also giving the persecuted community hope based on Jesus's repeated prophetic denunciations of the failed leadership of the Jewish authorities (1:9-11; 2:6-7; 5:1-6; cf. Matt. 23). Their theocratically rich oppressors will be judged shortly, "for the coming of the Lord is near" (5:8).

**3.** *The epistle of James does not mention a Gentile presence.*[83] *If the letter was written between the mid 40s and early 60s, which seem the most likely dates if James of Jerusalem is the author, it is odd that there is no discussion of Jew-Gentile relations, and no discussion at all as to how Gentiles are to live as Christians, as these were major issues for the church at this time.* While it is possible that the letter was written during this later period and simply did not deal with the issue, it is much more likely that the issue is not dealt with because the letter was written during a time when Jew-Gentile relations were not yet a looming problem—a time like the first years after the persecution of the Church mentioned in Acts 8, a time when James son of Zebedee would have been the most likely author.

---

82 McCartney, *James*, 8.

83 Robinson, *Redating*, 122. Robinson argues persuasively on this point, noting, "There is no suggestion throughout the epistle of a Gentile presence... Even within the church there is no sign of a Gentile mission, no mention of its claims, no evidence of the conflicts and tensions arising from it. Above all, there is no hint of Judaizing, as opposed to Jewish, attitudes...There is not a mention in the epistle of the issues that formed the heart of this controversy—of circumcision, dietary rules and ritual law."

If James son of Zebedee was in fact the author of the epistle of James, as does seem at least possible, then this is not merely an obscure academic issue. Indeed, if this assertion is true, then there are several important implications for interpretation of the book which we will now consider, each in turn.

**1.** *A new and more concrete setting for the letter.* If James was the author of the letter, and if the reference to diaspora in James 1:1 refers to the early Jewish persecution of the church, then we can postulate an audience for the letter that would have looked something like this: new Jewish converts to Christianity who had recently fled their homes in Jerusalem because of the threat posed by Jewish persecutors, and now faced a life marked by fear and poverty—all because of their decision to be baptized followers of Jesus Christ. Because most commentators assume a generic audience with no particular setting in mind they cannot see any coherence to the letter. It appears to be a loosely connected string of wisdom about various topics. In addition to that, the "foes" in the letter end up being the generic rich and wealthy land owners. If we, however, place the letter early as a response to the Jewish leaders pursuit and persecution of new Jewish converts to the Messiah Jesus, then we can make much more sense of the language used to describe them throughout the epistle. They are the theocratically rich authorities in Jerusalem, not simply wealthy people in general. This perspective gives us a helpful thread to understand how everything in the letter holds together.

**2.** *An explanation for meaning of the trials and sufferings addressed in the letter.* In the context of this setting, exhortations like "Count it all joy, my brothers, when you meet with trials of various kinds, for you know that the testing of your faith produces steadfastness" (1:2-3) or "Be patient, therefore, brothers, until the coming of the Lord" (5:7) take on new and richer meaning, for we can better imagine the circumstance to which they apply—a situation of physical persecution that would have demanded patient faith in the promises of their God. This context of suffering and persecution also provides a good explanation for the closing verses of James, "My brothers, if anyone among you wanders from the truth and someone brings him back, let him know that whoever brings back a sinner from his wandering will save his soul from death and will cover a multitude of sins" (Jm. 5:19-20). On the surface, this statement seems to be an odd way to end a letter. But if James is written to an audience that is experiencing physical persecution that prompted the temptations addressed by James—impatience, anger, violent aggression against their enemies, appeasing the authorities, and more— then James's exhortation is more easily understood. James was hoping that his letter would be used to win back erring brothers in their wandering from the truth.

**3.** *A clearer relationship between James and Paul's teaching on faith and works.* If James son of Zebedee is the author of the epistle, then we can confidently assert that James's discussion of faith and works in 2:14-26 predates Paul's teaching in Galatians and Romans on the subject. With this context in mind, we may dismiss the possibility that James's words are part of an intramural argument between himself and Paul. Because James's strong words about the necessity of works for true faith predate Paul's similarly strong admonition regarding the impossibility of salvation by "the works of the law/Torah" we can easily see that the two apostles are not arguing with each other, but merely approaching the topic of salvation from two different, but complementary, perspectives (and contexts). James's words therefore can be seen not as a threat to the biblical doctrine of salvation by grace alone through faith alone, but rather as advancing an important part of that doctrine—that is, the consequent works which are certain to flow from saving faith—a point that can then be eagerly applied to modern Christians.

Having briefly surveyed the evidence for the authorship of the epistle of James, we may now conclude at least that there is no firm reason to dismiss the candidacy of James son of Zebedee as summarily as recent commentators have done. Indeed, there is plenty of important evidence that supports his case that has not yet been seriously considered. In addition, if James son of Zebedee is the author of the epistle of James, then this reality points toward a new, more precise setting for the letter and sheds light on two of the most vexing interpretive problems in the letter—the nature of the trials and temptations experienced by its audience and the relationship between the teachings of James and Paul. What is being set forth in this essay is not a water-tight case for the authorship of James son of Zebedee (indeed, such a feat would likely prove to be impossible), but rather a strong nudge toward the possibility of his authorship, with the hope that the issue will be further considered—all in the interest of better understanding the context, audience and consequent theological and pastoral implications of the letter of James for the twenty-first century church.

# Bibliography

Brooks, James A. "Introduction to James," *Southwestern Journal of Theology* 43.11 (Fall 2000): 10-24.

Calvin, John. *Commentaries on the Catholic Epistles.* Translated by J. Owen. Reprint, Grand Rapids, MI: Zondervan, 1981.

Collins, C. John "James 5:14-16a: What is the Anointing For?" *Presbyterion* 23/2 (1997): 79-91.

Davids, Peter H. *The Epistle of James in the New International Greek Testament Commentary.* Grand Rapids, MI: Eerdmans, 1982.

Dreher, Rod. *The Benedict Option: A Strategy for Christians in a Post-Christian Nation.* New York: Penguin, 2017

Girard, René. *I See Satan Fall Like Lightning.* Translated by James G. Williams. Maryknoll, NY: Orbis Books, 2001.

Hansen, Collin, ed. *Revisiting "Faithful Presence": "To Change the World," Five Years Later.* Deerfield, IL: The Gospel Coalition, 2015.

Heil, John Paul. *The Letter of James: Worship to Live By.* Eugene, OR: Cascade Books, 2012.

Hengel, Martin. *The Zealots.* Translated by David Smith. Edinburgh: T&T Clark, 1989.

Hunter, James Davidson. *To Change the World: The Irony, Tragedy, and Possibility of Christianity in the Late Modern World.* Oxford: Oxford University Press, 2010.

Johnson, L. T. *The Letter of James.* Garden City: Double Day, 1995

Jordan, James B. *Primeval Saints: Studies in the Patriarchs of Genesis*. Moscow, ID: Canon Press, 2001.

Jordan, James B. "Rebellion, Tyranny, and Dominion in the Book of Genesis." In *The Tactics of Christian Resistance*. Ed. by Gary North. Tyler, TX: Geneva Press, 1983.

Kreidel, Alan. *The Patient Ferment of the Early Church: The Improbable Rise of Christianity in the Roman Empire*. Grand Rapids: Baker Academic, 2016.

Lange, John Peter. *A Commentary on the Holy Scriptures: James*. Translated by Philip Schaff. New York: Scribner, 1884.

Leithart, Peter J. *Delivered From the Elements of the World: Atonement, Justification, Mission*. Downers Grove, IL: InterVarsity Press Academic, 2016.

Leithart, Peter J. *The Four: A Survey of the Gospels*. Moscow, ID: Canon Press, 2010.

Martin, Ralph P. *James*. Waco, TX: Word, 1988.

Meyers, Jeffrey J. *The Lord's Service: The Grace of Covenant Renewal Worship*. Moscow, ID: Canon Press, 2003.

Meyers, Jeffrey J. *A Table in the Mist: Meditations on Ecclesiastes*. Monroe, LA: Athanasius Press, 2006.

McCartney, Dan. G. *James*. Grand Rapids, MI: Baker Academic, 2009.

Moo, Douglas. *The Letter of James*. Grand Rapids, MI: Eerdmans, 2000.

Motyer, J. A. *The Message of James*. Downers Grove: InterVarsity Press Academic, 1985.

Newbigin, Lesslie. *Foolishness to the Greeks: The Gospel and Western Culture*. Grand Rapids: Eerdmans, 1988.

Porter, Virgil V., Jr. "The Sermon on the Mount in the Book of James, Part 1," *Bibliotheca Sacra* 162(July-September): 344-60.

Poythress, Vern Sheridan. *Symphonic Theology*. Grand Rapids: Zondervan, 1987.

Riecke, Bo. *The Epistles of James, Peter, and Jude*. Volume 37 of The Anchor Bible. New York: Doubleday & Co., 1964.

Robinson, J. A. T. *Redating the New Testament*. Philadelphia: Westminster, 1976.

Scaer, David P. *James, The Apostle of Faith: A Primary Christological Epistle for the Persecuted Church*. Eugene, OR: Wipf & Stock, 2004.

Sevenster, J. N. *Do You Know Greek? How Much Greek Could the First Jewish Christians Have Known?* London: Brill, 1968.

Solzenhenitsyn, Aleksandr I. *The Mortal Danger*. New York: Harper & Row, 1980.

Taylor, Mark E. "Recent Scholarship on the Structure of James," *CBR* 3.1 (2004): 86-115.

Wenham, John. *Redating Matthew, Mark and Luke*. Downers Grove: Intervarsity Press, 1992.

Wright, N.T. *Jesus and the Victory of God*. Minneapolis: Fortress Press, 1996.

www.ingramcontent.com/pod-product-compliance
Lightning Source LLC
Chambersburg PA
CBHW071950070526
44583CB00015B/1133